First World War
and Army of Occupation
War Diary
France, Belgium and Germany

28 DIVISION
Divisional Troops
31 Brigade Royal Field Artillery
22 December 1914 - 31 October 1915

WO95/2271/4

The Naval & Military Press Ltd
www.nmarchive.com
Published in association with The National Archives

Published by

The Naval & Military Press Ltd

Unit 10 Ridgewood Industrial Park,
Uckfield, East Sussex,
TN22 5QE England
Tel: +44 (0) 1825 749494

www.naval-military-press.com
www.nmarchive.com

This diary has been reprinted in facsimile from the original. Any imperfections are inevitably reproduced and the quality may fall short of modern type and cartographic standards.

Contents

Document type	Place/Title	Date From	Date To
Heading	WO95/2271-4		
Heading	69th Batty. RFA. Vol I.		
War Diary	Winchester	22/12/1914	26/12/1914
War Diary	Coldeu Common	04/01/1915	04/01/1915
War Diary	Winchester Downs	12/01/1915	12/01/1915
War Diary	Colder Common	14/01/1915	18/01/1915
War Diary	Hazebrouck	19/01/1915	19/01/1915
War Diary	Noon Nr Strazeele	20/01/1915	22/01/1915
War Diary	Nr Strazeele	23/01/1915	27/01/1915
War Diary	Strazeele	28/01/1915	28/01/1915
War Diary	Ypres	29/01/1915	29/01/1915
War Diary	Strazeele	30/01/1915	31/01/1915
Heading	War Diary of 69th Battery R F A Volume II March 1915		
War Diary	Ypres	01/03/1915	07/03/1915
War Diary	Vlamertinghe		
War Diary	Ypres	14/03/1915	22/03/1915
Heading	War Diary of 69th Battery RFA. Volume I From 1st February 1915 to 28th February 1915		
War Diary	Strazeele	01/02/1915	01/02/1915
War Diary	Ypres	02/02/1915	28/02/1915
Heading	Feby 1915		
Heading	69th Battery RFA. April 1915		
War Diary	Ypres	01/04/1915	12/04/1915
War Diary	13th Zomebeke	14/04/1915	20/04/1915
War Diary	Zonnebeke	21/04/1915	30/04/1915
Heading	1915		
Heading	War Diary Of 1013 M T Coy R A M C		
Heading	War Diary Of 69th Battery RFA Volume III From 1st May 1915 to 31st May 1915		
War Diary	Zonnebeke	01/05/1915	03/05/1915
War Diary	N Ypres	04/05/1915	05/05/1915
War Diary	N. Ypres	06/05/1915	19/05/1915
War Diary	War Ypres	20/05/1915	24/05/1915
Miscellaneous	Ypres	25/05/1915	28/05/1915
War Diary	Abeele	29/05/1915	29/05/1915
War Diary	Herzelle	31/05/1915	31/05/1915
Heading	War Diary Of 69th Battery RFA Volume IV From 1st June 1915 to 30th June 1915		
War Diary	Herzeele	01/06/1915	17/06/1915
War Diary	Nr Dickebusch	17/06/1915	30/06/1915
Heading	War Diary of 69th Battery RFA Volume VII From 1st Sept 1915 to 30th Sept 1915		
War Diary	Nr Kemmel	01/07/1915	23/07/1915
War Diary	Nr Pradelles	24/07/1915	26/07/1915
War Diary	Nr Riez-Du-Vinage	26/07/1915	27/07/1915
War Diary	Nr Pt Levis U 11c 48	28/07/1915	29/07/1915
War Diary	Beuvry	29/07/1915	29/07/1915
War Diary	Vermelles	30/07/1915	30/07/1915

Heading	War Diary Of 69th Battery RFA Volume V From 1st July to 31st July 1915 Vol V		
War Diary	Nr Dickebusch	01/07/1915	16/07/1915
War Diary	Near Kemmel	17/07/1915	31/07/1915
Miscellaneous	A Form. Messages And Signals. Appendix 1	10/07/1915	10/07/1915
Miscellaneous	A Form. Messages And Signals. Appendix 11	10/07/1915	10/07/1915
Miscellaneous	Extract From Items Of General Interest. Appendix III	11/07/1915	11/07/1915
Heading	War Diary Of 69th Battery R F A Volume VI From 1st August to 31st Aug 1915		
War Diary	Nr Kemmel	01/08/1915	31/08/1915
Heading	War Diary. 28th Division Vol. No. 103rd Bty 31st Bde. R.F.A. From 22.12.14 To 31.1.15		
Miscellaneous	Cover for Documents. Nature of Enclosures.		
War Diary	Winchester	22/12/1915	31/12/1915
War Diary	Shaw Ford	04/01/1915	16/01/1915
War Diary	On Board S.S. Mount Temple	16/01/1915	16/01/1915
War Diary	On Board Mount Temple	17/01/1915	17/01/1915
War Diary	Havre	18/01/1915	19/01/1915
War Diary	Hazebrouck	20/01/1915	20/01/1915
War Diary	Nord Helf Near Strazeele	21/01/1915	21/01/1915
War Diary	Nord Helf	22/01/1915	01/02/1915
War Diary	Near Ypres	02/02/1915	02/03/1915
Heading	31st Brigade R.F.A. Dec 1914-Oct 1915		
Heading	31st Bde R.F.A. Vol I 22.12.14-31.1.15		
War Diary	Winchester	22/12/1914	08/01/1915
War Diary	Near Winchester	05/01/1915	20/01/1915
War Diary	Nord Helf	20/01/1915	29/01/1915
War Diary	Ypres	29/01/1915	31/01/1915
Heading	31st Bde RFA. Vol II 1-28.2.15		
War Diary	Nord Helf France	01/02/1915	01/02/1915
War Diary	Ypres	02/02/1915	28/02/1915
Miscellaneous	Appendix I	24/02/1915	24/02/1915
Miscellaneous	Appendix II	26/02/1915	26/02/1915
Heading	31st Bde RFA. Vol III 1-31.3.15		
War Diary	Ypres	01/03/1915	31/03/1915
Heading	31st Bde R.F.A. Vol IV 1-30.4.15		
War Diary	Ypres	01/04/1915	08/04/1915
War Diary	St Jan-Ter-Biezen	09/04/1915	10/04/1915
War Diary	Frezenberg	11/04/1915	23/04/1915
War Diary	84 Infantry Bde. Hqrs.	24/04/1915	24/04/1915
War Diary	Froienburg	24/04/1915	24/04/1915
War Diary	84th Infantry Bde Hqrs	25/04/1915	26/04/1915
War Diary	Frezenberg	27/04/1915	28/04/1915
War Diary	Sheet 28. 1/40000 D 25.b 6.2.	29/04/1915	29/04/1915
War Diary	D 25 b. 6.2	29/04/1915	30/04/1915
Heading	31st Bde. R.F.A. Vol V 1-31.5.15		
War Diary	D.25.b.6.2	01/05/1915	02/05/1915
War Diary	Ypres	03/05/1915	04/05/1915
War Diary	Potijze	05/05/1915	10/05/1915
War Diary	Dugouts On Stream	11/05/1915	13/05/1915
Miscellaneous	B Form. Messages And Signals.	14/05/1915	14/05/1915
War Diary		14/05/1915	18/05/1915
War Diary	Chateau	19/05/1915	28/05/1915
War Diary	Abeele	29/05/1915	31/05/1915
Heading	31st Bde. R.F.A. Vol VI 1-30-6-15		
War Diary		01/06/1915	17/06/1915

War Diary	Dickebusch H.34.a.6.10.	18/06/1915	19/06/1915
War Diary	Dickebusch	20/06/1915	30/06/1915
Heading	31st Bde R.F.A. Vol VII 1-31-7-15		
War Diary	Dickebusch	01/07/1915	17/07/1915
War Diary	Kemmel	17/07/1915	31/07/1915
Miscellaneous			
Miscellaneous	86th Battery RFA. War Diary		
Miscellaneous	C Form (Original). Messages And Signals.		
Miscellaneous			
Miscellaneous	C Form (Original). Messages And Signals.	10/11/1915	10/11/1915
War Diary	Kemmel	01/08/1915	31/08/1915
Heading	31st Bde R.F.A. Vol IX Sep 15		
War Diary	Kemmel	01/09/1915	30/09/1915
Operation(al) Order(s)	Operation Order No 26 by Major R.C Ramshen Cmdg 31st Brigade R.F.A. Appendix I	09/09/1915	09/09/1915
Operation(al) Order(s)	Operation Order No. 27 by Lt Col H.H Bond Cmdg 31st Brigade RFA Appendix II	11/09/1915	11/09/1915
Operation(al) Order(s)	Operation Order No. 28 by Lt Col H.H Bond Cmdg 31st Brigade RFA Appendix III	15/09/1915	15/09/1915
Heading	31st Bde R.F.A. Oct 1915 Vol X		
War Diary	Annequin	01/10/1915	31/10/1915
Operation(al) Order(s)	28th Divisional Artillery Operation Order No. 55	20/10/1915	20/10/1915
Miscellaneous	General Instructions for move of 28th Division.	20/10/1915	20/10/1915
Miscellaneous		20/10/1915	20/10/1915
Miscellaneous	28th Division. Programme Of Entraining Fouquereuil Station.		
Miscellaneous	28th Division. Programme Of Entraining. Lillers Station.		

A.2

28th division

121/4195

69th Batty: R F A.

Vol I.

Nil

Instructions regarding War Diaries and Intelligence Summaries are contained in F. S. Regs., Part II. and the Staff Manual respectively. Title pages will be prepared in manuscript.

WAR DIARY
or
INTELLIGENCE SUMMARY.
(Erase heading not required.)

Army Form C. 2118.

Hour, Date, Place	Summary of Events and Information	Remarks and references to Appendices
22/12/14 Winchester	69th Battery formed from L ½ 103rd Bty RFA	
26/12/14 Winchester till	Guns + wagons received to complete Bty to 4 gun est.	
	Mobilisation proceeding	
4/1/15 Colden Common	Bty moved out to billets 5 miles away from Winchester	
12/1/15 Winchester Downs	Inspection ~~Bty~~ Div^n by H.M. the King.	
14/1/15 Colden Common	Mobilisation completed	
16/1/15	Battery marched to Southampton embarked in S.S. "Kingstonian"	
18/1/15	Disembarked at Havre. Entrained Gare Maritime 10 pm.	
19/1/15 10 pm HAZEBROUCK	Detrained at.	
20/1/15 noon nr STRAZEELE	billetted at M DEMAREZ farm.	
21/1/15 "	Route march, raining	
22/1/15 " "	Routine fine	

Army Form C. 2118.

WAR DIARY
or
INTELLIGENCE SUMMARY.
(Erase heading not required.)

Instructions regarding War Diaries and Intelligence Summaries are contained in F. S. Regs., Part II. and the Staff Manual respectively. Title pages will be prepared in manuscript.

Hour, Date, Place	Summary of Events and Information	Remarks and references to Appendices
23/1/15 Nr STRAZEELE	gun pit digging. fine	
24/1/15 " "	" " " foggy	
25/1/15 " "	routine " foggy.	
26/1/15 " "	" " fine. Sentry fired at supposed spy at 10.35pm	but missed him
27/1/15 " "	" " fine	
28/1/15 STRAZEELE	Inspection By F.M. C.I.C. Cold snow showers	
29/1/15 YPRES.	B.C. + Lt Van Straubenzee proceeded to inspect positions	
30/1/15 STRAZEELE	returned Cold snow.	
31/1/15 " "	Routine Cold cloudy.	

Demarez Farm
31/1/15

E.P. Bedwell Major RA
Cmdg 69th Bty RA

(989) W4141—463. 400,000. 9/14. H.&J.Ltd. Forms/C. 2118/10.

Confidential

War Diary

of

69th Battery R.F.A.

Volume II

March 1915

From ~~1st March~~ 1915 to ~~30th April 1915~~

69th Bty R.F.A.

Instructions regarding War Diaries and Intelligence Summaries are contained in F. S. Regs., Part II. and the Staff Manual respectively. Title pages will be prepared in manuscript.

WAR DIARY
or
INTELLIGENCE SUMMARY.

(Erase heading not required.)

Army Form C. 2118.

Volume II

Hour, Date, Place	Summary of Events and Information	Remarks and references to Appendices
YPRES. 1st March	[illegible] Quiet. B.C.'s house shelled 11.30 pm Shrapnel through [illegible] ~~house~~ room [illegible] had a marvellous escape.	
2nd March	Bty shelled 1.30 am. by 6" howitzer. Four men wounded Gr. [illegible], Br. Lewis, Gr. Keech (dangerously), Br. [illegible]	
3rd March	Two or three shell near bty.	
4th March	B.C.'s house shelled again at night	
5th March	Quiet. Enemy shelled 118th Bty heavily. Very heavy fire at night from our heavy artillery in the distance	
6th March	[illegible] Quiet. Our heavies again busy at night. Battery [illegible] a line from 34 [illegible] to Bty [illegible] [illegible] very well.	

(73989) W4141—463. 400,000. 9/14. H.&J.Ltd. Forms/C. 2118/10.

Instructions regarding War Diaries and Intelligence Summaries are contained in F. S. Regs., Part II. and the Staff Manual respectively. Title pages will be prepared in manuscript.

WAR DIARY
or
INTELLIGENCE SUMMARY.
(Erase heading not required.)

Army Form C. 2118.

Hour, Date, Place	Summary of Events and Information	Remarks and references to Appendices
YPRES 7 March	Moved out to rest VLAMERTINGHE 10pm wet	
VLAMERTINGHE	building stables etc	
YPRES 14th	returned 5pm 4 rounds at 6.20. kept awake till 4 30am expecting to fire but nothing happened.	
" 15th	Quiet Fired a few rounds on German saps	
16th	Quiet same as day before.	
17	Quiet fire a few rounds daily	
18		
19		
20		
21		
22	To Vlamertinghe again	

Confidential

War Diary

of

69th Battery R F A.

Volume I

From 1st February 1915 to 28th February 1915.

121/5992

69th Bty RFA

Instructions regarding War Diaries and Intelligence Summaries are contained in F.S. Regs., Part II. and the Staff Manual respectively. Title pages will be prepared in manuscript.

WAR DIARY
or
INTELLIGENCE SUMMARY.
(Erase heading not required.)

Army Form C. 2118.

Volume I

Hour, Date, Place	Summary of Events and Information	Remarks and references to Appendices
8 am 1/2/15 STRAZEELE	Battery less one section marched with Divl Arty to YPRES halted 4 hours at VLAMERTINGHE. Guns in action $\frac{3}{4}$ m. S.E YPRES at 10.20 pm alongside 2 French guns 45th Bty (90 mm). French guns fired throughout night. 1st Line wagons + teams at VLAMERTINGHE	
2/2/15 YPRES	Fine + clear. Fired two rounds. L section arrived 10.30 pm. wet + misty	
3/2/15 YPRES	Fired 6 rounds in afternoon. Dull	
4/2/15 YPRES.	Fired 8 rounds in morning. 12 in afternoon at house supposed to have maxim in it. Heavy fire at night in infy trenches	
5/2/15 YPRES.	Fired 9 rounds in daytime. Arty of Divn bombarded German trenches at 9 pm for 40 minutes. Rate of our fire at first X.7 10 secs then finally X.F one min. Fired 110 rounds. roused at midnight + fired 15 more. Results not known but Germans kept quiet. fine	
6/2/15 YPRES	quiet no firing. Enemy shelled cross roads S.W of us intermittently all day. fine	

(73989) W4141—463. 400,000. 9/14. H.&J.Ltd. Forms/C. 2118/10.

Army Form C. 2118.

Instructions regarding War Diaries and Intelligence Summaries are contained in F. S. Regs., Part II. and the Staff Manual respectively. Title pages will be prepared in manuscript.

WAR DIARY
or
INTELLIGENCE SUMMARY.
(Erase heading not required.)

Hour, Date, Place	Summary of Events and Information	Remarks and references to Appendices
7/2/15 YPRES	Quiet, Dull. Germans still shelled cross-roads and the Lille gate. Taubes very busy last three days.	
8/2/15 YPRES	Quiet Cloudy Fired six rounds in the evening	

Instructions regarding War Diaries and Intelligence Summaries are contained in F. S. Regs., Part II. and the Staff Manual respectively. Title pages will be prepared in manuscript.

WAR DIARY
or
INTELLIGENCE SUMMARY.
(Erase heading not required.)

Army Form C. 2118.

Hour, Date, Place	Summary of Events and Information	Remarks and references to Appendices
15/2/15 YPRES	Wet Quiet.	
16/2/15 "	Fine quiet. aeroplanes (hostile over town)	
17/2/15	Germans shelled school, battery fired 140 rounds. Gr Droy wounded.	
18/2/15	School shelled again. Lt Van Straubenzee posted to RHA [illegible] to 1st Indian Cav Divn	
19/2/15	Quiet Lt CAL Brownlow joined. generally quiet. Germans fired a lot of blind shell at night. Windy + dull	
20/2/15	Battery fired 39 rounds at "Minenwerfer" House & got 6 direct hits in the morning. 4.30 to 5pm 117 Rds to support infantry. Germans almost got a direct hit on No1 gun. Their 5.9" howitzer busy at us. Br Newbery wound in thigh by a shell splinter. Thunderstorm in afternoon.	

Army Form C. 2118.

WAR DIARY
or
INTELLIGENCE SUMMARY.
(Erase heading not required.)

Instructions regarding War Diaries and Intelligence Summaries are contained in F. S. Regs., Part II. and the Staff Manual respectively. Title pages will be prepared in manuscript.

Hour, Date, Place	Summary of Events and Information	Remarks and references to Appendices
21/2/15	Fired 47 rounds 1 am 28 7 am. to support inf^y attacks. Rest of day Quiet Foggy.	
22/2/15	Quiet wet	
23/2/15	Quiet fine	
24/2/15	68 5.9" shell near Bty between 4.20 + 5.20 pm [illegible] Officers dug out had a very lucky escape. Decide to change position	
25/2/15	[illegible] new position [illegible]	
26/2/15	[illegible] New position [illegible] at 10 pm. [illegible] worked [illegible] + result [illegible] 2/Lt Simpson wounded in infantry trenches [illegible] fine + [illegible] cold at night	

Army Form C. 2118.

Instructions regarding War Diaries and Intelligence Summaries are contained in F. S. Regs., Part II. and the Staff Manual respectively. Title pages will be prepared in manuscript.

WAR DIARY
or
INTELLIGENCE SUMMARY.
(*Erase heading not required.*)

Hour, Date, Place	Summary of Events and Information	Remarks and references to Appendices
27th Ypres 28th Ypres	Dr Mackenzie joined Quiet cold strong wind Fired 8 rounds to silence enemies bty which was annoying the infantry. B.C's hutch collapsed. Storming at night.	
	[illegible] Cmdg 68th Bty [illegible]	

(73989) W4141—463. 400,000. 9/14. H.&J.Ltd. Forms/C. 2118/10.

FEBY
1916

6.9" Battery
R.F.A.
April
1915

Instructions regarding War Diaries and Intelligence Summaries are contained in F. S. Regs., Part II. and the Staff Manual respectively. Title pages will be prepared in manuscript.

WAR DIARY
or
INTELLIGENCE SUMMARY.
(Erase heading not required.)

Army Form C. 2118.

69" Battery RFA.

April 1915

Place	Date	Hour	Summary of Events and Information	Remarks and references to Appendices
Ypres.	1	1	Quick Fire few rounds	
	2		Good ~~Friday~~ Germans put 40 5"9" Shell in the School at noon. About 2.30 Crumps and Shrapnel. About 14. Lady in charge Officers billet wounded	
	3		Quiet Germans put shell on MENIN Road ½ mile E of us 103rd & 69" old posn shelled. Heavy Rifle fire at night	
	4		Generally Quiet. Shell on MENIN Road in afternoon	

D. D. & L., London, E.C.
(10340) Wt W5300/P713 750,000 3/18 E 2688 Forms/C/2118/16.

Army Form C. 2118.

Instructions regarding War Diaries and Intelligence Summaries are contained in F. S. Regs., Part II. and the Staff Manual respectively. Title pages will be prepared in manuscript.

WAR DIARY
or
INTELLIGENCE SUMMARY.
(Erase heading not required.)

Hour, Date, Place	Summary of Events and Information	Remarks and references to Appendices
28		
1	[illegible] Detachment at Ypres building new position	
29	Came into action new position work on which had been very well done by new [illegible] Sgt [illegible]	
30		
31	Quiet. Fire few rounds daily	
1		
2	Good Friday. Germans put 40 5'9" shell in the school at noon. About 2.30 Grump[s] and Shrapnel about 14 Lady in charge Officers billet wounded	
3	Quiet Germans put shell on MENIN ROAD ½ mile E Ypres. 103rd + 69th old pos[itio]ns shelled. Heavy rifle fire at night	
4th	Generally Quiet Shell on Menin road in afternoon	

Instructions regarding War Diaries and Intelligence Summaries are contained in F. S. Regs., Part II. and the Staff Manual respectively. Title pages will be prepared in manuscript.

WAR DIARY
or
INTELLIGENCE SUMMARY.
(Erase heading not required.)

Army Form C. 2118.

Hour, Date, Place	Summary of Events and Information	Remarks and references to Appendices
Ypres 5th	Germans shelled town [illegible], blew up house in [illegible] [illegible] [illegible] went [illegible] to inspect new positions [illegible] [illegible] French	
7th	Quiet	
8th	Quiet L × left position relieved by no section 123rd Bty	
9th	Quiet R × relieved. Bty went to position of rest ? W of Poperinghe	
10th	[illegible] went to see new wagon line	
11th	L × came into action near Zonnebeke relieving French Battery 37th [illegible] Regt	
12th	R × out of action. French position found [illegible] [illegible] [illegible] zone allotted this battery [illegible] [illegible] left of the [illegible] [illegible] — Enemy sent over 30 [illegible] at 5 p.m. nearly got [illegible].	

Instructions regarding War Diaries and Intelligence Summaries are contained in F. S. Regs., Part II. and the Staff Manual respectively. Title pages will be prepared in manuscript.

WAR DIARY
or
INTELLIGENCE SUMMARY.
(Erase heading not required.)

Army Form C. 2118.

Hour, Date, Place	Summary of Events and Information	Remarks and references to Appendices
13th Zonnebeke.	Registered. Enemy put 5.9" over for an hour 6 to 7 pm fired mainly on rly embankment, infantry dugouts, one shell nearly hit telephonists house. 70 shell 20 blind.	
14th "	Quiet registered some targets	
15th "	received instructions re changing position	
16th "	L. X changed + took over 149th position N of Zonnebeke road	
17th "	Major Bidwell sick. Major Willis took over R X changed & took over 149th position N of Zonnebeke Rd. Weather fine. Battery in new position without hitch.	Major Willis eventually remained in command – Major Bidwell being invalided to England.
18th –	Major Bidwell invalided home & struck off strength. Quiet.	
19th –	Capt The Hon Lyon Playfair joined from 126th Bty. Rds fired 45	
20th –	Capt Playfair killed by bullet whilst observing in trenches with 2/Lt MacKenzie. Weather fine. Fired several rounds with Latent discs on shells & found results unsatisfactory	

Instructions regarding War Diaries and Intelligence Summaries are contained in F. S. Regs., Part II. and the Staff Manual respectively. Title pages will be prepared in manuscript.

WAR DIARY
or
INTELLIGENCE SUMMARY.
(Erase heading not required.)

Army Form C. 2118.

Hour, Date, Place	Summary of Events and Information	Remarks and references to Appendices
21st Zonnebeke	Lt Barry joined from England to undergo instruction. Sergt Aves wounded by splinter in leg. 76 rounds fired and minenwerfer knocked out by us. BSM Deeks joined firing line from wagon line.	
22nd — —	Enemy employed poisonous gases. We fired 420 rounds repelled several infantry attacks. Weather fine.	
23rd — —	Lt Brink joined from 103rd temporarily. Fired 160 rounds 12 of which were H.E.	
24th — —	Major Wilks accompanied by Lt Brink and BSM Deeks reconnoitred ~~[illegible]~~ observing to left flank. At night Lt Barry along with BSM Deeks slept in dug-out on ridge but were unable to maintain telephonic communication owing to shell-fire. Weather wet. Fired 209 rounds repelling infantry attacks. Wagon line shelled. Br McCalfin and Dr Black wounded and 5 horses 4 of which were destroyed.	
25th →	Corpl. Holbrook wounded in trenches. Br Allen & Gr Simpson Gr Wilkins were wounded in action. Fired 174 rounds. Germans broke thro' at 25 trench suffering heavy losses	

Instructions regarding War Diaries and Intelligence Summaries are contained in F. S. Regs., Part II. and the Staff Manual respectively. Title pages will be prepared in manuscript.

WAR DIARY
or
INTELLIGENCE SUMMARY.
(Erase heading not required.)

Army Form C. 2118.

Hour, Date, Place	Summary of Events and Information	Remarks and references to Appendices
26th Zonnebeke	Wagon line shelled. Fired 174 rounds. Weather fine	
27th "	Quiet. Wagon line shelled & several horses killed & wounded. Fired 180 rounds.	
28th "	Wagon line shelled. Dr Richardson fatally wounded. Fired 83 rounds and position crumped by 5.9.	
29th "	Dr McGuinness Dr Monky wounded in wagon line. Lt Brink returned to 103rd. Fired 58 rounds.	
30th "	Gr Wilson killed at Battery. 4 limbers destroyed owing to barn being burnt. Fired 55 rounds. — On the Barn catching fire 2nd Lieut Swain, S.M. Meeks, Fitter St. Sergt Bates, & Gunner Mullins made several attempts to get into the barn to rescue the wounded of which there were several (infantry men) — but it was impossible to enter. — Gr Wilson was apparently from his attitude when found killed or severely wounded. — His remains were burned as were those of another man (infantry). — whose remains there were no means of identifying	
1st		S. M. [illegible] Major RFA

(73989) W4141—463. 400,000. 9/14. H.&J.Ltd. Forms/C. 2118/10.

MARCH & APRIL
1915

Confidential

War Diaries of

1013 MT Coy RASC

December 1918

January 1919.

September 1919

October 1919

Confidential

War Diary
of
69th Battery R F A

Volume III

From 1st May 1915 to 31st May 1915

69th Bty R.F.A.

WAR DIARY
or
INTELLIGENCE SUMMARY.
(Erase heading not required.)

Army Form C. 2118.

Volume III

Instructions regarding War Diaries and Intelligence Summaries are contained in F. S. Regs., Part II. and the Staff Manual respectively. Title pages will be prepared in manuscript.

Hour, Date, Place	Summary of Events and Information	Remarks and references to Appendices
1st May Zonnebeke	Quiet. Weather fine. Fired several rounds at Minnenwerfer, silencing same. Fired 96 rounds	
2nd — —	Gr Windmill wounded by rifle bullet at wagon line. Position under shrapnel fire. Fired 43 rds	
3rd — —	Very quiet. Weather fine. Fired 87 rounds. Left section retired to new position near Ypres at 8.50 pm and got guns in position under 2nd Lieuts Mackenzie & Swann	Mackenzie & Swann
4th — N Ypres	Gunner Stringer killed and Dr Wigglesford (ASC) wounded at wagon line. Right section rejoined Battery in new position* Fired 144 rds.	* under Major White. This was accomplished with unexpected ease — No shell came near the guns till Ypres was approached.
5th — —	Corpl Bird and S.S. Braybrook wounded by shrapnel at wagon line. Position heavily shelled all day. Fired 87 rounds. 17" inch dropping into the North end of Ypres ~~[illegible]~~ & inconveniently close from the north of our position at intervals all day.	

Instructions regarding War Diaries and Intelligence Summaries are contained in F. S. Regs., Part II. and the Staff Manual respectively. Title pages will be prepared in manuscript.

WAR DIARY
or
INTELLIGENCE SUMMARY.
(Erase heading not required.)

Army Form C. 2118.

Hour, Date, Place	Summary of Events and Information	Remarks and references to Appendices
6th May. N. Ypres	At 4 am. shell entered billet wounding Lt McElwain Corpl Pumpkin and Corpl McLachlan. Fired 219 rounds.	
7th ———	Busy day. Weather fine repelled several attacks firing 375 rounds — Fired twice during the night — at midnight & at about 3 a.m.	
8th ———	Commenced firing 6.30 am. and continued until one gun No 3 remained in action. Repaired guns & renewed firing until 11.30 pm with 2 guns. Fired 2398 rounds. Fire was very effective [illegible] [illegible] Gunners were splendid. Cpl Mullins & Cummins were wounded in action.	

(73989) W4141—463. 400,000. 9/14. H.&J.Ltd. Forms/C. 2118/10.

Instructions regarding War Diaries and Intelligence Summaries are contained in F. S. Regs., Part II. and the Staff Manual respectively. Title pages will be prepared in manuscript.

WAR DIARY
or
INTELLIGENCE SUMMARY.
(Erase heading not required.)

Army Form C. 2118.

Hour, Date, Place	Summary of Events and Information	Remarks and references to Appendices
9th May ~~1915~~ Nr Ypres	x Sgt J.A. Donnelly & Cpl Preedy x reported missing from previous day. Above were in firing trenches. 2Lt. F.W. SHORT. posted to Bty. ~~[illegible]~~ Fired 30 rounds.	'x' afterwards reported Prisoners of War in Germany.
10th May ——	Busy day. Fired 544 rounds	
11 " ——	Quiet. Fired 47 rounds.	
12 " ——	Fired 102 round. Right Section went out of action contemplating rest. Detailed to proceed to Abeele.	
13 " ——	German attacked heavily. Left X commenced firing at 5 am. & continued all day. Right X returned. Fired 832 rds. Weather very bad.	

(73989) W4141—463. 400,000. 9/14. H.&J.Ltd. Forms/C. 2118/10.

Instructions regarding War Diaries and Intelligence Summaries are contained in F. S. Regs., Part II. and the Staff Manual respectively. Title pages will be prepared in manuscript.

WAR DIARY
or
INTELLIGENCE SUMMARY.
(Erase heading not required.)

Army Form C. 2118.

Hour, Date, Place	Summary of Events and Information	Remarks and references to Appendices
14th May. N Ypres	Weather wet & cold. Fired 40 rounds.	
15th " —	~~[illegible]~~ Fired 151 rounds & registered several points.	
16th " —	Nothing unusual. Weather fine. Fired 38 rds.	
17th " —	L° except in morning when Battery was ~~[illegible]~~ shelled by* a 6in gun. Right section dug out had narrow escape as one shell came through roof & went blind. Weather wet. Fired no rounds	* From the direction of Polygon wood — about 20 or 30 rds. fired
18th " —	Weather wet. Fired late previous night & early in morning. Fired 64 rounds. ~~[illegible]~~	
19th " —	All quiet. ~~[illegible]~~. Fired no rounds.	

Instructions regarding War Diaries and Intelligence Summaries are contained in F. S. Regs., Part II. and the Staff Manual respectively. Title pages will be prepared in manuscript.

WAR DIARY
or
INTELLIGENCE SUMMARY.
(Erase heading not required.)

Army Form C. 2118.

Hour, Date, Place	Summary of Events and Information	Remarks and references to Appendices
20th May. Near Ypres	Quiet. Weather fine. Fired 8 rounds. Saw our aircraft-guns get direct hit on Enemy's aeroplane which appeared to fall in our lines. Amm^n now restricted to 12 rds per diem	
21st May — " —	quiet — weather fine — fired 11 rounds —	
22nd May — " —	Quiet. Fired 8 rounds. Very severe storm at night during which an attack was made against French troops on our left	
23rd May — " —	Quiet. Fired 11 rounds. Bty visited by Brig Genl Arbuthnot CRA 28th Divn. Weather fine	
24th May — " —	Attack by enemy about 3 AM. The attack started by gas fumes and heavy rifle fire. The enemy poured a tremendous shell fire on our Infy trenches and supports, afterwards turning their attention to our gun positions, aided by their airmen who were out very early and more daring than usual. Bty commenced firing about 3.10 AM and	

Army Form C. 2118.

Instructions regarding War Diaries and Intelligence Summaries are contained in F. S. Regs., Part II. and the Staff Manual respectively. Title pages will be prepared in manuscript.

WAR DIARY
or
INTELLIGENCE SUMMARY.
(*Erase heading not required.*)

Hour, Date, Place	Summary of Events and Information	Remarks and references to Appendices
24th Apr (Contd)	continued shelling enemy's positions at various points from 09° L to 22° 97 with scarcely a break until about 12 midnight firing a total of 1420 Rds. Very hard day in which all ranks worked splendidly. Several men suffered in the early morning from gas fumes and from gas shells. These men gradually got better and by evening were quite fit again. 2/Lt D.R. Mackenzie proceeded to Obs Stn at commencement of attack and was able to forward very useful information by telephone. As one wire of the Bty remained intact during most of the day this was the main source of ~~information from the~~ communication between the Bty on our post & and the 10th Inf Bde Hd Qrs, and was for some time the only ~~one~~ channel of communication. In addition	

Instructions regarding War Diaries and Intelligence Summaries are contained in F. S. Regs., Part II. and the Staff Manual respectively. Title pages will be prepared in manuscript.

WAR DIARY
or
INTELLIGENCE SUMMARY.
(Erase heading not required.)

Army Form C. 2118.

Hour, Date, Place	Summary of Events and Information	Remarks and references to Appendices
24th May (Contd)	to this Bty Hd Qtrs on more than one occasion succeeded in keeping the 16th Inf Bde & 6th Divn in communication. 2Lt D.P. Mackenzie's services on this day appeared to have been deserving of recognition. He was suffering from the effects of gas and while in this condition several times in conjunction with his telephonist No 78665 Gnr G. Owens mended the telephone wires under heavy shell fire. He collected much useful information and observed fire from a much shelled spot.	
	The guns stood the strain of firing well. Only one gun was temporarily out of action (owing to the control plunger having seized)	
	Weather fine	

(73989) W4141—463. 400,000. 9/14. H.&J.Ltd. Forms/C. 2118/10.

Army Form C. 2118.

WAR DIARY
or
INTELLIGENCE SUMMARY.
(Erase heading not required.)

Instructions regarding War Diaries and Intelligence Summaries are contained in F. S. Regs., Part II. and the Staff Manual respectively. Title pages will be prepared in manuscript.

Hour, Date, Place	Summary of Events and Information	Remarks and references to Appendices
0·45 AM 25th [illegible] Ypres	Ordered to continue firing at a slow rate on the last target engaged.	
1·0 AM — do —	Capt. [illegible] arrived with a [illegible] guns lent by the 146th [illegible], to replace the one with damaged buffer.	
2·30 AM — do —	Orders received to cease fire, the gunners then turned in. After this the day was comparatively quiet. A new zone having been allotted, a new [illegible] was reconnoitred and found, this time close to the Bty, and during the course of the day 300 Rds were fired on the enemy['s] working parties who were entrenching at the point where they had penetrated our line between the YPRES-MENIN road and the YPRES-ROULERS railway. As it could not be known that the change	

Instructions regarding War Diaries and Intelligence Summaries are contained in F. S. Regs., Part II. and the Staff Manual respectively. Title pages will be prepared in manuscript.

WAR DIARY
or
INTELLIGENCE SUMMARY.
(Erase heading not required.)

Army Form C. 2118.

Hour, Date, Place	Summary of Events and Information	Remarks and references to Appendices
25th May Nr YPRES	of zone was permanent and has communication with the Infy on the old zone NE of SAINT JEAN where our Infy had fallen back on to a new line was important 2Lt Short and a telephonist proceeded to the old Ob Stn at Battalion Hd Qtrs and remained there during the day. Weather fine	
7-0 AM 26th May — " —	Enemy shelled the ground around and behind the Bty with a 5.9" How. An aeroplane was observing and it is believed our anti aircraft guns were the objective. A large mill just in rear was set on fire being doubtless taken for an observation station. An enemys machine gun emplacement was observed in course of construction and a total of 28 rounds were fired at it during the course of the afternoon	

Instructions regarding War Diaries and Intelligence Summaries are contained in F. S. Regs., Part II. and the Staff Manual respectively. Title pages will be prepared in manuscript.

WAR DIARY
or
INTELLIGENCE SUMMARY.
(Erase heading not required.)

Army Form C. 2118.

Hour, Date, Place	Summary of Events and Information	Remarks and references to Appendices
26th May YPRES	In Camp [illegible] Weather fine	
27th May — do —	Several new trench lines in the zone referred to were registered, a total of 40 Rds being fired during day. ~~Weather fine~~	
9.0 P.M. — do —	The left section was withdrawn from action and sent to wagon line, being relieved by a section of 53rd Bty RFA Weather fine.	
28th May — do —	The enemys working parties and a machine gun emplacement were fired on at intervals during the day. 26 Rds were fired.	
[illegible] — do —	The left section marched to ABEELE distance about 10 miles from gun position.	
[illegible] — do —	The right section was withdrawn, being relieved by a second section of the 53rd Bty RFA, and marched to join remainder of Bty at ABEELE	

(73989) W4141—463. 400,000. 9/14. H.&J.Ltd. Forms/C. 2118/10.

Instructions regarding War Diaries and Intelligence Summaries are contained in F. S. Regs., Part II. and the Staff Manual respectively. Title pages will be prepared in manuscript.

WAR DIARY
or
INTELLIGENCE SUMMARY.
(Erase heading not required.)

Army Form C. 2118.

Hour, Date, Place	Summary of Events and Information	Remarks and references to Appendices
29th May '15 ABEELE	The Bty rested for the day. Weather remained fine.	
2 PM 30th " "	The Bty marched to HERZEELE [illegible] arriving there about 4-30 P.M. Distance about 8 miles.	
	Billets were found at farms, the weather being fine most men preferred to live in the open.	
31st " HERZELLE	Camp routine. Overhaul of equipment, harness, clothing etc. Weather fine.	
	An airship apparently a Zeppelin was observed at 8.50 P.M. travelling westerly.	
	[illegible] Major R.A.	

(73989) W4141—463. 400,000. 9/14. H.&J.Ltd. Forms/C. 2118/10.

Confidential

War Diary

of

69th Battery R.F.A.

Volume IV

From 1st June 1915 to 30th June 1915

69th Bty RFA

Instructions regarding War Diaries and Intelligence Summaries are contained in F. S. Regs., Part II. and the Staff Manual respectively. Title pages will be prepared in manuscript.

WAR DIARY
or
~~INTELLIGENCE SUMMARY.~~
(Erase heading not required.)

Army Form C. 2118.

Volume IV

Hour, Date, Place	Summary of Events and Information	Remarks and references to Appendices Initial	
1st June 1915 HERZEELE	Battery resting. Overhaul of equipment etc. Camp routine. Fine	FWS Lt.	Reference Maps. Belgium Sheets 28 NW & SW
2nd — do —	— do — — do —	FWS	
3rd — do —	His Majesty King George's Birthday. The Bty paraded in dismounted drill order at 12 noon, presented arms and gave three cheers. Fine. 2/Lt E. A. NODIN. posted to Bty.	FWS.	
4th — do —	The Bty paraded with the remainder of 31st Bde RFA at 11.45 am and were addressed by Major General Bulfin Commanding 28th Division B.E.F. Fine, passing clouds, light westerly wind at last.	FWS.	
5th — do —	Camp routine. Fine	FWS.	
6th — do —	— do — — do — Divine Service at 31st Bde RFA Ammn Column at 9 am.	FWS.	
7th — do —	Camp routine. Fine.	FWS.	
8th — do —	— do —	FWS.	

(73989) W4141—463. 400,000. 9/14. H.&J.Ltd. Forms/C. 2118/10.

Instructions regarding War Diaries and Intelligence Summaries are contained in F. S. Regs., Part II. and the Staff Manual respectively. Title pages will be prepared in manuscript.

WAR DIARY
or
~~INTELLIGENCE~~ SUMMARY.
(Erase heading not required.)

Army Form C. 2118.

Volume IV

Hour, Date, Place	Summary of Events and Information	Remarks and references to Appendices
9th June/15 HERZEELE	Camp routine. Heavy thunderstorm during afternoon	JWS
10th —do— —do—	—do— Fine Showery	JWS
11th —do— —do—	—do— Fine	JWS
12th —do— —do—	—do— Fine	JWS
13th —do— —do—	—do— Fine	JWS
14th —do— —do—	—do— Fine but chilly	JWS
15th —do— —do—	—do— —do—	JWS
16th —do— —do—	—do— Fine. Major WILLIS accompanied by Lt. MACKENZIE rode to DICKEBUSCH to reconnoitre position occupied by A Bty 48th Bde RFA, with a view to taking it over. Orders received at 11 P.M. to be prepared to move on following day.	JWS
17th —do— —do—	Orders received about mid-day to move one section to position near DICKEBUSCH. Lt. SHORT proceeded in advance to arrange wagon line.	

(73989) W4141—463. 400,000. 9/14. H.&J.Ltd. Forms/C. 2118/10.

Instructions regarding War Diaries and Intelligence Summaries are contained in F. S. Regs., Part II. and the Staff Manual respectively. Title pages will be prepared in manuscript.

WAR DIARY
or
INTELLIGENCE SUMMARY.
(Erase heading not required.)

Army Form C. 2118.

Volume IV

Hour, Date, Place	Summary of Events and Information	Remarks and references to Appendices
4-30 pm 17th June. HERZEELE	The Right section under Major WILLIS and Lt NODIN marched to new position, about 14 miles, arriving there about 10-30 pm. The guns were at once put into action to replace Left section of A Bty 48th Bde, withdrawn, under command of Major ERSKINE. RFA.	
12 Midnight — DICKEBUSCH	A message was received from our Infy to the effect that Bombs and a Trench mortar were worrying them. No 3 gun fired 5 rounds in co-operation with A Bty 48th Bde, and the enemy were silenced.	JWS
	Battery position H 35 D. 6. 4. – An old French position with well built dug outs alongside a red farm still partially standing and just South of the ETANG DE DICKEBUSCH. The front of the Bty entirely screened from observation by the enemy by a long ridge. The Obs Stn about 500 yds away, a dug out and a cottage close by, the latter however, used by several Batteries. The view from the Obs Stn over the spur on which ST ELOI stands, very extensive, and only a small	

Instructions regarding War Diaries and Intelligence Summaries are contained in F. S. Regs., Part II. and the Staff Manual respectively. Title pages will be prepared in manuscript.

WAR DIARY
or
INTELLIGENCE SUMMARY.
(Erase heading not required.)

Army Form C. 2118.

Volume IV

Hour, Date, Place	Summary of Events and Information	Remarks and references to Appendices
17th June 15 Nr DICKEBUSCH (Contd)	portion of the zone allotted was concealed, (by BOIS CONFLUENT) and had to be observed from our front trenches, to which three telephone wires run a distance of about three miles, the approach fairly safe. The wagon line is about 2 miles in rear of position, between DICKEBUSCH and RENINGHELST. Situation very quiet. The weather remained fine but chilly.	JWS.
18th — do — do —	Registration was carried out during the morning on enemy's front line trenches near ST ELOI, a total of 12 rounds being fired. Major WILLIS assumed command of the position at mid-day. The left section under Lt MACKENZIE marched from HERZEELE at 4-30 PM and joined Bty in action at 9-30 PM relieving Right section of A Bty 4th Bde RFA. Weather still fine though chilly.	JWS.

(73989) W4141—463. 400,000. 9/14. H.&J.Ltd. Forms/C. 2118/10.

Instructions regarding War Diaries and Intelligence Summaries are contained in F. S. Regs., Part II. and the Staff Manual respectively. Title pages will be prepared in manuscript.

WAR DIARY
or
INTELLIGENCE SUMMARY.
(Erase heading not required.)

Army Form C. 2118.

Volume IV

Hour, Date, Place	Summary of Events and Information	Remarks and references to Appendices
19th June Nr DICKEBUSCH	Registration carried out during morning from front line trenches by Lt MACKENZIE, 11 Rounds being fired. Enemy very quiet weather bright but chilly, northerly wind.	FWS.
20th — do — — do —	Major WILLIS reconnoitred front line trenches and interviewed Battalion Comdrs. Suffolks (Trenches P2. 3 + 4) Northumberland Fusiliers (Trench P1) and also arranged for relaying of telephone wires to P2 and P3 trenches.	
5.30PM — do — do —	Received information that enemy were supposed to be withdrawing a portion of their troops from our front and was asked whether the Officer could confirm it. No movement of any sort is however could be detected.	FWS.
11.30PM — do — do —	Warning received that Infy Bde on our left would fire (rapid) at 2.30AM to ascertain enemy's strength. The message did not say how the desired information would be obtained from this procedure.	

Instructions regarding War Diaries and Intelligence Summaries are contained in F. S. Regs., Part II. and the Staff Manual respectively. Title pages will be prepared in manuscript.

WAR DIARY
or
INTELLIGENCE SUMMARY.
(Erase heading not required.)

Army Form C. 2118.

Volume IV

Hour, Date, Place	Summary of Events and Information	Remarks and references to Appendices
20th June Nr DICKEBUSCH (Contd)	Weather fine but cold wind northerly. 4 rounds fired.	FWS
21st 2·30 AM — do — do —	Infy rapid fire took place and drew considerable gun fire from the enemy and men working in communicating trenches suffered.	
9·30 AM — do — do —	OC reconnoitred proposed new alternative gun position with OC 31st Bde RFA, in square N 3 A 5.3	
3·50 PM — do — do —	OC P3 trench asked for help against snipers in PICCADILLY FARM and 5 rounds were fired.	FWS
7·40 PM — do — do —	Registered two targets. 9 rounds fired.	
11·0 PM — do — do —	The Infy were very active during the night and the Bde on our right opened fire.	
	Weather fine and much warmer.	
4·45 AM 22nd June — do —	Enemy sent several shell near Bty position	
9·0 AM — do — do —	Desultory shelling by a 4" How continued till at this hour the Bty opened fire on enemy's gun position previously	FWS

Instructions regarding War Diaries and Intelligence Summaries are contained in F. S. Regs., Part II. and the Staff Manual respectively. Title pages will be prepared in manuscript.

WAR DIARY
or
INTELLIGENCE SUMMARY.
(*Erase heading not required.*)

Army Form C. 2118.

Volume IV

Hour, Date, Place	Summary of Events and Information	Remarks and references to Appendices
22nd June 15 Nr DICKEBUSCH (Contd)	registered by aeroplane observation, when the enemy's fire which was principally directed on the DICKEBUSCH - VIERSTRAAT road, died down. Rounds fired. 4.	H.S.
7.30 Pm — do —	Heavy firing was heard to the north east.	
	Day fine and hot. Wind north to north west	
23rd June 15 Nr DICKEBUSCH	Day very quiet	
3-10 Pm — do — — do —	Infantry at S2 Trench asked for a few rounds to be fired at enemy's front line. This was done, three rounds being fired	H.S.
9.50 Pm — do — — do —	Three rounds were fired at a bombing party of the enemy in PICCADILLY FARM O.8.A.3.7. This took place at the request of the Infy who observed the fire as effective	
[illegible] — do	Weather fine until evening when a little rain fell.	
2.20 AM 24th June 15 — do —	A call was received from the Infy (Royal Fusiliers) asking us to fire on enemy's machine guns in front of S4 Trench.	

(73989) W4141—463. 400,000. 9/14. H.&J.Ltd. Forms/C. 2118/10.

Instructions regarding War Diaries and Intelligence Summaries are contained in F. S. Regs., Part II. and the Staff Manual respectively. Title pages will be prepared in manuscript.

WAR DIARY
or
INTELLIGENCE SUMMARY.
(Erase heading not required.)

Army Form C. 2118.

Volume IV

Hour, Date, Place	Summary of Events and Information	Remarks and references to Appendices
24th June 15 By DICKEBUSCH (Contd)	4 rounds were fired and two holes were blown in the enemys trench. Our Infy laid two machine guns on the damaged trenches but no attempt was made to repair them.	
9-15 AM — do —	As a reply to the enemy shelling our front with crumps, four rounds were fired at enemys Bty in O15 B68, which had previously been located by aeroplane. This had the desired effect.	JHS.
5-40 PM — do —	Registration was carried out on various objectives. 11 rounds being fired.	
	Quiet day. Weather overcast with occasional sunshine. Slight rain during afternoon.	
11-55 PM — do —	Five rounds were fired at request of Infy at a trench mortar which was very busy in O2 0 65. The effect could not be ascertained with accuracy but the trench mortar did not trouble us any more during the night.	JHS.

(73989) W4141—463. 400,000. 9/14. H.&J.Ltd. Forms/C. 2118/10.

Instructions regarding War Diaries and Intelligence Summaries are contained in F. S. Regs., Part II. and the Staff Manual respectively. Title pages will be prepared in manuscript.

WAR DIARY
or
INTELLIGENCE SUMMARY.
(Erase heading not required.)

Army Form C. 2118.

Volume IV

Hour, Date, Place	Summary of Events and Information	Remarks and references to Appendices
12·12 AM June 24th fr. DICKEBUSCH (Contd)	A machine gun was troubling our Infy, said by them to be in PICCADILLY FARM. One round was fired and the machine gun silenced.	
10 30 AM June 25th — do —	Divine service conducted by Rev. H Royse C.F. was held in Bty position	
1·37 pm — do —	Registration of new zone. 6 rounds were fired at enemy trenches in front of BOIS QUARANTE, 078. The Bty having been detailed to cover all the trenches occupied by the Royal Fusiliers, trenches O3 and O4 were brought into our zone, in addition to all the P trenches.	H.W.S.
3·30 pm — do —	4 rounds were fired at PICCADILLY FARM. Snipers were very active in this neighbourhood, and machine guns were also said to be there.	
	Very wet day, particularly during the afternoon and evening.	
10·30 AM June 26th — do —	The enemy fired a few light shrapnel at the ridge in front of Bty, whilst a hostile aeroplane was about dropping smoke balls.	

Instructions regarding War Diaries and Intelligence Summaries are contained in F. S. Regs., Part II. and the Staff Manual respectively. Title pages will be prepared in manuscript.

WAR DIARY
or
~~INTELLIGENCE~~ SUMMARY.
(Erase heading not required.)

Army Form C. 2118.

Volume IV

Hour, Date, Place	Summary of Events and Information	Remarks and references to Appendices
June 26th Nr DICKEBUSCH (Contd)	One man of 118th Bty was wounded and a few splinters fell to right of Bty.	
5·15 to 6·5 PM — do —	Registration was carried out on enemys support and communication trenches. 13 rounds being fired.	
10·50 PM — do —	1 round fired at machine gun in front of P4 trench, at request of Infy	FHS.
	Fine warm day. slight rain in the evening.	
9·10 AM 27th June — do —	Fired 12 rounds on enemy's support trenches at request of our Infy, as a reprisal.	
11·55 PM — do —	2 rounds fired at enemys machine guns in front of P4 trench	FHS.
11·45 PM — do —	1 round fired on the last target. All the above firing was at the request of Infy, who sent a message of thanks, saying the fire was effective.	
	Very wet day	
28th June — do —	Very quiet day. Cold and showery.	FHS.

Instructions regarding War Diaries and Intelligence Summaries are contained in F. S. Regs., Part II. and the Staff Manual respectively. Title pages will be prepared in manuscript.

WAR DIARY
or
INTELLIGENCE SUMMARY.
(Erase heading not required.)

Army Form C. 2118.

Volume IV

Hour, Date, Place	Summary of Events and Information	Remarks and references to Appendices
1-15-1.35 Pm 29th June 15 Nr DICKEBUSCH	Enemy shelled Infy trenches with Whiz bangs. 6 rounds were fired on enemy trenches as a reprisal.	
3-40 Pm —do—	Shelled enemy's support trenches in front of P2 line. 22 rounds fired. Effective	H.S.
6-10 Pm —do—	Enemy observed repairing above trenches, 8 rounds were fired at the new work.	
	Weather fair. Heavy rain during evening.	
30th June 15 —do—	Enemy shelled DICKEBUSCH during the afternoon which caused several casualties amongst civilian population.	H.S.
4-25 Pm —do—	Shelled enemy's communication trenches, four rounds being fired	
	Fine but cloudy during morning, afternoon very clear.	[illegible] Major R.A.

28th Division

Confidential

121/7170

War Diary
of
69th Battery RFA
Volume VII

From 1st Sept 1915 to 30th Sept 1915

Appendix I to III

Instructions regarding War Diaries and Intelligence Summaries are contained in F. S. Regs., Part II. and the Staff Manual respectively. Title pages will be prepared in manuscript.

WAR DIARY
or
~~INTELLIGENCE SUMMARY.~~
(Erase heading not required.)

Army Form C. 2118.

Volume VII

Place	Date	Hour	Summary of Events and Information	Remarks and references to Appendices
Nr KEMMEL	Sept 1st	10 AM	Several large H E Shell were fired by enemy towards KEMMEL about N 27 B 5 9. where a new work appeared to be in progress of construction. Considerable movement after shelling began and as this point is in view of the enemy, probably some movement drew the fire.	Reference Maps BELGIUM, SHEET 28 NW and SW.
— do —	— do —	11 AM	3 Heavy Shrapnel struck KEMMEL HILL. No damage was done.	
— do —	— do —	11.30 AM	A working party was engaged at N 30 A 4 5. 5 Rds were fired which appeared effective and the work stopped.	
— do —	— do —	3.3 PM	3 Rds were fired at a working party at O 26 B 2 1. These also appeared effective	H.H.
— do —	— do —	5.30 PM to 6.3 PM	Our own 8" guns commenced shelling PECKHAM FARM, the fourth round was very effective as a party of about 9 of the enemy persistently tried to extricate someone or something in the farm yard. 14 Rds of Shrapnel was fired at intervals by the Bty and appeared very effective, several of the enemy being seen to fall. The enemy retaliated by sending 6" and 8" shells over J 5 trenches. They did not appear to do any damage. Two salvos of four shrapnel were also fired which burst near 103rd Bty. Lt WEBER of 1/Welsh took bearings of troughs and a hole in a hedge made by these shell. They were 102° Mag taken from a point 40 yds SE of DOCTORS HOUSE N 21 C 6 7. Rain fell at intervals during the day	

Instructions regarding War Diaries and Intelligence Summaries are contained in F. S. Regs., Part II. and the Staff Manual respectively. Title pages will be prepared in manuscript.

WAR DIARY
or
~~INTELLIGENCE SUMMARY~~.
(Erase heading not required.)

Army Form C. 2118.

Volume VII

Place	Date Sept	Hour	Summary of Events and Information	Remarks and references to Appendices
Mt KEMMEL	2nd	11-30AM	Heavy shelling by enemy on some point invisible to the right front and also heavy shrapnel near HANNARTS FARM. The OC 31st Bde RFA ordered retaliation for this on enemys front	
— do —	— do —	12·30PM	line trenches. After 12 rounds had been fired the shrapnel fire ceased, but a few rounds from a whiz bang were fired at F5 trenches.	
— do —	— do	3·30PM	A few shrapnel were again fired at F5 trenches. At about this hour some very heavy shelling was heard and seen in the direction of HOOGE and a considerable amount of shrapnel fire N of YPRES. It was impossible to say definitely whose shell was seen at HOOGE but fighting went on in that direction practically all the afternoon.	
— do —	— do —	5.30PM to 6.15PM	A considerable amount of shell of sorts (about 13) were fired at KEMMEL HILL and air lines a good deal damaged. Some very heavy shell probably 8" fell on the forward slope, below Obs Stns, the remainder, apparently 4", were about crest sides and back of hill. The Artly Observers on the Hill had rather an an anxious time. It has been stated this is the most serious shelling of the Hill since Nov '14.	Hd
— do —	— do —	6.45PM	Just at dusk a mine was exploded by the enemy, in or near G2 trench. The explosion was preceded by a heavy shell and was followed by a considerable amount of shelling of all sorts, of which some fell very close to F5 trench. Luckily this was seen from KEMMEL	

2353 Wt. W2544/1454 700,000 5/15 D. D. & L. A.D.S.S. Forms/C 2118.

Instructions regarding War Diaries and Intelligence Summaries are contained in F. S. Regs., Part II. and the Staff Manual respectively. Title pages will be prepared in manuscript.

WAR DIARY
or
~~INTELLIGENCE SUMMARY~~.
(Erase heading not required.)

Army Form C. 2118.

Volume VII

Place	Date Sep	Hour	Summary of Events and Information	Remarks and references to Appendices
Mt KEMMEL	2nd Contd	6.45pm	as owing to neglect at the Infy end, the Bty was out of telephone communication, except through Battalion Hd Qtrs. In retaliation 6 rounds were fired in section salvos at BLACK REDOUBT. Very little rifle fire was heard and the shelling died down about 7 pm.	
— do —	— do —	7.20pm	A heavy cannonade was again started in the HOOGE direction, apparently by the enemy. Flashes were angled, bearing 89° and 97° Mag taken from dugout at N26 B19, the latter flash being from a big gun. This information was forwarded in progress report in the hope it might be of use to locate enemy's guns.	
			Heavy rain during the afternoon and most of the evening.	
			Great difficulty experienced in keeping up direct telephonic communication with trenches. The two lines, one to G2 & one to J3 trenches continually being broken, usually between Batt Hd Qtrs & the firing trenches. The Infy are responsible for these portions but very little effort is made to keep them in working order. On several occasions lately our linesman has repaired the line between the above points, and ~~on two~~ at least twice not more than 100 yds from fire trenches.	
— do —	3rd		Heavy rain practically all night and day. No movement seen and no firing done. Wonderful to relate, it was reported by Adjt 1/Welsh that no casualties occurred at the	

2353 Wt W2544/1454 700,000 5/15 D. D. & L. A.D.S.S. Forms/C 2118.

Instructions regarding War Diaries and Intelligence Summaries are contained in F. S. Regs., Part II. and the Staff Manual respectively. Title pages will be prepared in manuscript.

WAR DIARY
or
~~INTELLIGENCE SUMMARY.~~

(Erase heading not required.)

Army Form C. 2118.

Volume VII

Place	Date	Hour	Summary of Events and Information	Remarks and references to Appendices
	Sept Contd			
Nr KEMMEL	3rd		mine explosion and bombardment of previous evening	
— do —	— do —	7.12pm	It was reported that we would explode a mine from G2 trench. The Bty was prepared to assist if necessary. No call was received and at 10.20pm a message was received to say the mine had been exploded. No further facts are known	G.S.
— do —	4th		Raining practically all day. No movement was seen on firing line	H.L.
— do —	5th	10 am	Registration carried out on a dug out at N25 A10 6 supposed to be an observing station 5 Rds fired	
— do —	— do —	3 pm	A regrettable accident occurred in the Bty gun line. BSM Decks with several other NCOs and men attempted to take a blind german shell to pieces with the result that the fuze exploded. The following were severely injured, BSM Decks, Sgt Roberts, Fitter Sergt Bates & Gnr Styles, slightly injured, Gnr Goulethorn.	G.S.
— do —	— do —	4 pm	A working party in communicating trench at N30 A92 was seen and 4 Rds were fired at them stopping the work.	
— do —	— do —	5.30pm	The 9.2" How shelled SPANBROEKMOLEN. Shell appeared effective. The Bty was standing by in case any Germans should be visible. Nothing could be seen	
— do —	— do —	6.30pm	The enemy replied at 6.30pm with 7 4" HE Shell about the rear of F2 trench	

Army Form C. 2118.

WAR DIARY
or
~~INTELLIGENCE SUMMARY.~~
(Erase heading not required.)

Volume VII

Instructions regarding War Diaries and Intelligence Summaries are contained in F. S. Regs., Part II. and the Staff Manual respectively. Title pages will be prepared in manuscript.

Place	Date	Hour	Summary of Events and Information	Remarks and references to Appendices
Mt KEMMEL	Sept 5th	9-0 PM to 9.30 PM	A searchlight was seen working from about the direction of WARNETON.	JMS
			A lot of rain fell during the morning, the afternoon however was very fine and clear	
— " —	6th	12.40 PM	The enemy put about 10 small shell on SCHERPENBURG HILL. Several shell were seen to fall close to the MOLEN but it is doubtful if any damage was done as the gun was almost at extreme range.	
— " —	— " —	5.30 PM	A working party was observed in support trench at O 25 B 6 2 and fired on. 3 rds dispersed the enemy.	JMS
— " —	— " —	6 PM	Enemy retaliated for fire on BLACK REDOUBT by sending a few 6" HE on J 4 & J 5 trenches	
			Fine day though cloudy. Aeroplanes very active, our own in particular	
— " —	7th	10.30 AM	A lot of HE and heavy shrapnel were fired by the enemy, about N 10 & N 14. Results not known. An aeroplane was over at the time, dropping smoke balls	
— " —	— " —	1-40 PM	4 Rds were fired at BOIS L'ENFER (O 25 D 0 9) in retaliation for enemy shelling	JM
			Enemy aeroplanes very active during the afternoon and evening, one particularly so, coming a long way over in rear of KEMMEL	
			Fine day, though the light was not good	
— do —	8th	10.45 AM	A message was received from sniping post of 6/Welsh reporting a working party at SPANBROEK	

2353 Wt. W2544/1454 700,000 5/15 D. D. & L. A.D.S.S. Forms/C 2118.

Instructions regarding War Diaries and Intelligence Summaries are contained in F. S. Regs., Part II. and the Staff Manual respectively. Title pages will be prepared in manuscript.

WAR DIARY
or
INTELLIGENCE ~~SUMMARY~~.
(Erase heading not required.)

Army Form C. 2118.

Volume VII

Place	Date	Hour	Summary of Events and Information	Remarks and references to Appendices
	Sept			
N. KEMMEL	8th		MOLEN. It was too misty to see from Observing station. 4 Rds were fired and reported by Infy as being effective	[illegible]
— do —	— do —	5. P.M.	3 Rds Registration were fired at a trench, O.25.A.7.3	
— do —	— do —	5.35 P.M.	3 large H.E. Shell were seen to fall in rear of F4 trench. F4 & F5 trenches appear to receive these shell as a daily 'hate' from the enemy, probably in return for our daily bombardment of BLACK REDOUBT.	[illegible]
— do —	— do —	7.30 P.M.	A large fire was seen in rear of German trenches and to the right of SPANBROEK MOLEN. Fine day but the light was very bad for Observation	
— do —	9th	1. P.M.	Enemy fired 3 H.E. Shell and 12 Whiz bangs near F4 trench apparently doing no damage.	
— do —	— do —	2.45 P.M.	Orders having been received to assist in bombardment of BLACK REDOUBT, 4 Rds were fired to verify registration.	Appendix I
— do —	— do —	5.15 P.M.	5 H.E. Shell and 5 Shrapnel were fired on above target. Fire appeared very effective. The enemy replied with 3 H.E. Shell in rear of F4.	
— do —	— do —	8.5 P.M.	A sharp burst of rifle fire along our front. Nothing could be ascertained as to cause until the fire had died down, when G2 trench reported it was presumed a mine had been exploded near H trenches. Fine day light bad except during a portion of afternoon	[illegible]

Instructions regarding War Diaries and Intelligence Summaries are contained in F. S. Regs., Part II. and the Staff Manual respectively. Title pages will be prepared in manuscript.

WAR DIARY
or
~~INTELLIGENCE SUMMARY.~~
(Erase heading not required.)

Army Form C. 2118.

Volume VII

Place	Date	Hour	Summary of Events and Information	Remarks and references to Appendices
	Sept			
Nr KEMMEL	10th	1.30 pm	6 whizz bangs fell near F4 trench, but did not appear to do any damage.	
—do—	—do—	4. pm	A working party was observed in work at O 25 A 9 8½. 3 Rds were fired and two at intervals later. The latter two rounds were seen to burst right among party and it seemed almost certain they must have had some casualties.	JWS.
—do—	—do—	4.30 pm	2 large H.E. Shell fell in rear of F5 trench. Two similar shell fell in the same place at 5.35 pm the latter apparently in reply to our Howitzers firing on BLACK REDOUBT. Fine day with exceptionally good light in the afternoon.	
—do—	11th	3.50 pm	Enemy dropped 5 HE Shell in rear of F5 trench. Reported by F4 that no damage was done. This was no doubt in return for Howitzers on BLACK REDOUBT and 18 pdrs firing on SPAN BROEK MOLEN	
—do—	—do—	4.30 pm to 4.45 pm	Enemy put about 12 heavy shrapnel in region of KEMMEL HILL. A mounted trench Officer and Orderly were seen on top of the Hill and probably these had been seen by the enemy. The light was bad during the greater portion of the day and no movement was seen. Fine day.	JWS.
—do—	12th	10 AM	Working party seen and fired on at N 30 A 2 1. 5 Rds fired and the work stopped.	

2353 Wt. W2544/1454 700,000 5/15 D. D. & L. A.D.S.S. Forms/C 2118.

Instructions regarding War Diaries and Intelligence Summaries are contained in F. S. Regs., Part II. and the Staff Manual respectively. Title pages will be prepared in manuscript.

WAR DIARY
or
~~INTELLIGENCE SUMMARY.~~
(Erase heading not required.)

Army Form C. 2118.

Volume VII

Place	Date	Hour	Summary of Events and Information	Remarks and references to Appendices
	Sept.			
Nr KEMMEL	12th	10-35am	Working party observed at about O19 D 32. 6 Rds were fired and the party dispersed	
— do —	— do —	11-10am	Registration was carried out on some houses about O19 D 71 where the above party were seen to disappear. 12 Rds fired	
— do —	— do —	11-50am	Orders having been received for the Bty to take part in combined shoot on BLACK REDOUBT 5 Rds were fired to verify fuzes etc	H.L.
— do —	— do —	4-0pm	5 Rds H.E. and 5 Rds Shrapnel were fired on BLACK REDOUBT in combination with other Batteries. Fire appeared very effective. The enemy replied with a few whizbangs in rear of 4·5 trucks	Appendix II
— do —	— do —	6-20pm	A house in our lines about N 29 b was seen to be burning furiously. Fine day with splendid light most of day	
— do —	13th	4-30pm	Working party again seen at O19 D 32. As the Bty was waiting for Balloon to register some points fire could not be opened.	
	— do —	5-25pm	Information received that the balloon was not available fire was opened on the above party. 3 Rds were fired and the party dispersed. Fine day fairly good light	H.L.
— do —	14th	10-30am	Large puffs of smoke were observed behind SPANBROEK MOLEN. This is thought to be the engine of a steam excavator. A Bty fired Shrapnel in this direction and no more smoke was seen	

2353 Wt. W2544/1454 700,000 5/15 D. D. & L. A.D.S.S. Forms/C. 2118.

Instructions regarding War Diaries and Intelligence Summaries are contained in F. S. Regs., Part II. and the Staff Manual respectively. Title pages will be prepared in manuscript.

WAR DIARY
or
~~INTELLIGENCE SUMMARY.~~
(Erase heading not required.)

Army Form C. 2118.

Volume VII

Place	Date	Hour	Summary of Events and Information	Remarks and references to Appendices
	Sept			
Nr KEMMEL	12th	10-35AM	Working party observed at about O19 D 32. 6 Rds were fired and the party dispersed	
— do —	— do —	11-10AM	Registration was carried out on some houses about O19 D 71 where the above party were seen to disappear. 12 Rds fired	
— do —	— do —	11-30AM	Orders having been received for the Bty to take part in combined shoot on BLACK REDOUBT	THL
			5 Rds were fired to verify fuzes etc.	
— do —	— do —	4-0PM	5 Rds HE and 5 Rds Shrapnel were fired on BLACK REDOUBT in combination with other Batteries. Fire appeared very effective. The enemy replied with a few whiz bangs in rear of F4 F5 trenches	Appendix II
— do —	— do —	6-20PM	A house in our lines about N29 B was seen to be burning furiously.	
			Fine day with splendid light most of day.	
— do —	13th	4-35PM	Working party again seen at O19 D 32. As the Bty was waiting for Balloon to register some points, fire could not be opened.	
— do —	— do —	5-35PM	Information received that the Balloon was not available, fire was opened on the above party. 3 Rds were fired and the party dispersed	THL
			Fine day, fairly good light.	
— do —	14th	10:30AM	Large puffs of smoke were observed behind SPANBROEK MOLEN. This is thought to be the engine of a steam excavator. A Bty fired Shrapnel in this direction and no more smoke was seen	

2353 Wt. W2544/1454 700,000 5/15 D. D. & L. A.D.S.S. Forms/C 2118.

Instructions regarding War Diaries and Intelligence Summaries are contained in F. S. Regs., Part II, and the Staff Manual respectively. Title pages will be prepared in manuscript.

WAR DIARY
or
~~INTELLIGENCE SUMMARY~~.
(Erase heading not required.)

Army Form C. 2118.

Volume VII

Place	Date	Hour	Summary of Events and Information	Remarks and references to Appendices
	Sept			
[illegible]	14th	12.55pm	Our Howitzers fired a few rounds HE on BLACK REDOUBT. Fifteen minutes later the enemy retaliated with three large shell on F5 trench. The last two shells seemed to burst on our parapet but on enquiry it was ascertained that no damage had been done.	
— do —	— do —	3.5 pm	In accordance with orders from OC 3rd Bde RFA, the Bty registered three points with Balloon Observation at G20A39, G25A102 and G26B32. 16 Rds being fired	FWS.
do	do	4.5 pm	Open work was observed being done on Hill 70 and about G19C32.	
do	do	4.30pm	3 large shrapnel fell in rear of F5 trench.	
			Fine day, but the light indifferent except between 3 and 4 pm	
— do —	15th	12.30pm	How's fired two rounds on BLACK REDOUBT. Enemy replied with 3 HE Shell in rear of F4.	FWS.
— do —	— do —	12.40pm	The crossroads and cutting at G20C44 was registered by Balloon Observation, 10 Rds being fired	
			Fine day	
— do —	16th	9.45am	Several light shrapnel were fired by the enemy at the neighbourhood of H27A25	FWS
— do —	— do —	11.5am	6 [illegible] shrapnel fell over F4 & F5 trenches, very high bursts	
— do —	— do —	12.58pm	Having orders having been received (Appendix III) 4 Rds were fired on BLACK REDOUBT	

Instructions regarding War Diaries and Intelligence Summaries are contained in F. S. Regs., Part II. and the Staff Manual respectively. Title pages will be prepared in manuscript.

WAR DIARY
or
~~INTELLIGENCE SUMMARY~~.
(*Erase heading not required.*)

Volume VII

Army Form C. 2118.

Place	Date	Hour	Summary of Events and Information	Remarks and references to Appendices
	Sept	Cont'd		
Nr KEMMEL	16th	12-5 PM	trench lines and fuze.	
			Boards were observed in BLACK REDOUBT, evidently the enemy are still persevering with it in spite of continual bombardment.	
— do —	— do —	4-30 PM	Owing to extremely bad light, the combined bombardment was postponed.	HS.
— do —	— do —	8-10 PM	The Infy reported a few shell fell in rear of F5 trench presumably at a working party.	
			Fine day but very misty especially during the afternoon.	
— do —	17th	2-45 PM	A working party was observed about O25A88. 2 Rds fired and the party dispersed	
— do —	— do —	4-0 PM	The bombardment arranged for the 16th was carried out. The Bty fired 16 Rds. The whole of the shooting appeared very effective.	Appendix III
— do —	— do —	4-30 to 5-40 PM	The enemy retaliated by firing about 20 four and six inch HE on F4 & F5 trenches.	
			Communication was kept up with the Infy. Frequent messages were received. The last said "No material damage was done".	HS.
			Fine day though the light again was not good.	
— do —	18th	1-PM	12 four inch shrapnel burst very high somewhere about N14 C & D in salvos of 3 evidently searching for the 9-2 Howitzers	
— do —	— do —	1-30 PM	14 six inch HE shell fired on F4 & F5 trenches for which in retaliation 4 Rds.	

2353 Wt. W2544/1454 700,000 5/15 D. D. & L. A.D.S.S. Forms/C. 2118.

Instructions regarding War Diaries and Intelligence Summaries are contained in F. S. Regs., Part II. and the Staff Manual respectively. Title pages will be prepared in manuscript.

WAR DIARY
or
INTELLIGENCE ~~SUMMARY~~.
(Erase heading not required.)

Army Form C. 2118.

Volume VIII

Place	Date	Hour	Summary of Events and Information	Remarks and references to Appendices
	Sept			
Nr KEMMEL	18th	1.30pm	were fired on BLACK REDOUBT and 12 Rds on SPANBROEKMOLEN.	
— do —	"	2.30 to 4pm	About 30 eight or eleven inch shell were fired by salvos of 3, and a few whiz bangs at F2, F4 & F5 trenches. 6 Rds were fired in retaliation into LENFER WOOD but without result	HJ
— do —	"	4.30 to 5pm	About 8 eight or eleven inch shell were fired over the H trenches. No report could be heard and the direction from which the shells came could not be ascertained. Fine day but light very indifferent. Very misty in the morning.	
— do —	19th	4.30pm	A few whiz bangs and four 8" HE shell were fired on F5 trench. The Bty retaliated on the trenches south of PECKHAM N30A55, where they are in enfilade. No more 8" was fired in this area. 5 Rds fired	HJS
— do —	— do —	6.30pm	3 Rds were fired from a whiz bang on F2 trenches and the Bty again retaliated on the PECKHAM trenches. 3 Rds fired. Fine day and clear.	
— do —	20th		Very quiet day. No firing by enemy and no movement seen. Fine day.	HJS
— do —	21st		Fine day but very misty. No movement seen and no firing done.	HJS
— do —	22nd		Orders having been received that the Bty was to be withdrawn, preparations were made	

2353 Wt. W2544/1454 700,000 5/15 D. D. & L. A.D.S.S. Forms/C. 2118.

Instructions regarding War Diaries and Intelligence Summaries are contained in F. S. Regs., Part II. and the Staff Manual respectively. Title pages will be prepared in manuscript.

WAR DIARY
or
~~INTELLIGENCE SUMMARY.~~
(Erase heading not required.)

Army Form C. 2118.

Volume VII

Place	Date	Hour	Summary of Events and Information	Remarks and references to Appendices
	Sept			
Nr KEMMEL	22nd	7.40 PM	during the day and at night the Bty marched to wagon line near LOCRE. M24 D 38. Orders were given not to fire during the day unless necessary owing to the reliefs going on. Fine day	JHS
	23rd	9.0 AM	The Bty marched with remainder of 31st Bde RFA to billets near PRADELLES via LOCRE – ST JANS CAPPEL – METEREN – FLETRE – STRAZEELE, arriving at billets about 3 PM. Distance about 12 miles. Very tedious and slow march, owing to traffic on the roads and ~~the~~ a very warm day.	Ref Map HAZEBROUK 5A JHS
			The Bde was inspected en route by Brig Genl Arbuthnot, the turn out being very satisfactory.	
			Orders received "to be ready to move at one hours notice". This order was altered about 9 PM "to be ready to move at short notice."	
Nr PRADELLES	24th		Camp routine. The Bty remained in a state of readiness all day. Raining most of day	JHS
– do –	25th		——— do ———	JHS.
– do –	26th	9.0 AM	Bty marched with remainder of 31st Bde RFA and 85th Infy Bde to billets at the road triangle P26 between LE CORNET MALO and the AIRE LA BASSEE CANAL. Marched via VIEX BERQUIN – NEUF	Ref Map FRANCE BETHUNE (Combined Sheet) 1/40000

Army Form C. 2118.

Instructions regarding War Diaries and Intelligence Summaries are contained in F. S. Regs., Part II. and the Staff Manual respectively. Title pages will be prepared in manuscript.

WAR DIARY
or
INTELLIGENCE SUMMARY.
(Erase heading not required.)

Place	Date	Hour	Summary of Events and Information	Remarks and references to Appendices
	Sept			
Nr RIEZ-DU-VINAGE	26th Contd		BERQUIN-MERVILLE, arriving about 2 pm. Distance about 14 miles. Tedious and slow march due to continuous stoppages in front. Orders received to be ready to move at one hours notice. Fine day.	JHS
— do —	27th	2-30 pm	Btty marched to billets on canal bank near HINGES about O11 C 48. About 3 miles. Commenced to rain en route and continued most of the evening.	JHS
Nr PT LEVIS O11 C 48	28th		Remained at billets all day. Camp routine and drill. Raining most of day.	
— do —	29th	1-20 pm	Btty ordered into action at VERMELLES. Marched to wagon line position at BEUVRY CHATEAU via ESSARS, arriving there at 4-30 pm. About 6 miles.	JHS
BEUVRY	- do -	6 0 pm	Firing Btty marched to position at VERMELLES about G 8 A 28 getting guns into position by 9-45 pm. Raining nearly all day. Incessant ~~Shell~~ gun fire from our Btys already in position of which there were a large number including 2 9.2 How about 10 yds in rear of Btty. Good position but rather confused and crowded.	Ref Trench Maps. Sheet 36 B NW 1 and Sheet 36 C NW 3 and part B 1
			The Btty was now attached to 2nd Divn, temporarily. The 28th Divl Infy being covered by 2nd Divn guns who were already in position and knew the ground	
VERMELLES	30th		Gun and wagon positions improved and cleaned. Telephone lines laid to an Observing Station behind support trenches and Battalion Hd Qtrs of the Infy the Btty covers. The zone allotted being from point 48 in A 28 C to point 15 in A 28 D	

Instructions regarding War Diaries and Intelligence Summaries are contained in F. S. Regs., Part II. and the Staff Manual respectively. Title pages will be prepared in manuscript.

WAR DIARY
or
~~INTELLIGENCE SUMMARY~~.
(Erase heading not required.)

Volume VII

Army Form C. 2118.

Place	Date	Hour	Summary of Events and Information	Remarks and references to Appendices
	Sept			
VERMELLES	30th	3 Bty	Registration was carried out on the enemys front trenches wherever they could be identified 69 Rds being fired Fine day until evening when heavy rain fell.	
			Violent Arty bombardment of enemys lines by our guns all day with very little reply	JM.
			Observation was exceptionally difficult owing to our trenches being at the foot of a convex slope. The slopes further concealed the German trenches on our immediate front opposite MADAGASCAR from our own front trenches. At the period at which the Bty came into action the situation as far as known was this. The enemy had reoccupied all his front line trenches in front of GIVENCHY and AUCHY as far as LITTLE WILLIE an advanced trench connecting HOHENZOLLERN Redoubt with his main trench line N of it, which we were in occupation of. The enemy held HOHENZOLLERN Redoubt, we held his advanced trench BIG WILLIE running out of it SE. and thence to the chalk pits which were continually changing hands. We held (GUN TRENCH) formerly belonging to the enemy facing HULLUCH which we had had to evacuate ~~the~~ Thence our line ran E of LOOS which had been consolidated, LITTLE WILLIE, the DUMP at FOSSE No 8 & the chalk pits were almost hourly scenes of desperate fighting and were constantly changing hands.	

2353 Wt. W2544/1454 700,000 5/15 D. D. & L. A.D.S.S. Forms/C. 2118.

1/10/15

S. Ward[?]
Major RGA
Comdg 69th Bty RGA

28th Division

Confidential

121/6529

War Diary
of
69th Battery R.F.A.

Volume V

From 1st July to 31st July 1915.

Vol V

Instructions regarding War Diaries and Intelligence Summaries are contained in F. S. Regs., Part II. and the Staff Manual respectively. Title pages will be prepared in manuscript.

69th Bty RFA

WAR DIARY
or
INTELLIGENCE SUMMARY.
(Erase heading not required.)

Army Form C. 2118.

Volume V

Hour, Date, Place	Summary of Events and Information	Remarks and references to Appendices Initial	
12-8 Pm 1st July 16 Nr DICKEBUSCHE	4 Rounds were fired at a working party of the enemy near PICCADILLY FARM.		Reference Maps. BELGIUM Sheets 28 NW & SW.
3-40 Pm — do —	Enemys front line at O7c46 & O7c27 were registered, 9 rounds being fired.		
4-25 — do —	5 Rounds were fired at enemy's front and support trenches in front of P4 & P2a trenches. At the request of Infy to retaliate for a "whiz bang". Enemy's shelling ceased.	H.S.	
	Fine but cloudy. Quiet day		
8-30 Pm 2nd July — do —	One round fired as a test as to quickness of Bty in supporting Infy.		
	Fine day and very clear in afternoon. Very Quiet	H.S.	
9-22 am to 11-30 am 3rd July — do —	8 Rounds were fired on enemy's support trenches as a reprisal for them shelling ours. On each occasion we fired the enemy stopped firing at once.		
4-55 Pm — do — do —	2 Rounds were fired on enemys support trenches to retaliate for shelling of our communication trenches	H.S.	
4-58 Pm — do — do —	1 Round test. (Time 15")		
5-33 Pm — do — do —	Registration was carried out on Sunk road (O9 B82) and a portion of trench, 14 Rounds being fired.		
	Fine warm and generally clear day.		
1-22 am 4th July — do —	1 Round test (Visual signalling from trenches to Bty) Time 1'-15"		
1-10 Pm — do —	A trench mortar was worrying our Infy in P2 trenches. At their request 6 rounds were fired which silenced the mortar.	H.S.	
	Very quiet day. Fine and very warm.		
10-03 am 5th — do — do —	Enemy Artillery very active. They first shelled the region of CHATEAU at H36c27 and then switched to BRASSERIE at N6a and on to RIDGEWOOD		

(73989) W4141—463. 400,000. 9/14. H.&J.Ltd. Forms/C. 2118/10.

Instructions regarding War Diaries and Intelligence Summaries are contained in F. S. Regs., Part II. and the Staff Manual respectively. Title pages will be prepared in manuscript.

WAR DIARY
or
~~INTELLIGENCE~~ SUMMARY.
(Erase heading not required.)

Volume V

Army Form C. 2118.

Hour, Date, Place	Summary of Events and Information	Remarks and references to Appendices Initial
5th July Nr DICKEBUSCH (Contd)	at N5. This last fire appeared to be among our Infy dug-outs and in retaliation 4 rounds were fired at the back of BOIS QUARANTE* where the enemy were reported to have a lot of dug-outs. This had the desired effect, the enemy immediately stopped shelling.	* 07
10.17am — do —	Registration carried out on corner of BOIS QUARANTE at 07A, fire being observed by Major RAMSDEN 100th Bty RFA, a total of 4 rounds being fired	[initials]
12.35pm — do — 1.10pm — do —	6 Rounds were fired at enemy's working party at O 26 71. This fire was effective the enemy scattered in all directions	
	Fine warm day, cloudy.	
6th July — do —	Heavy bombardment in the North heard between 4 & 6 AM.	
7.45pm — do —	The enemy shelled the VIERSTRAAT - HALLEBAST road with heavy shrapnel.	[initials]
	Weather fair, cloudy, slight rain afternoon and evening	
2.10AM 7th July — do —	Information received from Infy in our zone (The Buffs 2nd West Kents) that their working parties were being bombarded by Minenwerfer, fired from a point slightly N of PICCADILLY FARM. The Infy requested the Bty to "blow down 20 yards or so" of the enemy parapet at this point. Ammunition not being allowed to comply with this request, 3 rounds were fired at the point named and the mortar ceased firing.	[initials]
8.0pm — do —	6 rounds were fired at enemy's front line trench at BOIS QUARANTE as a reprisal for them shelling O Trenches.	
5.40pm — do —	Registration carried out on buildings not shewn on map (O9B55)	

Instructions regarding War Diaries and Intelligence Summaries are contained in F. S. Regs., Part II. and the Staff Manual respectively. Title pages will be prepared in manuscript.

WAR DIARY
or
~~INTELLIGENCE~~ SUMMARY.
(Erase heading not required.)

Army Form C. 2118.

Volume V

Hour, Date, Place	Summary of Events and Information	Remarks and references to Appendices
		Initial
7th July 15 Nr DICKEBUSCH (Contd)	7 rounds being fired	
	Cold gusty & cloudy day with rain at intervals	
10-5 AM 8th July 15 to 12-30 PM — do —	Smoke from a fire lighted in enemys support trench was observed and occasional rounds fired on this portion, a total of 7 rounds were fired	
6-0 PM — do —	Enemy shelled crossroads at N 23 with high explosive	
6-30 PM to 7-25 PM — do —	There was much movement of men up and down new communicating trench running NW of through Sq. O 9 A, during the evening. 9 rounds were fired at intervals and it is thought most of them must have been effective	F.W.S.
8 PM — do —	1 round was fired at a trench mortar in PICCADILLY FARM.	
	Cold windy day	
11-15 PM 9th July — do —	3 rounds were fired on enemys trench mortar near PICCADILLY FARM at request of Infy. The last two of these rounds were reported effective and the mortar gave no further annoyance during the night.	
	A British aeroplane was brought down by the enemy and the aviator killed near DICKEBUSCH during the morning.	F.W.S.
	Apart from a few rounds fired by enemy on DICKEBUSCH, the day was very quiet	
	Cold rainy and generally dull day.	
3-30 AM 10th July 15 — do —	Mining operations were brought to a successful conclusion ~~on~~ at ST ELOI MOUND by the 5th Divn, the enemy having many casualties.	
9-35 AM to 9-40 AM — do —	Five heavy shrapnel (woolly bears) were fired by the enemy on RIDGEWOOD (N 5).* Two time fuzes were shown to Bty, both set at 4700 metres. Bearings	* 2 men of 2nd Buff being wounded.

Instructions regarding War Diaries and Intelligence Summaries are contained in F. S. Regs., Part II. and the Staff Manual respectively. Title pages will be prepared in manuscript.

WAR DIARY
or
~~INTELLIGENCE SUMMARY~~.
(*Erase heading not required.*)

Army Form C. 2118.

Volume V

Hour, Date, Place	Summary of Events and Information	Initial	Remarks and references to Appendices
10th July 15 Nr DICKEBUSCH (Contd)	were taken from the fall of the shell and the enemy's battery located about O 16 A 36.		
9-40 AM — do —	In reply to above fire, two rounds were fired on enemy's dug-outs behind BOIS QUARANTE. This appeared to have the desired effect as they did not trouble us any more		
12-50 PM — do —	The above information was forwarded to Adjt. 31st Bde RFA.		
1-30 PM — do —	DICKEBUSCH was heavily shelled by the enemy with long range guns. As far as known one man of 3rd Hussars and one woman ~~were~~ severely wounded were the only casualties. Several houses were burned. Possibly this was a little "hate" in reply to mining operations of the morning.	THS.	
5-40 PM — do —	Enemy observed passing up & down communicating trench at O 9 A 55. 6 rounds were fire as opportunity occurred.		
6-30 PM — do —	Registration carried out on building O 9 B 55 near communicating trenches. 7 rounds fired		
	A fine message of appreciation of work done and a report on the fire of the Bty was received during the evening from O C 85th Infy Bde.		Appendix I & II attached
	Fine day but rather chilly.		
1-25 AM to 2-10 AM 11th July 15 — do —	Trench mortars were busy from the region of PICCADILLY FARM. At the request of Infy 5 rounds were fired at intervals which silenced them.		
5-0 AM — do —	Enemy shelled our trenches at P2 A & P4 with heavy shell, evident from a 5.9 fuze received from Infy. 9 rounds were fired on enemy trenches in retaliation	THS.	
6-10 AM — do —	2 rounds were fired on enemy observed in communicating trench at O 9 A 55		
4-50 PM — do —	3 rounds fired on preceding target as large numbers of enemy presented themselves.		

Instructions regarding War Diaries and Intelligence Summaries are contained in F. S. Regs., Part II. and the Staff Manual respectively. Title pages will be prepared in manuscript.

WAR DIARY
or
~~INTELLIGENCE SUMMARY.~~
(Erase heading not required.)

Army Form C. 2118.

Volume V

Hour, Date, Place	Summary of Events and Information	Remarks and references to Appendices
10.40 & 11.35 pm 11th July 15 Hq. DICKEBUSCH (Contd)	Two rounds fired on enemy's trench mortar near PICCADILLY FARM at request of Infty.	
	The enemy heavily shelled the trenches near ST ELOI MOUND during the morning and the cross roads N2B in the evening.	JWS
	Fine day but dull	
5 pm to 5.30 pm 12th July 15 — do —	A lot of movement was observed in communicating trench at O9A55, at least 50 men seen going to trenches.* 3 rounds were fired as opportunity offered.	* most of these men carried white sand bags
6.0 pm — do —	Enemy shelled DICKEBUSCH, some civilians being killed.	
	The enemy's aircraft were very busy about this time and the remainder of evening	JWS
8.30 pm — do —	6 rounds fired at a working party of the enemy near PICCADILLY FARM.	
10.55 pm — do —	2 rounds fired at trench mortars at request of Infy again near above farm	
	Heavy rain in the early morning, afterwards fine.	
12.15 am 13th — do —	5 rounds fired at preceding target and another trench mortar on P3 line	JWS
1.30 pm — do —	4 rounds fired at dug out at back of BOIS QUARANTE to endeavour to discourage a 'whizz bang' gun by taking reprisals. This gun had been reported by the Infy (East Surreys) to be behind BOIS QUARANTE. Lt MACKENZIE and Lt SHORT proceeded to trenches to endeavour to	

Instructions regarding War Diaries and Intelligence Summaries are contained in F. S. Regs., Part II. and the Staff Manual respectively. Title pages will be prepared in manuscript.

WAR DIARY
or
~~INTELLIGENCE SUMMARY.~~
(Erase heading not required.)

Army Form C. 2118.

Volume V

Hour, Date, Place	Summary of Events and Information	Initial	Remarks and references to Appendices
13th July '15 N. DICKEBUSCH (Contd)	locate this gun. It could not be seen but from information received as to flashes, it was thought to be about O 7 D 4 7. Other useful information re trench mortars and rifle grenades of the enemy was also obtained.		
2.30 pm — do —	Enemy shelled BRASSERIE cross roads (N 6 A) wounding seven men. This region and intervening ground to MOATED GRANGE (O 1 A) was heavily shelled during the afternoon. A complete shell was obtained from near the BRASSERIE. This had been blind and partly taken to pieces by an adventurous man before coming into our possession. As it was a very peculiar fuze and one which had not been seen before by us, a sketch and description was made by Major WILLIS, and forwarded to Adjt 31st Bde.	H.S.	
	Remarks of G.O.C. 2nd Div and Divisional Commander were received in 'Items of General Interest', on the wires received by the Bdg on the 16th July, and are attached.		Appendix III
10.25 pm — do —	5 rounds fired at enemy working party near PICCADILLY FARM. Heavy firing to the north was heard during the evening and gas fumes could be smelled.		
12.45 pm 14th July '15 — do —	Finer day than usual, very threatening during the afternoon. DICKEBUSCH again shelled with high explosive, about 6 rounds only.	H.S.	
3.15 pm — do —	NEW FARM through which our telephone wires pass to trenches was shelled and set on fire by the enemy		

(73989) W4141—463. 400,000. 9/14. H.&J.Ltd. Forms/C. 2118/10.

Instructions regarding War Diaries and Intelligence Summaries are contained in F. S. Regs., Part II. and the Staff Manual respectively. Title pages will be prepared in manuscript.

WAR DIARY
or
INTELLIGENCE SUMMARY.
(Erase heading not required.)

Army Form C. 2118.

Volume V

Hour, Date, Place	Summary of Events and Information	Remarks and references to Appendices
14th July 15 DICKEBUSCH (Contd)	Very heavy rain through the evening and most of the night.	
	During the night the 2nd Northumberland Fusiliers took over the trenches in our zone.	HS
5th 15th 5.35 — do —	Large numbers of the enemy observed passing along communicating trench 09A55. 8 rounds were fired as targets presented themselves.	
	Orders received to move to new position near KEMMEL. Major WILLIS proceeded there to reconnoitre.	HS
3-10 Pm 16th July — do —	Fine day showery at intervals	
	Enemy's front line trench at 02664 reported by 5th Div to be damaged and that men were visible. 5 rounds fired, the effect of which could not be ascertained.	HS
9.30 Pm — do —	The 1st section left for new position under Lt SHORT. Very heavy rain and a very dark night, the guns were got into action under difficulties. All ranks worked well and cheerful, the guns being ready to open fire about 11-30 Pm.	
	Very rainy from the afternoon onward & through most of following night	
11-0 AM 17th July to noon Near KEMMEL.	Major WILLIS arrived at Observing Station and registered the section on portions of enemy's trench line from 030A47 to 030A33, 22 rounds being fired	HS
2 Pm — do —	Section registered on MAEDELSTEDE FARM N24673 8 rounds fired.	

Instructions regarding War Diaries and Intelligence Summaries are contained in F. S. Regs., Part II. and the Staff Manual respectively. Title pages will be prepared in manuscript.

WAR DIARY
or
~~INTELLIGENCE SUMMARY.~~
(Erase heading not required.)

Army Form C. 2118.

Volume V

Hour, Date, Place	Summary of Events and Information	Remarks and references to Appendices
10.30pm 17th July 15 N. KEMMEL	The 2nd Section under Lt MACKENZIE arrived from old position near DICKEBUSCH having been relieved by the 123rd Bty RFA. Still raining and very dark, the guns were put into action and were ready soon after 1 a.m. The Btys position is at N21A96, relieving the 3rd Bty (North Riding) of the Northumbrian Bde (Territorials). Fine position among willows with plenty of natural and artificial cover. Splendid Observing Station on KEMMEL HILL with good dug outs. Visual communication to Bty by night & day practicable from both ends. 31st Bde Hd Qtrs visible but no signalling can be carried out from Ob Stn. Our own trenches clearly visible throughout the length of zone allotted. Zone O30A33 to PECKHAM FARM — Trenches F5 & 6 which are at present occupied by different Battalions. Telephones to 9 H Q2 trenches. Wagon line at M24D47. Raining practically all day.	H.S.
10-30am 18th July 15 — do —	Registration continued on various points, 16 rounds being fired. Registration very difficult owing to numbers of batteries firing as well as irregularity of enemy's line. Fine but cloudy. Situation very quiet.	H.S.
19th July 15 — do —	Registration carried out on various points. Rounds fired 16. Fine warm day. Situation very quiet except to north where heavy firing was heard in the evening.	H.S.
20th July 15 — do —	Situation very quiet. Fine day.	H.S.

(73989) W4141—463. 400,000. 9/14. H.&J.Ltd. Forms/C. 2118/10.

Army Form C. 2118.

Instructions regarding War Diaries and Intelligence Summaries are contained in F. S. Regs., Part II. and the Staff Manual respectively. Title pages will be prepared in manuscript.

WAR DIARY
or
~~INTELLIGENCE SUMMARY.~~
(Erase heading not required.)

Volume V

Hour, Date, Place	Summary of Events and Information	Remarks and references to Appendices
6 PM 21st July 15 nr KEMMEL	About 12 of the enemy ~~[illegible]~~ carrying boards at least 10 feet long, seemed passing along trenches from about O36A105 to O36A87. This was reported to Adjt 3rd Bde RFA and the 103rd Bty RFA who engaged the target. A message was received from Adjt 3rd Bde saying the Infy had reported the enemy very active about SPANBROEKMOLEN (O30C28). Possibly the above had connection with mining operations being carried on at this place	HLS
6.20 PM — do —	3 rounds fired at machine gun emplacement opposite F5 trench	
	Quiet day. Fine and warm.	
3.45 PM 22nd July 15 — do —	5 rounds fired at enemy trenches near SPANBROEKMOLEN and 2 rounds	
6.30 PM — do —	at N30A44 (machine gun emplacement) to discourage working parties.	
	The enemy working parties were very busy during the day about above positions in spite of being continually shelled.	HLS
	Situation fairly quiet. Fine during morning but heavy rain fell during the evening and night.	
~~[illegible]~~	Heavy firing heard from direction of YPRES at about 10 PM but the flashes could not be located except one which gave the range as 11000 yds.	
10 PM — do —	Large fire was noticed from direction of MESSINES or beyond.	
11 AM 23rd July 15 — do —	10 rounds fired on enemy communicating trench at O25A104 for registration	HLS
	Quiet day. Heavy showers most of day.	

(73989) W4141—463. 400,000. 9/14. H.&J.Ltd. Forms/C. 2118/10.

Instructions regarding War Diaries and Intelligence Summaries are contained in F. S. Regs., Part II. and the Staff Manual respectively. Title pages will be prepared in manuscript.

WAR DIARY
or
INTELLIGENCE SUMMARY.
(Erase heading not required.)

Volume V

Army Form C. 2118.

Hour, Date, Place	Summary of Events and Information	Remarks and references to Appendices
11.30AM to 12.10PM 24th July 15 Nr KEMMEL	Registration on trenches near LONE TREE O24D36 to O24D25. 11 rounds fired, trenches near MAEDELSTEDE O24C04 6 rounds fired. The enemy then fired about 12 (4 in.?) shell on F4 & F5 trenches.	
12.35PM — do —	Enemy fired 4 Heavy shell on POPERINGE Road about N.20 C causing some casualties among the British Cavalry digging trenches.	
5.30PM — do —	Additional rounds having been allotted, registration was continued on PECKHAM FARM and SPANBROEKMOLEN, 11 rounds fired.	H.S.
	A large German encampment of bell tents was observed from KEMMEL Hill. These appeared about 12000 yds away and could only be seen with a powerful glass. Direction about O30 or beyond.	
	Fine day except for occasional showers.	
11AM 25th July Nr KEMMEL	Gun line visited by Brig Genl ARBUTHNOT	
10PM — do —	3 rounds fired at machine gun emplacement (N30A44) at request of Infy. Fire apparently effective as gun did not open fire again during the night.	
	Enemy very quiet except aircraft. A German aircraft thought to be a ~~Taube~~ Fokker was over about 7PM flying fairly low & dropped 3 lights one red one green & one white. Apparently he was mistaken for a Morane scout as our antiaircraft guns did not open for a long time, probably being deceived by his lights. Several other German aircraft were over, mostly at great heights.	H.S.

(73989) W4141—463. 400,000. 9/14. H.&J.Ltd. Forms/C. 2118/10.

Instructions regarding War Diaries and Intelligence Summaries are contained in F. S. Regs., Part II. and the Staff Manual respectively. Title pages will be prepared in manuscript.

WAR DIARY
or
~~INTELLIGENCE SUMMARY.~~
(Erase heading not required.)

Army Form C. 2118.

Volume V

Hour, Date, Place	Summary of Events and Information	Remarks and references to Appendices
25th July 15 Nr KEMMEL (Contd)	Very misty morning and afterwards showery	
2-15 pm 26th —	3 rounds fired at working party N 30 A 4.4, work stopped	
3-15 pm — do —	2 rounds fired at O 24 B 5.4 as a test	HuS.
4-30 pm — do —	3 rounds fired at O 29 D 0.3, registration.	
	Quiet day, rain in early morning, afterwards fine.	
27th — do —	Considerable movement of wagons and small parties of enemy visible at a range of 8000 or 9000 yds.	
	Severe shelling by enemy of for about two hours, on the old position of 118th Bty near DICKEBUSCH.	
	Brigade test was carried out under Col. H.H. Bond who had recently assumed command of 3rd Bde RFA on Col G.H. White rejoining RHA.	HuS.
	Various targets were engaged in test during the afternoon, 9 rounds being fired with satisfactory results.	
	Again rainy during morning, remainder of day fine.	
4-30 pm 28th — do —	Registration 9 rounds fired	
5-35 pm — do —	Shoot in co-operation with A/49 How Bty to drive off working party near SPANBROEKMOLEN. 2 rounds fired and the work stopped	HuS.
	Situation very quiet. Fine day	
4-15 & 4-30 pm 29th — . —	Tests by Col Bondy from J5 & G2 Trenches	
3-15 pm — do —	Our 9.2 & 60 prs shelled the HOSPICE at WYTSCHAETE. Enemy replied	

Instructions regarding War Diaries and Intelligence Summaries are contained in F. S. Regs., Part II. and the Staff Manual respectively. Title pages will be prepared in manuscript.

WAR DIARY
or
~~INTELLIGENCE SUMMARY.~~
(Erase heading not required.)

Army Form C. 2118.

Volume V

Hour, Date, Place	Summary of Events and Information	Remarks and references to Appendices
4-35 PM 29th July Nr KEMMEL	by shelling KEMMEL Village. This village had been very little damaged as the enemy had previously refrained from shelling it. Shelling went on with heavy shrapnel and crumps until about 5-35 PM. Very little damage was done, some cattle being hit, a few houses damaged and as far as known 1 man of Cheshires wounded	HS
7. PM — do —	Some heavy shrapnel was fired in direction of cross roads N 20 B and it is believed some men of the Oxfordshire Hussars (Yeomanry) were killed and wounded	
	Fine day.	
12-15 AM 30th July Nr KEMMEL	4 rounds fired at request of Infy at N 30 C 19 on a working party. Work stopped	
1-15 PM — do —	Registration carried out on O 25 A 73, 5 rounds fired.	HS
6-0-7-0 PM — do —	J4, 5 & 6, Y2 Trenches heavily shelled with crumps, Infy reported very little damage done.	
	Heavy firing in direction of Hill 60, at 2-15 AM, which finally died away about 6-0 AM. Firing continued about 2 PM, probably a counter attack.	
	Fine day	
2-15 PM 31st — do —	Request from A.G. 3rd Bde to fire 20 Rds on LENFER in retaliation for enemy shelling Infy dugouts. Fire was effective & enemy ceased. 8 rounds fired in Registration, O 25 A. Fine warm day	

1/8/15

St. [illegible] Major RGA
Comdg 6?4 Bty RGA

(73989) W4141—463. 400,000. 9/14. H.&J.Ltd. Forms/C. 2118/10.

"A" Form. Army Form C. 2121.

MESSAGES AND SIGNALS.

No. of Message

Prefix SM Code EIP m.

Office of Origin and Service Instructions.

Z.H.E

Words 83 | Charge

Sent
At m.
To
By

This message is on a/c of: Appreciation I Service.

(Signature of "Franking Officer.")

Recd. at m.
Date
From
By

TO			
O	C	31ST	BDE

Sender's Number.	Day of Month	In reply to Number	
* BM 617	10TH		AAA

G.O.C.	hopes	that	you	will
express	to	the	69th	Bty
the	appreciation	of	their	fire
felt	by	men	in	the
trenches	AAA	This	fire	at
once	stops	the	enemy's	trench
mortar	when	it	attempts	to
trouble	us	at	night	and
the	excellent	results	obtained	encourage
our	men	very	considerably	AAA
From	personal	observation	G.O.C.	can
testify	to	the	interest	taken
in	the	firing	of	the
Bty	by	the	infantry	in
the	trenches			

From	85TH	INF	BDE
Place		2.40	PM
Time			

The above may be forwarded as now corrected. (Z)

Censor. Signature of Addressor or person authorised to telegraph in his name.

* This line should be erased if not required.

(T1809) Wt. 14142—641. 4500) pads. 4/15. Sir J. C. & S.

"A" Form. Army Form C. 2121.

MESSAGES AND SIGNALS. No. of Message ....

Prefix .... Code .... m. Office of Origin and Service Instructions.	Words / Charge	*This message is on a/c of:* Appendix II .... *Service.*	Recd. at .... m.
	Sent At .... m. To .... By	(Signature of "Franking Officer.")	Date .... From .... By ....

TO O C 69TH BATTERY

Sender's Number.	Day of Month	In reply to Number	AAA
* BM 623	10TH		

P. I reports our guns making splendid practice today

From	75TH	INFANTRY	BDE
Place			
Time		6.50	PM

The above may be forwarded as now corrected. (Z)

Censor. Signature of Addressor or person authorised to telegraph in his name.

* This line should be erased if not required.

(T1809) Wt. 14142—641. 45000 pads. 4/15. Sir J. C. & S.

Extract from items of General Interest

Appendix III.

d/- 11.7.15

x x x x x x x x

5 It gives the C R A great pleasure to have the following correspondence published.

(a) Wire from 85th Infy Bde to O C 31st Bde RFA
(See Appendix I to War Diary)

(b) (See Appendix II to War Diary)

(c) Comments of Divisional Commander.
"I have heard of the prompt and substantial support given by the guns of the 31st Bde to the Infy in the zones their guns are covering and I am glad to read the message from GOC 85th Bde."

Sd I V Ferguson Major RA
Bde Major 28th Division

Confidential

28th Division

War Diary

of

69th Battery R F A.

Volume VI

From 1st August to 31st Aug 1915.

69th Bty RFA.

Instructions regarding War Diaries and Intelligence Summaries are contained in F. S. Regs., Part II. and the Staff Manual respectively. Title pages will be prepared in manuscript.

WAR DIARY
or
~~INTELLIGENCE SUMMARY.~~
(Erase heading not required.)

Army Form C. 2118.

Volume VI

Hour, Date, Place	Summary of Events and Information	Remarks Initial	and references to Appendices
			Reference Maps BELGIUM Sheets 28 NW & SW.
5.35 PM 1st Aug '15 Nr KEMMEL	6 rounds fired on enemy's work at N30A45.		
6.30 PM — do —	Enemy heavily shelled F trenches probably in return for 68th firing on theirs. Fine day.	H.W.S.	
5.30 PM 2nd Aug '15 — do —	Registration on comtg trench O25A79. 10 Rds fired. Fine until evening when heavy rain fell.	H.W.S.	
11.45 AM 3rd Aug '15 — do —	31st Bde RFA test on various targets 5 Rds fired		
8.30 PM — do —	Enemy exploded a mine in G2 trench. No call for assistance was received from our Infy although they had numerous casualties. Generally quiet. Raining practically all day	H.W.S.	
4th Aug '15 — do —	Rain early morning, bad light all day, no rounds fired	H.W.S.	
2.35 PM 5th — do —	Registration on enemy work at O25B20 8 Rds fired		
3.40 PM — do —	— do — O19C93 6 — do		
5.15 PM — do —	Fired on a vehicle concealed in enemy's work O25A109. 7 Rds fired. Effective but no direct hit obtained	H.W.S.	

(9 29 6) W4141—463 100,000 9/14 H W V Forms/C. 2118/10

Instructions regarding War Diaries and Intelligence Summaries are contained in F. S. Regs., Part II. and the Staff Manual respectively. Title pages will be prepared in manuscript.

WAR DIARY
or
~~INTELLIGENCE SUMMARY.~~
(Erase heading not required.)

Volume VI

Army Form C. 2118.

Hour, Date, Place	Summary of Events and Information	Remarks and references to Appendices Initial
6·31 Pm 5th Aug 15 Nr KEMMEL	Fired on sap head decorated with French flags N30 A1.8. 6 Rds fired. Fine day.	H.L.
4·20 Pm 6th Aug 15 — do —	3rd Bde Test on various targets. 7 Rds fired	
5·Pm — do —	Registration and to try No 85 Fuzes. 11 Rds fired but the results obtained with new fuzes not satisfactory. Threatening day with rain in morning and at intervals later	H.L.
7th Aug 15 — do —	Very quiet and dull day. no movement visible. Fine but cloudy.	H.L.
5·40 Pm 8th Aug 15 — do —	Registration of KRUISSTRAAT CABT (N36B28) 7 Rds fired. Capt A G DICKSON and 6 NCOs & Men of 123rd Bde RFA were attached from 37th Div for 8 days instruction. Fine day but poor light.	H.L.
9th Aug 15 — do —	Orders were received to bombard SPANBROEKMOLEN as an attack was to take place by the 6th Div at HOOGE.	
3·AM — do —	Fire was opened for 10 minutes, 10 rounds being fired.	

(9 29 6) W4141—463 100,000 9/14 H W V Forms/C. 2118/10

Instructions regarding War Diaries and Intelligence Summaries are contained in F. S. Regs., Part II. and the Staff Manual respectively. Title pages will be prepared in manuscript.

Army Form C. 2118

WAR DIARY
or
~~INTELLIGENCE SUMMARY.~~

(Erase heading not required.)

Volume VI

Hour, Date, Place		Summary of Events and Information	Remarks and references to Appendices
3·20 AM	9th Aug 15 Nr KEMMEL	Fire was again opened for 20 minutes, 30 rounds being fired.	
3·20 PM	— do —	A working party was observed in above position, probably repairing damage done by bombardment. One round was fired and the point registered. The enemy disappeared, but in anticipation of their return the gun was reloaded and layed. The	JHS.
3·38 PM	— do —	party recommenced work and the gun fired. A beautiful round which burst right among them. One man wearing a white shirt was seen to fall and no doubt several more were hit. It afterwards leaked out that the Commander in Chief witnessed this shoot.	
		Fine day.	
5·40 PM	10th Aug 15 — do —	Registration was carried out with No 85 fuzes but the results could not be called satisfactory	
		Fine warm day	
	11th Aug 15 — do —	The attached Officer Capt DICKSON was taken to proposed	

(9 29 6) W 4141—463 100,000 9/14 H W V Forms/C. 2118/10

Instructions regarding War Diaries and Intelligence Summaries are contained in F. S. Regs., Part II. and the Staff Manual respectively. Title pages will be prepared in manuscript.

WAR DIARY
or
~~INTELLIGENCE SUMMARY.~~
(Erase heading not required.)

Volume VI

Army Form C. 2118.

Hour, Date, Place	Summary of Events and Information	Remarks and references to Appendices
11th Aug 15 Nr KEMMEL	forward gun position and Infy trenches, by 2Lt SHORT. Owing to the mine recently exploded by the enemy, the direction from G1 to G2 trenches was not clear and a guide took the party a wrong way, the result was they found themselves on the edge of the crater and in full view of the German lines. After an exciting time and a considerable amount of crawling on their stomachs, the party, however, reached safety without being observed.	H.W.
4.0 pm — do —	3 rounds were fired at a working party near BLACK REDOUBT (N30 A44)	
4.10 pm — do —	14 Rds with No 85 fuzes fired for Registration on various targets. Enemy's aircraft very busy during the evening. Fine day	H.W.
4 pm to 6 pm 12th Aug 15 — do —	Registration continued with No 85 fuzes. 22 rounds fired. Fine warm day	
4.45 pm 13th Aug 15 — do —	Enemy heavily cramped the region of KEMMEL. Very little damage	

(9 29 6) W4141—463 100,000 9/14 H W V Forms/C. 2118/10

Instructions regarding War Diaries and Intelligence Summaries are contained in F. S. Regs., Part II. and the Staff Manual respectively. Title pages will be prepared in manuscript.

WAR DIARY
or
INTELLIGENCE SUMMARY.
(Erase heading not required.)

Army Form C. 2118.

Volume VI

Hour, Date, Place	Summary of Events and Information	Remarks and references to Appendices
13th Aug 15 Nr KEMMEL (Contd)	done except to a few houses.	
2.4 Pm —do—	Bde Test on SPANBROEKMOLEN. Time 15 sec	HS
	Raining day	
10.30 AM to 12 noon 14th Aug 15 —do—	Enemy heavily shelled Btys old position near DICKEBUSCH, with 6" or 8" How. Direction apparently from WERVICQ.	A gun was hit but the detachments had been removed.
3.30 Pm —do—	2 Rds fired on a working party near SPANBROEKMOLEN. Enemy stopped work.	
7.15 Pm —do—	Test call from G2 Trench. Time 1 minute	
9 Pm —do—	A mine was fired in gallery of German mine near G2 trench. This caused very little noise or disturbance. Except for a little nervousness in the German lines all was quiet and no call for assistance was received from our Infy	HS
	Fine clear day with a very good light	
3.20 Pm 15th Aug 15 —do—	A Brit Test was carried out, 4 rounds being fired at trenches near PECKHAM and 4 at SPANBROEKMOLEN. Some shell from	

Army Form C. 2118.

Instructions regarding War Diaries and Intelligence Summaries are contained in F. S. Regs., Part II. and the Staff Manual respectively. Title pages will be prepared in manuscript.

WAR DIARY
or
~~INTELLIGENCE SUMMARY.~~
(Erase heading not required.)

Volume VI

Hour, Date, Place	Summary of Events and Information	Remarks and references to Appendices
15th Aug M. KEMMEL (Contd)	enemy fell on F5 trench during the test.	
4-0 pm — do —	Capt DICKSON of 123rd Bde attached for instruction, carried out two series on N24 D61 and O25 A52. 12 rounds being fired on difficult targets, the results being very good.	HWS.
	Heavy rain during morning afterwards fine.	
7.40 pm 16th Aug 15 — do —	Test call received from G2 trench. A gun was immediately fired but on asking for the time it was discovered that the call had been sent in error.	HWS.
	The morning was so dull and the afternoon so misty that no firing was done.	
17th Aug 15 — do —	Capt A.G. DICKSON and the men of 123rd Bde RFA left to rejoin their own Divn	
12-20 pm — do —	2 Rds were fired at a working party of the enemy at O25 B86. The party dispersed.	HWS.
3-10 pm — do —	Registration on PETIT BOIS (N24 A86) 12 Rds fired	
	Heavy firing and unrest all evening on our left.	

Instructions regarding War Diaries and Intelligence Summaries are contained in F. S. Regs., Part II. and the Staff Manual respectively. Title pages will be prepared in manuscript.

WAR DIARY
or
~~INTELLIGENCE SUMMARY.~~
(Erase heading not required.)

Army Form C. 2118.

Volume VI

Hour, Date, Place	Summary of Events and Information	Remarks and references to Appendices
17th Aug 15 – Nr KEMMEL (Contd)	Heavy thunderstorm during morning, dull and cloudy remainder of day.	
18th — do —	Raining most of the early morning. Very quiet. No firing done. Heavy bombardment heard and seen in the direction of HOOGE during the evening.	YHS.
12.15 a.m. 19th — do —	Disc Test. One round fired at trenches near PECKHAM delayed owing to line being under repairs. Time 2 minutes.	YHS.
3 P.M. — do —	Registration on enemy's work O 31 B 55. 9 Rds fired. Fine but cloudy.	
1-50 P.M. 20th — do —	Owing probably to some movement near KEMMEL TOWER the enemy started a desultory shrapnel fire, sending over about 7 shell. There were some narrow escapes among Arty Observing Officers on the Hill.	YHS.
3 P.M. — do —	Three willow trees were blown up in the enemy's trench facing G2 and the Infy suspecting that positions for trench mortars were being prepared there, called up and asked for	

(9 29 6) W 4141—463 100,000 9/14 H W V Forms/C. 2118/10

Army Form C. 2118

Instructions regarding War Diaries and Intelligence Summaries are contained in F. S. Regs., Part II. and the Staff Manual respectively. Title pages will be prepared in manuscript.

WAR DIARY
or
~~INTELLIGENCE SUMMARY.~~
(Erase heading not required.)

Volume VI

Hour, Date, Place	Summary of Events and Information	Remarks and references to Appendices
2nd Aug 15 (Contd)	the spot to be registered, which was done. 8 rounds were fired, an Officer in the trench giving valuable assistance. The shooting at this point is difficult owing to the trenches being so close, so the portion of our trench was partially cleared.	[illegible]
3.30pm, 2nd Aug 15 [illegible]	Registration on enemy's work at O28 A 101. Successful, no second round brought retaliation. 7 Rds fired.	
	Fine but again cloudy	
	Infty reported that two men in armour could be seen working an excavation at [illegible]. Nothing could be seen of this from our Observing Station, however.	[illegible]
9.15pm —do—	OC B2 Trench reported that a mine was believed to exist under his trench and requested the Bty to be ready to fire on its afternoon registration if required.	
3.40pm 3rd Aug 15 —do—	5 Rds were fired at a party of the enemy, probably an Observing party at O25 A 109. They dispersed.	[illegible]
4.0pm —do—	Brigade Test on various targets 12 Rds fired	

(9 29 6) W 4141—463 100,000 9/14 H W V Forms/C. 2118/10

Army Form C. 2118.

Instructions regarding War Diaries and Intelligence Summaries are contained in F. S. Regs., Part II. and the Staff Manual respectively. Title pages will be prepared in manuscript.

WAR DIARY
or
~~INTELLIGENCE SUMMARY.~~
(Erase heading not required.)

Volume VI

Hour, Date, Place	Summary of Events and Information	Remarks and references to Appendices
4.26 pm Aug 21st 15 Nr KEMMEL	Registration on a sap or listening post at N 30 C 1 9. 7 Rds fired with good results.	
5.30 pm — do —	Two rounds only, were fired by a German field gun from between points O 25 A 3 8 and N 30 B 6 5, the objective being apparently G 2 Trench close by PECKHAM. As there is a mine under that trench it is suggested that a gun had been brought forward to assist when it should be exploded and that it fired two rounds by daylight to register. Information was sent to 1/Welsh as the point ranged on is probably his danger zone. Unfortunately the exact spot where the above gun was concealed could not be determined. It did not fire again during the evening.	T.W.
8.20 pm — do —	It was thought that smoke was seen in G 2 trench, no report however was heard. This turned out to be a counter mine exploded by our own people, apparently a successful operation	
9.[illegible] pm — do —	Heavy firing heard in the direction of HOOGE or HILL 60.	

(9 29 6) W 4141—463 100,000 9/14 H W V Forms/C. 2118/10

Army Form C. 2118.

Instructions regarding War Diaries and Intelligence Summaries are contained in F. S. Regs., Part II. and the Staff Manual respectively. Title pages will be prepared in manuscript.

WAR DIARY
or
~~INTELLIGENCE~~ SUMMARY.
(Erase heading not required.)

Volume VI

Hour, Date, Place	Summary of Events and Information	Remarks and references to Appendices
(Contd) 9.30pm 21st Aug 15 Nr KEMMEL	Two red flares could be seen floating in the air in that direction.	HLd
	Fine day.	
12.10pm 22nd Aug 15 —do—	Searching fire was carried out on the suspected area O25B58 for whizz bang gun. 8 Rds fired. This had the effect of temporarily silencing it.	
5.15pm —do—	A red balloon, at a great height was observed travelling SE very fast. It appeared to have no car. It had a highly polished surface which made observation difficult. About 12 large shrapnel in all was fired at our observation balloon near LOCRE, during the course of the afternoon. All ineffective.	HLd
	Fine bright day, which brought out a good many aircraft. Several german machines came some distance over our lines. A large number of shell was fired at them but none appeared to be hit.	
2pm 23rd Aug 15 —do—	A working party in enemy's front line trench near PECKHAM was	

Army Form C. 2118

Instructions regarding War Diaries and Intelligence Summaries are contained in F. S. Regs., Part II. and the Staff Manual respectively. Title pages will be prepared in manuscript.

WAR DIARY
or
INTELLIGENCE SUMMARY.
(Erase heading not required.)

Hour, Date, Place	Summary of Events and Information	Remarks and references to Appendices
23rd Aug 15 Nr KEMMEL (Contd)	fired on and at intervals during the afternoon. 9 Rds were fired many of which appeared effective.	H.S.
4.30pm —— do ——	2 Rds fired on BLACK REDOUBT in retaliation for a Whiz bang.	
	Fine day.	
24th Aug 15 —— do ——	Enemy's heavy guns were were very active during the day, the support trenches in rear of F4 & F2 receiving most attention	H.S.
	The day was dull and very misty. No movement was seen and no rounds fired by the Bty	
5.30pm 25th Aug 15 —— do ——	4 Rds fired at a working party at N30C54 and the work stopped This with another Bty firing near PECKHAM brought on a lot of 'hate' from a Whiz bang and heavy Howitzer. Again our support trenches were the enemy's objective	H.S.
	Fine day but again dull and misty	
4pm 26th Aug 15 —— do	Two peculiar black holes were observed in hedges O19c41. These were suspected to be positions for Whiz bangs. Registration was carried out 16 Rds being fired	H.S.
10.10pm —— do ——	An aeroplane or airship could be heard passing over and the flash of	

Instructions regarding War Diaries and Intelligence Summaries are contained in F. S. Regs., Part II. and the Staff Manual respectively. Title pages will be prepared in manuscript.

WAR DIARY
or
~~INTELLIGENCE~~ SUMMARY.
(Erase heading not required.)

Volume VI

Army Form C. 2118.

Place	Date	Hour	Summary of Events and Information	Remarks and references to Appendices
		(Contd)		
Nr KEMMEL	Aug/15 26	10-10 pm	anti-aircraft shell further north could be seen. Twenty minutes later it passed over again from North west to South east and could be heard for some time afterwards.	
— do —	— do	10-30 pm	Infantry in F4 trench requested fire to be opened on a working party at SPANBROEK MOLEN. Two rounds were fired and were reported by Infy as very effective.	FWS
— do —	— do	11-30 pm	The above party again started work. Two rounds were fired and the work stopped. Fine day but misty.	
— do —	27th	5-30 pm	Planks could be seen being carried about between PECKHAM and MAEDELSTEDE. It was thought this might be stuff as the planks were carried back to a ~~position~~ point in rear and then carried up again. Nothing seen worth firing at. Fine day with the light much clearer.	FWS
— do —	28th	12-40 pm	Test from F5 trench. Time 40 secs. Delayed a little owing to some Staff Officers in front of guns	
— do —	— do	4-15 pm	4 Rds Registration fired at a point near SPANBROEKMOLEN. Fine day with better light.	FWS
— do —	29th	11-0 am	Registration carried out on various points, 23 Rds being fired.	
— do —	— do	3-40	— do — 6 Rds fired. Rain most of day with very poor light	FWS

2353 Wt. W2544/1454 700,000 3/15 D. D. & L. A.D.S.S. Forms/C. 2118.

Instructions regarding War Diaries and Intelligence Summaries are contained in F. S. Regs., Part II. and the Staff Manual respectively. Title pages will be prepared in manuscript.

WAR DIARY
or
~~INTELLIGENCE SUMMARY.~~
(Erase heading not required.)

Army Form C. 2118.

Volume VI

Place	Date	Hour	Summary of Events and Information	Remarks and references to Appendices
	Aug 15			
Mt KEMMEL	30th	3 P.M.	6 Rds fired at a working party at N30A42. Work stopped.	
— do —	— do —	3.20 P.M.	New communicating trench at N24B.1.2 was Registered. 7 Rds fired	
			Communicating trench at O31B44 was registered and identified. 7 Rds fired.	[illegible]
			Fine day. Good light though fitful	
do	31st		No movement seen or rounds fired.	[illegible]
			Dull day with slight rain at intervals.	

1st Sept 1915

[illegible] Major RGA
Comdg 69th Bty RGA

2353 Wt. W2544/1454 700,000 5/15 D. D. & L. A.D.S.S. Forms/C. 2118.

Volume No.

BRITISH SALONIKA FORCE

WAR DIARY.

28th Division

Vol. No.	Unit	PERIOD From	To
1.	103rd Bty. 31st Bde. R. F. A.	22. 12. 14.	31. 1. 15
2.	do.	1. 2. 15	28. 2. 15.

A.P. & S.D., Alex./No. 752/8:5:17/3000 (5004IG/53) W. M. & Co.

W. 15517—M. 141. 250,000. 1/16. L.S.&Co. Forms/W 3091/2.

Army Form W. 3091.

Cover for Documents.

Nature of Enclosures.

Notes, or Letters written.

Army Form C. 2118.

Vol 1

Instructions regarding War Diaries and Intelligence Summaries are contained in F. S. Regs., Part II. and the Staff Manual respectively. Title pages will be prepared in manuscript.

WAR DIARY

or

~~INTELLIGENCE SUMMARY.~~

(Erase heading not required.)

Hour, Date, Place	Summary of Events and Information	Remarks and references to Appendices
1915 Winchester ~~22nd December~~ to 3rd Jan	Battery in process of mobilizing as part of 31st F.A. Bde of 28th Division Having thrown off its offshoot (the 69th Battery), is now being made up as a 4-gun Battery Commander Major J. W. Hope, R.F.A. Three subalterns:— Lieut K. A. Ireland, 2nd Lieut (Spec Reserve) C. R. Cumming and 2nd Lieut A. C. Kennedy (Spec Reserve). Billeted in Winchester.	SALONIKA ARMY D.A.A.G. 13 FEB 1917 THIRD ECHELON
SHAWFORD 4th Jan — 11th Jan	moved to billets at Shawford. Lieut Ireland is posted as Adjutant 31st Brigade RFA. 2nd Lieut. W. C. Hetton joined the Battery in his place	
12th January	Took part in review on Fawley Down of the 28th Divn by H M the King.	
13th to 15th January	Completed mobilization. ~~Shipped~~	
16th January	Marched off at 10 AM from SHAWFORD, strength 4 Officers, 134 other ranks x, 127 horses Arrived Southampton ~~at~~ Docks at 2 PM and embarked on board the MOUNT TEMPLE with 84th Infantry Brigade HQ and the — Batt. Suffolk Regt.	x. 5 short of establishment ~~##~~ 1 Fitter & 1 Trumpeter deficient. 1 deserter 2 sick

(73989) W4141—463. 400,000. 9/14. H.&J.Ltd. Forms/C. 2118/10.

Instructions regarding War Diaries and Intelligence Summaries are contained in F. S. Regs., Part II. and the Staff Manual respectively. Title pages will be prepared in manuscript.

WAR DIARY
or
~~INTELLIGENCE~~ SUMMARY.
(Erase heading not required.)

Army Form C. 2118.

2

Hour, Date, Place	Summary of Events and Information	Remarks and references to Appendices
16/1/15 on board S. S. MOUNT TEMPLE	Ship left quai about 5PM. 2 men slipped away for refreshment and were left behind. 7 horses were detained for Veterinary reasons, and only 4 could be obtained to replace from Remount Depot on Dock. Anchored for the night in the SOLENT.	
17/1/15 on board MOUNT TEMPLE	Remained anchored all day; weighed anchor & sailed at about 7 PM.	
18/1/15 HAVRE	Arrived off HAVRE in early morning, got into our berth at about 11 AM, & commenced disembarking. The 2 absentees reported themselves having come over on another ship. Marched off about 4.30 p.m to No. 2 Rest Camp, about 4 miles. Very steep hill and cobbled roads gave some trouble. Settled down in camp in the dark.	
19/1/15 HAVRE	Rain storms at intervals. Marched off 11.45 a.m about 5 miles to Entraining station GARE MARITIME and entrained with part of Ammunition	

(73989) W4141—463. 400,000. 9/14. H.&J.Ltd. Forms/C. 2118/10.

Instructions regarding War Diaries and Intelligence Summaries are contained in F. S. Regs., Part II. and the Staff Manual respectively. Title pages will be prepared in manuscript.

WAR DIARY
or
~~INTELLIGENCE SUMMARY.~~
(Erase heading not required.)

Army Form C. 2118.

3

Hour, Date, Place	Summary of Events and Information	Remarks and references to Appendices
	Column, 2 platoons Welsh Regt. & 2 platoon Cheshires all deficiencies in horses made good. Started 5.30 p.m.	
HAZEBROUCK. 20/1/15.	Arrived at our detraining point, HAZEBROUCK, at about 4 PM. Could not commence detraining until 5 P.M, and marched off at about 6 PM. [One horse a casualty and left at HAZEBROUCK] Our only guide was a man of the 69th Battery who assured us that he knew the way, but succeeded in leading us about 4 miles out of our way. When it was quite clear that he had lost the way, I sent Cumming on to reconnoitre and we eventually reached STRAZEELE, where I enquired from the headquarters 84th Infantry Brigade, and was given a new guide, who took us to NORD HELF[illegible], the Headquarters of the 31st F.A. Bde, and we commenced settling down into our billets, the horses and vehicles in a muddy field, and the Officers & men in a Farm, the whole of the men being crowded in a barn. This operation not completed until 1 AM in drizzling rain.	

(73989) W4141—463. 400,000. 9/14. H.&J.Ltd. Forms/C. 2118/10.

Instructions regarding War Diaries and Intelligence Summaries are contained in F. S. Regs., Part II. and the Staff Manual respectively. Title pages will be prepared in manuscript.

WAR DIARY
or
INTELLIGENCE SUMMARY.
(Erase heading not required.)

Army Form C. 2118.

Hour, Date, Place	Summary of Events and Information	Remarks and references to Appendices
NORD HELF near STRAZEELE. 21/1/15.	Spent the day squaring up and settling down more comfortably. Moved ~~the~~ D Subsection personnel into another farm about 600 yards away; steady rain all day. Intermittent fire from heavy guns heard during the day. One or two rifle shots from snipers heard close to us during the night before.	
NORD HELF 22/1/15.	The Battery moved out in F.S. marching order to drill and in the afternoon some practice in entrenching was done. A cold frosty and sunny day. Some excitement caused by seeing bouquets of shells in the air fired at an aeroplane, but whether ~~is~~ ours or the enemy's was not certain.	
NORD HELF. 23/1/15.	Cold frosty, fine day. Battery gundrill and driving drill in the forenoon; practised entrenching in the afternoon. Firing of heavy artillery from the direction of YPRES very audible all day; more puffs seen of shots fired at aeroplanes. ~~[illegible]~~ gunners and 2 drivers	

5

Instructions regarding War Diaries and Intelligence Summaries are contained in F. S. Regs., Part II. and the Staff Manual respectively. Title pages will be prepared in manuscript.

WAR DIARY
or
INTELLIGENCE SUMMARY.
(Erase heading not required.)

Army Form C. 2118.

Hour, Date, Place	Summary of Events and Information	Remarks and references to Appendices
	and one horse supplied from the Ammunition Column, completing our establishment less one Fitter; one of these drivers takes the place of the 2nd Trumpeter who cannot be supplied.	
NORDHOLF 24/1/15	Cold raw day. Took some Officers and N.C.Os to practise reconnaissance in the forenoon. After dark the Battery practised entrenching for about 2 hours.	
25/1/15	Cold raw day. Battery gun drill and driving drill in the forenoon. Laying for gunners in the afternoon. Entrenching practise for two hours after dark. Took the guns into the epaulments prepared.	
26/1/15	Frosty morning. Battery gun drill in the epaulments in the forenoon. Various parades in the afternoon including lecture by Medical Officer on First Aid. Orders received in the evening to hold ourselves	

6

Instructions regarding War Diaries and Intelligence Summaries are contained in F. S. Regs., Part II. and the Staff Manual respectively. Title pages will be prepared in manuscript.

WAR DIARY
or
INTELLIGENCE SUMMARY.
(Erase heading not required.)

Army Form C. 2118.

Hour, Date, Place	Summary of Events and Information	Remarks and references to Appendices
	in readiness to turn out at short notice during the night as tomorrow is the Kaiser's birthday. Two horses died of cold and exposure; replaced by Ammunition Column.	
NORD HELF 27/1/15.	Frosty day, fine. Paraded Battery in Field Service Marching Order to test how we are to carry the horse rugs when we move up to the Front. Officers and Nos 1 went to inspect the gun epaulments of the 100th Battery. In the afternoon practised entrenching. Cumming took some N.C.Os out for reconnaissance and Kennedy practised sending back angles and observations from forward observing station.	
28/1/15	Hard frost. The Battery paraded in F.S.M.O. dismounted and marched to STRAZELEE where the C. in C. Field Marshal Sir John French inspected all the troops in the 84th Infantry Brigade area.	

(73989) W4141—463. 400,000. 9/14. H.&J.Ltd. Forms/C. 2118/10.

7

Instructions regarding War Diaries and Intelligence Summaries are contained in F. S. Regs., Part II. and the Staff Manual respectively. Title pages will be prepared in manuscript.

WAR DIARY
or
INTELLIGENCE SUMMARY.
(Erase heading not required.)

Army Form C. 2118.

Hour, Date, Place	Summary of Events and Information	Remarks and references to Appendices
NORD HELF	The II Army Commander General Smith Dorrien, and our Corps (5th) Commander, General Plummer as well as the Divl Comdr were present. H.H. The Prince of Wales was on the C in C's Staff. In the afternoon, the C.R.A. held a conference of all Battery Commanders to discuss programme for our move into the Firing Line.	
29/1/15	Hard frost with light snow on the ground. The ~~C.R.A. and~~ Brigade and Battery Officers with some subalterns for observation duties were taken in a motor bus to YPRES and spent 24 hours with the French Batteries which are to be relieved, reconnoitring sites, observing stations, etc.	

8

Army Form C. 2118.

Instructions regarding War Diaries and Intelligence Summaries are contained in F. S. Regs., Part II. and the Staff Manual respectively. Title pages will be prepared in manuscript.

WAR DIARY
or
INTELLIGENCE SUMMARY.
(Erase heading not required.)

Hour, Date, Place	Summary of Events and Information	Remarks and references to Appendices
[illegible]	~~[illegible]~~	
30/1/15.	The ~~[illegible]~~ Officers returned to their Commands. Entrenching and gun drill practised. Thaw set in.	
31/1/15	Fall of snow and thaw. Church parade service was ordered at MERRIS, but on arrival of our Detachment there it was cancelled and they marched back. Preparations being made for march tomorrow	

[illegible]
Major RFA
Comdg 103 Battery RFA.
1/2/15.

(73989) W4141—463. 400,000. 9/14. H.&J.Ltd. Forms/C. 2118/10.

Instructions regarding War Diaries and Intelligence Summaries are contained in F. S. Regs., Part II. and the Staff Manual respectively. Title pages will be prepared in manuscript.

Vol. 9

WAR DIARY
or
INTELLIGENCE SUMMARY.
(*Erase heading not required.*)

Army Form C. 2118.

IX

Hour, Date, Place	Summary of Events and Information	Remarks and references to Appendices
1/2/15. NORD HELF	The ~~Battery marched off~~ Right Section with O.C. Battery Staff etc, and Lieuts Cumming & Kennedy marched off at 8 AM, and, after joining the rest of the Divisional Artillery we moved via BAILLEUL – LOCRE – RENINGHELST to VLAMERTINGE, whence we moved into our positions by night, relieving sections of the French Batteries. Heavy firing was in progress in front of us while we were moving in. Spent the rest of the night improving gunpits & settling in.	
2/2/15 near YPRES	A dull rainy day. We fired 10 registration shots during the day. The Left Section, under Lieut Gretton, arrived at about 11 PM. and we got them settled down in place of the French guns. Lieut Cumming went off to represent 31st F.A. Bde at Hd Qrs 84th Inf. Bde., Lieut Gretton went back to Wagon Line.	
3/2/15 near YPRES.	Carried out registration during the forenoon. Fine day. Many hostile aeroplanes reconnoitring close to us, which necessitated men taking cover a great deal.	
4/2/15 near YPRES	Fine sunny day. Aeroplanes very active; no registration done. Lieut. Cumming returned to the Battery and Lieut Kennedy went out to the Infantry trenches as Brigade Observer. In the evening after dark we fired	Fired 12 rounds at range of about 6000 at a hostile Battery reported.

(73989) W4141—463. 400,000. 9/14. H.&J.Ltd. Forms/C. 2118/10.

Army Form C. 2118.

WAR DIARY
or
INTELLIGENCE SUMMARY.
(Erase heading not required.)

Instructions regarding War Diaries and Intelligence Summaries are contained in F. S. Regs., Part II. and the Staff Manual respectively. Title pages will be prepared in manuscript.

Hour, Date, Place	Summary of Events and Information	Remarks and references to Appendices

Instructions regarding War Diaries and Intelligence Summaries are contained in F. S. Regs., Part II. and the Staff Manual respectively. Title pages will be prepared in manuscript.

WAR DIARY
or
~~INTELLIGENCE SUMMARY.~~
(Erase heading not required.)

Army Form C. 2118.

XI

Hour, Date, Place	Summary of Events and Information	Remarks and references to Appendices
	flank of the 100th Battery to hold the personnel of both batteries when we are subjected to heavy shell fire. We also reconnoitred for fresh battery positions, which are difficult to find as the ground is so exposed, all the ground being saturated with moisture.	
[illegible] YPRES 7/2/15	Commenced work at the splinterproof in the morning at 5.45 AM & went on more or less all day as it was misty. Lieut Cumming was up at the Infantry Trenches all day, but we did not fire. Half the Gunners are now back at the wagon line, resting.	
8/2/15	Commenced work at 5.45 AM. & by sunrise had completed the wood structure of the splinterproof & covered the roof over with brushwood & sods to conceal it from Aeroplanes. In the evening Major Hope was summoned to Divisional Artillery Headquarters to ~~[illegible]~~ confer with Aeroplane Observer re registration for following day of two hostile batteries.	
~~9/2/15~~	Lieut Hess R.H.A. joined the Battery on attachment in exchange with Lieut. Kennedy, in order to have a more	

Army Form C. 2118.

XII

Instructions regarding War Diaries and Intelligence Summaries are contained in F. S. Regs., Part II. and the Staff Manual respectively. Title pages will be prepared in manuscript.

WAR DIARY
or
INTELLIGENCE SUMMARY.
(Erase heading not required.)

Hour, Date, Place	Summary of Events and Information	Remarks and references to Appendices
	experienced Officer with Battery to take Major's place if necessary.	
9/2/15	Windy & cloudy day. Aeroplane observation found to be impracticable so our registration did not come off. At about 12.45 PM the forward observing Officer reported a point to register on, and, though Major Hope was temporarily away at the house in rear having lunch, ~~[illegible]~~ the O.C. Brigade ordered ranging to be commenced, sending ranges etc. from Brigade Hd Qrs. Major Hope arrived just before the conclusion of the series which was brought to an abrupt close by a report that three shells had fallen into our own trenches.	
	In the evening a man of the 100th Battery was wounded in the hand by a sniper from one of the outhouses near the white house Officer's billet. Both batteries sent some men with rifles & under Major Ramsden & Lieut Bretton, searched the premises	

(73989) W4141—463. 400,000. 9/14. H.&J.Ltd. Forms/C. 2118/10.

Instructions regarding War Diaries and Intelligence Summaries are contained in F. S. Regs., Part II. and the Staff Manual respectively. Title pages will be prepared in manuscript.

WAR DIARY
or
~~INTELLIGENCE SUMMARY.~~
(Erase heading not required.)

Army Form C. 2118.

XIII

Hour, Date, Place	Summary of Events and Information	Remarks and references to Appendices
	with no result, but the whole of the inmates of the White house were placed under a guard & the Provost Sergeant & an Interpreter came to investigate, with however no result.	
Near YPRES. 10.2.15.	Continued work at the splinterproof in the early morning. At about 8 AM. some shells began to fall close to the battery, apparently shrapnel from a howitzer, some bursting on graze & some in air: No casualties.	
	At about 10.45 AM the British aeroplane arrived and we commenced ranging on a hostile battery. Fired 23 rounds one of which was reported to be a direct hit.	
	At about noon some of the enemy's shells fell unpleasantly close to the battery. In the afternoon we got ready to range on another battery with aeroplane, but it did not come off for some reason probably the haze.	Rain fell during the night
11/2/15	The 100th Battery commenced registration with aircraft [illegible] at about 9 AM and we got ready to follow them,	

(73989) W4141—463. 400,000. 9/14. H.&J.Ltd. Forms/C. 2118/10.

Instructions regarding War Diaries and Intelligence Summaries are contained in F. S. Regs., Part II. and the Staff Manual respectively. Title pages will be prepared in manuscript.

WAR DIARY
or
INTELLIGENCE SUMMARY.
(Erase heading not required.)

Army Form C. 2118.

XIV

Hour, Date, Place	Summary of Events and Information	Remarks and references to Appendices
near YPRES.	but aeroplane observation appeared to be difficult and we did not get to work. ~~At~~ 2.15 pm we registered a hostile battery by means of our forward observer, firing 20 rounds, concluding with two rounds of High Explosive shell (TROTYL), but observations appeared to be difficult. At 4.15 PM received information that the hostile battery which we had registered yesterday was harassing the Cavalry trenches on our left and we fired four rounds of H.E. shell at ~~them~~ it. Lieut Bretton went to wagon line and Lieut Cummings returned to the Guns.	
12/2/15	Dull, misty day. Worked at improving gun positions, and dug a new gun pit about 200 yards to our left front. At 12 10 PM. we were ordered to fire at a length of road between points 1.35 C 17 and 1.35 a 42. Fired 20 rounds section fire 10 seconds, with lines of fire opened out 1 degree and sweeping 1 degree.	
13/2/15.	Cold, rainy day. At 8.10 am ~~we fired~~ under orders from Brigade Headquarters, we fired four rounds of time shrapnel at the usual objective of the battery (Point C)	

Instructions regarding War Diaries and Intelligence Summaries are contained in F. S. Regs., Part II. and the Staff Manual respectively. Title pages will be prepared in manuscript.

WAR DIARY
or
~~INTELLIGENCE~~ SUMMARY.
(Erase heading not required.)

Army Form C. 2118.

XV

Hour, Date, Place	Summary of Events and Information	Remarks and references to Appendices
	In the afternoon we were subjected to some sniping. Major Hope went out with a party to search, but the sniper could not be located, and the shots seemed to come from various directions.	
Near YPRES. 14/2/15	Cold, dull, rainy day. Several shell, both High Explosive and time shrapnel burst near the Battery during the day. At 4.45 PM, under orders from Brigade Headquarters we opened fire on target X. Square I.35, B.43, (Battery) and fired 20 shrapnel and 4 High Explosive at it. During the evening there was heavy firing to the south. Some heavy high explosive shell fell close to the Battery at night.	
15/2/15	Cold, dull, rainy day. Ordered to open fire a slow rate of fire at our normal points at "the first glimmer of dawn," which, on enquiry was 5.45 AM. After firing about 25 rounds we were informed that the C.R.A. meant 6.20 am when he used the expression above referred to, so we stopped firing and recommenced at that time and went on firing for one hour, fired altogether 111 rounds time shrapnel, searching from 3700 to 4000 yards and sweeping ½ degree with lines opened out ½ degree.	

(73989) W4141—463. 400,000. 9/14. H.&J.Ltd. Forms/C. 2118/10.

Instructions regarding War Diaries and Intelligence Summaries are contained in F. S. Regs., Part II. and the Staff Manual respectively. Title pages will be prepared in manuscript.

WAR DIARY
or
INTELLIGENCE SUMMARY.
(Erase heading not required.)

Army Form C. 2118.

XVI

Hour, Date, Place	Summary of Events and Information	Remarks and references to Appendices
15/2/15. (continued)	At 12 noon, under orders from Brigade Headquarters fired four rounds at hostile battery in Square I.35 B 43 and four at the houses square I.35. A. 56. In the evening there was a general stillness, and attack seems to be expected.	
Near YPRES. 16/2/15	Fine day with a touch of frost. Aeroplanes active again.	
(10.45 am)	Under orders from Brigade Headquarters fired 6 rounds of fuze shrapnel at German breastwork on railway (I.35. B.17), ranges 3700 to 3800 corrector 154. Appeared range rather long. The unusual quiet still continues, and we are warned to hold ourselves in readiness for hostile attack at any moment.	
	At about 9.15 P.M. under orders from Bde Hd Qrs we fired 27 rounds at our normal point C.	
17/2/15	Cold, windy, rainy day. Commenced digging a new dug-out by the railway to take shelter from shell fire. At 10 am we were ordered to open fire on Germans in a wood in the zone of the 146th Brigade, where they had captured one of our trenches on which we were now making a counterattack. Fired 83 rounds at this target. Subjected to ~~[illegible]~~ rather severe shell fire in the early afternoon. About 3 P.M. we were	

(73989) W4141—463. 400,000. 9/14. H.&J.Ltd. Forms/C. 2118/10.

Instructions regarding War Diaries and Intelligence Summaries are contained in F. S. Regs., Part II. and the Staff Manual respectively. Title pages will be prepared in manuscript.

WAR DIARY
or
INTELLIGENCE SUMMARY.
(Erase heading not required.)

Army Form C. 2118.

XVII

Hour, Date, Place	Summary of Events and Information	Remarks and references to Appendices
	ordered to open fire to repel a hostile attack along the railway cutting on the left of our zone, and fired 38 rounds. Later commenced firing occasional single shots of high explosive into the railway cutting, but after two shots orders received to cease firing as the supposed concentration for attack was found to be improbable. Much gratified to hear that the counterattack which we supported this morning was successful in recapturing the lost piece of trench, and that our support had been most effective.	
near YPRES. 18/2/15.	Fine day. Under orders from Brigade Headquarters, fired 20 rounds at a battery square I. 35 & 42. at 1.5 P.M. At 4.45 pm we fired 10 rounds at a very slow rate at the same point. In the afternoon some big shell fell ~~Dull misty day.~~ close to us, four of them practically on the railway line, cutting a rail, and very close to our mess dug-out, which seems hardly worth going on with.	
~~19/2/15~~		

(73989) W4141—463. 400,000. 9/14. H.&J.Ltd. Forms/C. 2118/10.

Instructions regarding War Diaries and Intelligence Summaries are contained in F. S. Regs., Part II. and the Staff Manual respectively. Title pages will be prepared in manuscript.

WAR DIARY
or
~~INTELLIGENCE SUMMARY.~~
(Erase heading not required.)

Army Form C. 2118.

XVIII

Hour, Date, Place	Summary of Events and Information	Remarks and references to Appendices
near YPRES. 19/2/15	Windy day, but fairly fine. At 2.30 pm we were ordered to open a slow rate of fire single shots at the hostile battery Square I.35 b.4.3. Fired altogether 11 rounds during the afternoon.	
20/2/15.	Rainy day. Between 4 and 5 pm we were subjected to some rather close shell fire from high explosive shell estimated to be 6-inch howitzer, most of which fell just to the left of the Battery. Withdrew the men to dug outs on the right of 100th Battery for a short time. At 9 P.M. we were ordered to hold ourselves in readiness to open fire as the Infantry in the trenches in front were being relieved by a fresh Brigade. The night however passed quietly.	
21/2/15.	Fine day. Absolute quiet all day. Ordered to be ready to open fire during night while Infantry Brigade on our right was being relieved	
22/2/15.	Frosty morning, and thick mist all day. Quiet all day. Did some physical training in the early morning. In the evening we were ordered to be ready to turn fire on to point I.29.d 60 (road junction), but nothing happened.	[signature] Major Comdg 103rd Battery RFA.
23/2/15.		

(73989) W4141—463. 400,000. 9/14. H.&J.Ltd. Forms/C. 2118/10.

Instructions regarding War Diaries and Intelligence Summaries are contained in F. S. Regs., Part II. and the Staff Manual respectively. Title pages will be prepared in manuscript.

WAR DIARY
or
INTELLIGENCE SUMMARY.
(Erase heading not required.)

Army Form C. 2118.

XIX

Hour, Date, Place	Summary of Events and Information	Remarks and references to Appendices
Near YPRES 23 2/15	Fine day – physical training in the course of the morning & re-drilling for N.C.Os & signallers – laying & fuze setting in the afternoon – Before dusk [illegible] lines of fire on the normal lines – [illegible] quiet night	
24 2/15	Fine morning, ~~physical~~ but misty up to 9 a.m. Opened fire at 11.30 a.m. on a wood I 29 b. searching the wood – fired about 20 rds. – opened fire again at about 1 p.m. on the same point & fired about 10 rds – again at about 2 p.m. – At about 3.15 p.m heavy shelling by a German 6 inch started & the battery stopped firing & took cover, by	[illegible]
	the Germans had the range & line. – No 4 wagon was hit & blew up – 2 signallers Bdr King & Gr Smith were killed in the covered trench at that point. – Major Hope – 2Lieut Cumming & 2Lieut Hess were in the same trench – 2Lieut Hess being just outside the door.	

(73989) W4141—463. 400,000. 9/14. H.&J.Ltd. Forms/C. 2118/10.

Instructions regarding War Diaries and Intelligence Summaries are contained in F. S. Regs., Part II. and the Staff Manual respectively. Title pages will be prepared in manuscript.

WAR DIARY
or
INTELLIGENCE SUMMARY.
(Erase heading not required.)

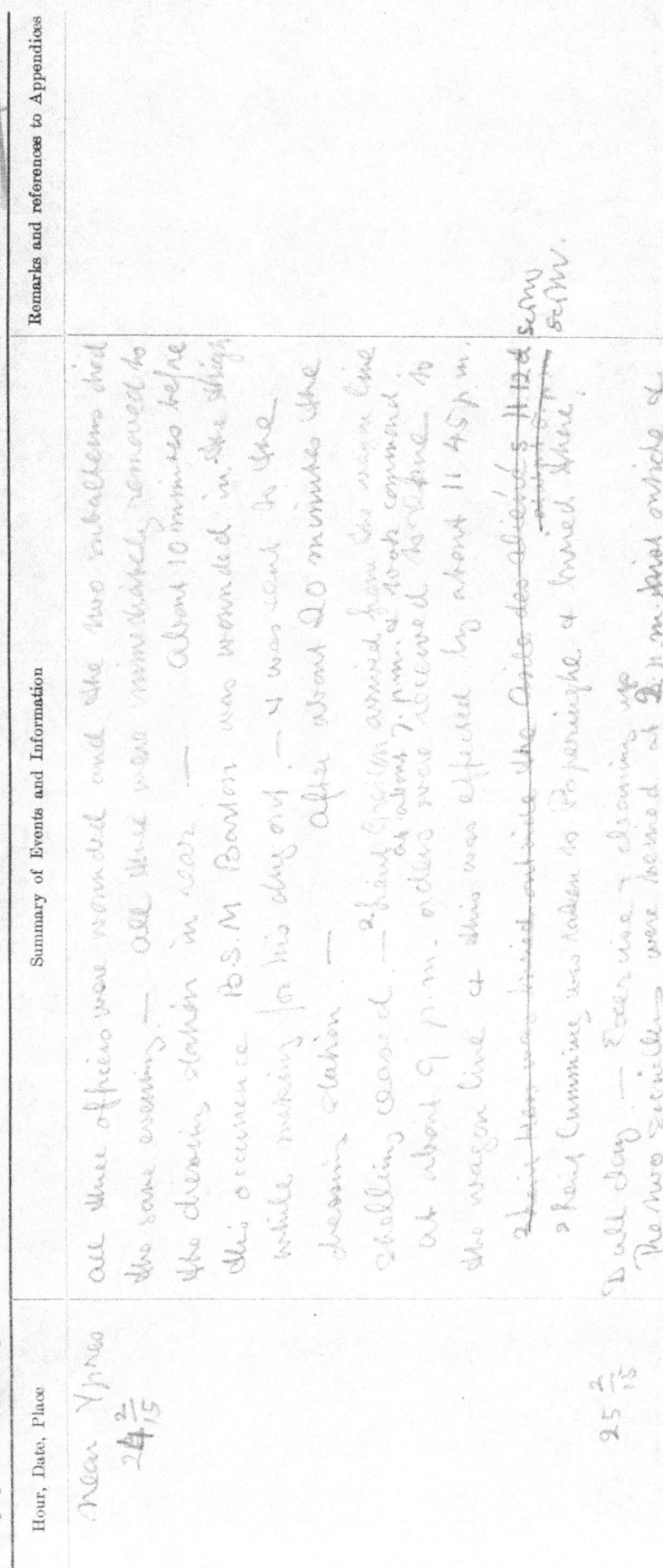

Army Form C. 2118.

XX

Hour, Date, Place	Summary of Events and Information	Remarks and references to Appendices
Near Ypres 24/2/15	all three officers were wounded and the two subalterns died the same evening. — All three were immediately removed to the dressing station in rear. — About 10 minutes before this occurrence B.S.M Barton was wounded in the thigh while making for his dug out. — & was sent to the dressing station. — After about 20 minutes the shelling ceased. — 2 Lieut Gratton arrived from the wagon line at about 7. p.m. & took command. At about 9 p.m. orders were received to retire to the wagon line & this was effected by about 11 45 p.m.	
	~~2 Lieut Hess was buried outside the Asile des Aliénés H 12 d~~	S.C.M.
	2 Lieut Cumming was taken to Poperinghe & buried there.	S.C.M.
25/2/15	Dull day — Exercise & cleaning up. The two signallers were buried at 2 p.m. just outside & north of the Churchyard I 8. b. 5. 5. 2 Lieut Hess was buried outside the Asile des Aliénés H. 12 d. at about 5 p.m. Lieut Brownlow arrived from 69th Battery, attached to take command temporarily in the evening	

(73989) W4141—463. 400,000. 9/14. H.&J.Ltd. Forms/C. 2118/10.

Instructions regarding War Diaries and Intelligence Summaries are contained in F. S. Regs., Part II. and the Staff Manual respectively. Title pages will be prepared in manuscript.

WAR DIARY
or
INTELLIGENCE SUMMARY.
(Erase heading not required.)

Army Form C. 2118.

XXI

Hour, Date, Place	Summary of Events and Information	Remarks and references to Appendices
near Ypres. 26 2/15	Fine day. — occupied in overhauling gear & inventorying ~~Sent~~ One gun sent to Poperinghe for overhauling	
27 2/15	Fine day. — spent in a similar manner. Inspection of horses by the P.V.O.	
28 2/15	Fine day. — exercise & stables —	
~~24~~ 1 3/15	~~Fine day~~ — Dull day turning to rain & sleet in the evening. — One section inspected in F.S. Marching order. — Every man was taken to the bathing place & had a wash. Major Willis joined at about 5 p.m. & took command	
2 3/15	One section in F.S. Marching order — day spent in looking over & checking. — 11 horses received to replace casualties from 31st Bde Ammn Column.	

J. W. [illegible] Capt.
Cmdg 103rd Bty RFA

(73989) W4141—463. 400,000. 9/14. H.&J.Ltd. Forms/C. 2118/10.

28TH DIVISION
DIVL ARTILLERY

31ST BRIGADE R.F.A.

DEC 1914-OCT 1915

XI

A 2
Ab. 6

28th Division

121
4195

31st Bde: R. F. A.

Vol I. 22.12-14 — 31.1.15

31st Brigade R.F.A.

Instructions regarding War Diaries and Intelligence Summaries are contained in F. S. Regs., Part II. and the Staff Manual respectively. Title pages will be prepared in manuscript.

WAR DIARY
or
INTELLIGENCE SUMMARY.
(Erase heading not required.)

Army Form C. 2118.

Hour, Date, Place		Summary of Events and Information	Remarks and references to Appendices
Winchester	22/12/14	Orders for mobilisation received.	
"	23/12/14	31st Brigade R.F.A. formed of three batteries, 69th, 100th & 103rd on a new 4 gun basis. The 103rd Battery on a 6 gun basis split into the 69th and 103rd Batteries on a 4 gun basis. The 100th battery had already done so when the 27th Division was mobilised, with which their off-shoot Battery went; they were therefore already on a 4 gun basis. Lt. A.B. van Straubenzee acting Adjutant.	
	24/12/14.	Lt-Col. H.E.T Kelly posted to command the Brigade, and Capt. H.J. King appointed ~~temporarily~~ to command the Brigade Ammunition Column. This commenced to form forthwith. Lt. Col. Kelly joined from the 47th Brigade R.F.A., New Army. Guns arrived from Devonport to complete the 69th Battery. Brigade H.Q. established at STAR HOTEL, High Street	
	26/12/14.	All batteries completed in guns and Ammunition wagons. Considerable difficulty experienced in doing any training of recruits posted owing to the billets being necessarily scattered, and the consequent difficulty of getting hold of the men.	
"	27th Decr 1914 to Jan 3rd 1915	Mobilisation continued. Batteries practically completed in clothing, personnel, horses, and harness; and S.A.A. Cleaning materials for harness, dubbin for boots had to be purchased locally in small quantities as an issue was	

31st Brigade R.F.A.

Instructions regarding War Diaries and Intelligence Summaries are contained in F. S. Regs., Part II. and the Staff Manual respectively. Title pages will be prepared in manuscript.

WAR DIARY
or
INTELLIGENCE SUMMARY.
(*Erase heading not required.*)

Army Form C. 2118.

Hour, Date, Place	Summary of Events and Information	Remarks and references to Appendices
Winchester Jan 3rd 1915	not obtainable. Only a small proportion of 18 pr. Q.F. ammunition received, for the most part plugged Ammunition from India.	
Jan 4th 1915.	The Brigade had to change billets to make room in Winchester for Infantry. The 69th Battery moved to COLDEN COMMON (5 miles), the 103rd to SHAWFORD (3 miles), and the Brigade Ammunition Column to TWYFORD (4 miles) out of WINCHESTER. The 100th Battery remained in its former billets in WINCHESTER adjoining Brigade Headquarters, established in the College (since January 2nd). All batteries in telephonic communication with Bde H.Q.S. but owing to pressure of work at the Exchange, considerable delay experienced in getting touch when required.	
Jan 5th to 8th	Mobilisation continued under considerable difficulties owing to distance of Batteries from Headquarters, and the scattered nature of the individual billets. One officer per battery occupied almost continuously in adjusting claims and payments of billets. Dial Sights belonging to 103rd Battery - brought from India - had to be handed over to 3rd Brigade, constituted Emergency Brigade; the result being the training of layers entirely stopped. No dummy shell being available, & bar indicators not having been issued	

(73989) W4141—463. 400,000. 9/14. H.&J.Ltd. Forms/C. 2118/10.

31st Brigade R.F.A.

Instructions regarding War Diaries and Intelligence Summaries are contained in F. S. Regs., Part II. and the Staff Manual respectively. Title pages will be prepared in manuscript.

WAR DIARY
or
INTELLIGENCE SUMMARY.
(Erase heading not required.)

Army Form C. 2118.

Hour, Date, Place	Summary of Events and Information	Remarks and references to Appendices
near Winchester Jan 5th to 8th.	training in fuze setting done under difficulties. Recruits received were very backward in gun drill, and owing to necessary promotions, inexperienced N.C.O.'s filling the more responsible positions very noticeable.	
Jan 9th	Lieut K.G. Ireland from 103rd Battery R.F.A. appointed Adjutant. Lieut A.B. van Straubenzee from Acting Adjutant to 69th Battery, Lieut W.E. Gritton from 69th Battery to 103rd Battery.	
	R.S.M. Cork joined ~~on~~ posting from T.F. permanent staff.	
Jan 11th	Batteries and Ammunition Column held practice marching order parades fully mobilised as far as possible. Ammunition Column had considerable difficulty owing to shortage of portions of harness etc. and their shortage in artificers, none being available for posting to them, particularly saddlers and farriers.	
Jan. 12th	Division reviewed by H. M. The King ~~and~~ accompanied by Lord Kitchener. The Brigade paraded with Firing Batteries only, and Staffs. Division formed up in 2 lines while His Majesty walked round and then units wheeled right & marched past batteries at close interval.	
Jan 13th - 15th	mobilisation completed except for certain small stores	

(73989) W4141—463. 400,000. 9/14. H.&J.Ltd. Forms/C. 2118/10.

3/1st Brigade R.F.A.

Instructions regarding War Diaries and Intelligence Summaries are contained in F. S. Regs., Part II. and the Staff Manual respectively. Title pages will be prepared in manuscript.

WAR DIARY
or
INTELLIGENCE SUMMARY.
(Erase heading not required.)

Army Form C. 2118.

Hour, Date, Place	Summary of Events and Information	Remarks and references to Appendices
	indented for only 1098. Brigade short of Artificers throughout. Several absentees - sick & deserters - reduce personnel.	
Winchester Jan. 16th	The 31st Brigade with 84th Infantry Brigade marched out of WINCHESTER. Headquarters, 69th and 100th Batteries passing COLDEN COMMON at 11 am en route for Southampton 103rd Battery following 20 minutes later, and Brigade Ammunition Column one hour later.	
	Sick and distressed horses changed by Remounts en route at SWAYTHLING.	
	Units arrived SOUTHAMPTON DOCKS at 2 p.m. Headquarters of the Brigade, 69th Battery, and Ammunition Column embarked immediately on KINGSTONIAN, 100th Battery on AUSTRALIND, 103rd Battery on the MOUNT TEMPLE. A large number of horses, inspected by Veterinary Officer, were cast as unfit by him, and were not replaced by sufficient number (cases of catarrh chiefly). Headquarters embarked one horse short, Ammunition Column 17 horses short. Embarkation completed by 5 p.m. KINGSTONIAN cast off 6 p.m. and moved out into the stream and anchored. Rations and forage in plenty had been placed on board ship.	

(73989) W4141—463. 400,000. 9/14. H.&J.Ltd. Forms/C. 2118/10.

31st Brigade R.F.A.

Instructions regarding War Diaries and Intelligence Summaries are contained in F. S. Regs., Part II. and the Staff Manual respectively. Title pages will be prepared in manuscript.

WAR DIARY
or
INTELLIGENCE SUMMARY.
(*Erase heading not required.*)

Army Form C. 2118.

Hour, Date, Place	Summary of Events and Information	Remarks and references to Appendices
At Sea January 17th	KINGSTONIAN ~~cast~~ shipped anchor at 8 a.m. & moved out off BEMBRIDGE POINT, and lay to till 8 p.m. ~~Cast~~ Shipped anchor at 8 p.m. and crossed. Weather calm, but cold.	
January 18th	Arrived HAVRE 8 a.m. but could not enter harbour till 10 a.m. Got alongside dock at 11 a.m. and proceeded to disembark. Each unit told off to an area on dock where men, horses, and vehicles were parked. Warm clothing drawn up forthwith. Horses made up by Remounts. Headquarters proceeded to entraining point with 69th Battery at 7 p.m. Rations and forage for 2 days, and iron rations drawn up on platform. Entrained immediately. Completed by 10.30 p.m. Horses & men in cattle trucks.	
January 19th	Train left at 1.30 a.m. 103rd Battery, after spending night in rest camp entrained 2 p.m. 100th Battery and Brigade Ammunition column entrained 6.30 a.m. Headquarters & 69th Battery arrived HAZEBROUCK 10 p.m. Delay of 2 hours while Surrey Yeomanry completed detraining. ~~Commenced to detrain~~	
January 20th	Commenced detraining 12.30 a.m. Clear of Station by 3 a.m. and proceeded to adjoining field	

Army Form C. 2118.

Instructions regarding War Diaries and Intelligence Summaries are contained in F. S. Regs., Part II. and the Staff Manual respectively. Title pages will be prepared in manuscript.

WAR DIARY
or
INTELLIGENCE SUMMARY.
(Erase heading not required.)

Hour, Date, Place	Summary of Events and Information	Remarks and references to Appendices
January 20th	when horses and vehicles were parked. Rain was falling steadily, and the field was extremely muddy. Men billetted for the night in a half built hospital at	
	4.30 am.	
	10.30 am. Brigade Headquarters and 69th Battery left billets in HAZEBROUCK	
	10.30 am. 100th Battery billetted in NORDHELF near STRAZEELE	
	12.30 pm. Brigade Headquarters and 69th Battery reached their billets at NORDHELF ~~and~~	
NORDHELF	4 pm. Brigade Ammunition Column reached their billet, having detrained at and marched from CASSEL.	
	9.30 pm. 103rd Battery reached their billet. They detrained at HAZEBROUCK at 4.30 pm. but their guide missed his way in the dark, and led them 5 miles out of their way.	
	Arrangements by billetting party were inferior throughout. This was undoubtedly due to the fact that special men were not selected at WINCHESTER for the purpose, as ~~the fact~~ it was not made clear by Headquarters that the party to be detailed would proceed on ahead as a billetting party.	

Instructions regarding War Diaries and Intelligence Summaries are contained in F. S. Regs., Part II. and the Staff Manual respectively. Title pages will be prepared in manuscript.

WAR DIARY
or
INTELLIGENCE SUMMARY.
(Erase heading not required.)

Army Form C. 2118.

Hour, Date, Place	Summary of Events and Information	Remarks and references to Appendices
NORDHELF Jany 21st	The Batteries proceeded on Route marches. Brigade Head-quarters laid a telephone wire by wagon past all Battery Headquarters. Batteries tapped in.	
— " — Jan. 22nd to — " — January 26th	Batteries training in digging and concealment of the guns by day and by night. Telephonic communication established by Brigade Headquarters with Headquarters of 84th Infantry Brigade at STRAZEELE on January 23rd. – Horse rugs issued at the rate of 1 per horse on January 24th. In spite of this horses suffering from exposure – Weather very cold, but fine on the whole – occasional Snow Storms. Ground very wet and heavy but quite passable anywhere for troops after frost. Water reached 2 feet from surface when digging.	
— " — January 27th	~~[illegible]~~ 31st Brigade detailed as Emergency Brigade in conjunction with 84th Infantry Brigade to be ready to move at 3 hours notice from 9 a.m. for the subsequent 24 hours. The 27th being the ~~[illegible]~~ Kaiser's birthday, orders were received from Divisional Headquarters to be prepared to move a short notice, if required, from 1 a.m. to ~~take part in~~ assist in dealing with any demonstration by the enemy, and the Brigade remained in readiness for an immediate move – Baggage wagons were packed as far as possible.	

Army Form C. 2118.

Instructions regarding War Diaries and Intelligence Summaries are contained in F. S. Regs., Part II. and the Staff Manual respectively. Title pages will be prepared in manuscript.

WAR DIARY
or
INTELLIGENCE SUMMARY.
(Erase heading not required.)

Hour, Date, Place	Summary of Events and Information	Remarks and references to Appendices
NORDHELF January 25th	Sanction granted for drawing of 1 G.S. wagon for hay per Battery, and one single horse cart per battery and Brigade Headquarters to replace the one G.S. wagon for cooks allowed by War Establishments.	
	*Braziers and wood for charcoal drawn	* 7 per brigade.
	2 dummy guns per Brigade drawn from O.C. R.E. Park STRAZEELE	
	31st Brigade paraded dismounted with 84th Infantry Brigade at 11.30 a.m. at STRAZEELE for inspection by the Field-Marshal Commander-in-Chief –	
	Slight fall of snow –	
January 29th	Brigade and Battery Commanders with their observation officers proceeded by motor bus from STRAZEELE at 7.30 a.m. to inspect the positions round YPRES with a view to taking over from the French –	
	Arrived YPRES 11.30 a.m. 31st Brigade to take over three positions occupied by French 90 mm Batteries; Battery Commanders and their observing officers spent the next 18 hours with the corresponding French officers noting details of objectives, ranges, angles of sight and general information likely to prove useful	

(73989) W4141—463. 400,000. 9/14. H.&J.Ltd. Forms/C. 2118/10.

Instructions regarding War Diaries and Intelligence Summaries are contained in F. S. Regs., Part II. and the Staff Manual respectively. Title pages will be prepared in manuscript.

WAR DIARY
or
INTELLIGENCE SUMMARY.
(Erase heading not required.)

Army Form C. 2118.

Hour, Date, Place	Summary of Events and Information	Remarks and references to Appendices
YPRES January 29th	~~Battery commanders spent~~ The French control of fire being on a different system from ours, fresh wires for telephonic communication from observers to Batteries will have to be laid	
	The positions of the Batteries and their headquarters appear to be known to the enemy as both were shelled during the night with considerable accuracy.	
January 30th	~~Batt~~ The party returned, leaving YPRES 10 a.m., to their billets –	
January 31st	Heavy Snow blizzard in the morning: thaw setting in. Brigade commenced preparations for leaving billets.	

28th Division.

121
4506

31st Bde: RFA.

Vol II. 1 – 28. 2. 15

Nil

Instructions regarding War Diaries and Intelligence Summaries are contained in F. S. Regs., Part II. and the Staff Manual respectively. Title pages will be prepared in manuscript.

WAR DIARY
or
INTELLIGENCE SUMMARY.
(*Erase heading not required.*)

Army Form C. 2118.

Hour, Date, Place	Summary of Events and Information	Remarks and references to Appendices
8 am. ~~3/~~ 1/2/15 NORDHELF FRANCE	31st Brigade Headqrs, three Batteries less a section each and half the Brigade Ammun.n Column left their billets at NORDHELF and marched via BAILLEUL ~~—~~ LOCRE – OUDERDOM to VLAMERTINGHE, reaching the latter at 12.30 pm. An area was allotted to the Brigade for billetting, and had to be reconnoitred and subdivided.	All references ~~—~~ to places are taken from map of Belgium Sheet 28 1/20000 squared
3.45 pm	Brigade Headquarters staff & observing Officer, started for Ypres. Two aeroplane Bombs dropped near road in VLAMERTINGHE, no damage. VLAMERTINGHE – YPRES road, and billetting area shelled periodically without result.	
7 p.m.	~~Both~~ Section of each Battery left VLAMERTINGHE to take over French positions near Ypres.	
9 p.m.	Commenced laying telephone wire from Observing Officer in trenches to Bde. HQS.	
10 pm.	Batteries passed through Ypres having been held up by Infantry in busses, and column of supply lorries. All sections in action and teams clear of positions by 11.10 pm.	KJA.
2/2/15. YPRES.	Communication by telephone established between Brigade HQS., observing post, and Batteries.	

Instructions regarding War Diaries and Intelligence Summaries are contained in F. S. Regs., Part II. and the Staff Manual respectively. Title pages will be prepared in manuscript.

WAR DIARY
or
INTELLIGENCE SUMMARY.
(*Erase heading not required.*)

Army Form C. 2118.

Hour, Date, Place	Summary of Events and Information	Remarks and references to Appendices
2/2/15 Ypres.	Batteries fired a few registration rounds on points located by observer. Remaining half batteries arrived at night and all were in action by 11 p.m., and ready to open fire.	K.G.
3/2/15 – 4/2/15 4/2/15	Hostile aeroplanes very active. Attack on infantry expected at dawn but did not develop. At request of 84th Infantry Bde. batteries opened fire on positions of hostile guns to check their fire; it had ceased however before our batteries opened.	
5/2/15.	11 a.m. 100th Battery opened fire on German trench from which there was considerable sniping. Range quickly obtained and several shell struck parapet of trench. 6.30 p.m. 69th Battery turned onto a hut supposed to contain machine gun. A direct hit was not obtained; only six rounds fired. 7 p.m. All batteries fired a few rounds to verify their lines on registered points A, B and C. (German support trenches, cross roads etc.) 7 p.m. Under orders from G.O.C. R.A. all batteries bombarded German support trenches; searching and sweeping fire	K.G.

(73989) W4141—463. 400,000. 9/14. H.&J.Ltd. Forms/C. 2118/10.

Instructions regarding War Diaries and Intelligence Summaries are contained in F. S. Regs., Part II. and the Staff Manual respectively. Title pages will be prepared in manuscript.

WAR DIARY
or
INTELLIGENCE SUMMARY.
(Erase heading not required.)

Army Form C. 2118.

Hour, Date, Place	Summary of Events and Information	Remarks and references to Appendices
Ypres. 5/2/15	employed - Bombardment in support of attack by 83rd Infantry Brigade. Orders to cease fire miscarried owing to communications with 83rd Bde, being cut. Fire continued for 40 minutes until stopped by order of the G.O.C 84th Infantry Bde. Ammunition expended 436 rds.	KGI.
6/2/15	Batteries opened fire 12.5 am. at request of Infantry in front line of trenches where apparently counter-attack (local) was in progress - After 10 minutes fire was stopped.	KGI
7/2/15.	Weather during past week on the whole fine and sunny, light wind, no rain. Slight showers 7/2/15. Hostile aeroplanes very active especially in the afternoons.	KGI
8/2/15	Sniping from the rear round battery positions after dark	
9/2/15	Further sniping occurred after dark, and one man of 100th Battery slightly wounded in hand - Sniper escaped.	KGI
	11.30 pm. 100th Battery opened fire on German Battery flashes of which were visible to Observing officer. The position of this battery had not been registered in conjunction with aeroplane observation. Range and line taken from	

(73989) W4141—463. 400,000. 9/14. H.&J.Ltd. Forms/C. 2118/10.

Instructions regarding War Diaries and Intelligence Summaries are contained in F. S. Regs., Part II. and the Staff Manual respectively. Title pages will be prepared in manuscript.

Army Form C. 2118.

WAR DIARY
or
~~INTELLIGENCE SUMMARY.~~
(Erase heading not required.)

Hour, Date, Place	Summary of Events and Information	Remarks and references to Appendices
9/2/15	map. Range about 3500 yds. The German Battery ceased fire while 100th Battery was firing, but effect of our fire could not be ascertained.	KGl
10/2/15	8.0 am. 100th and 103rd Battery shelled (Shrapnel) for 15 minutes. Effect of German fire nil; their line was inaccurate, falling mostly to the left of the 103rd Battery, and the shell either burst on graze or very high.	
	10.30 am Aeroplane arrived to register gun targets with 103rd Battery; the first objective was a hostile Battery about 100 yards in rear of German trenches. The range 3900 yards & line were found – aeroplane then went away before second target was registered.	
	Hostile aeroplanes very active in the afternoon. Weather fine and dry.	KGl
11/2/15	Aeroplane arrived for registering objectives with 100th Battery: the Battery opened fire at 10.40 am. on position of hostile battery to be registered. Aeroplane only recorded 2 observations, the second one being direct hit	

(73989) W4141—463. 400,000. 9/14. H.&J.Ltd. Forms/C. 2118/10.

Instructions regarding War Diaries and Intelligence Summaries are contained in F. S. Regs., Part II. and the Staff Manual respectively. Title pages will be prepared in manuscript.

WAR DIARY
or
INTELLIGENCE SUMMARY.
(Erase heading not required.)

Army Form C. 2118.

Hour, Date, Place	Summary of Events and Information	Remarks and references to Appendices
	but as some 10 rounds had been fired, the Battery Commander was unable to ascertain to which ones the observations related to. The aeroplane then went away, the observer reporting subsequently that he had been unable to see the 100th battery firing, and surmised they had stopped.	
	2 p.m. 103rd Battery opened fire on battery position as reported by aeroplane immediately in rear of German trenches. The objective adjoined a house visible to observing officer in the trenches. Range found to be 3700 yards.	KGA
12/2/15	Town shelled by heavy Artillery apparently from direction of OOSTAVERNE during night 11th – 12th.	
	At 12 noon on receipt of orders from G.O.C. R.A., 69th and 100th Battery opened sweeping fire on road in rear of German trenches, covering about 500 yards of the road – About 50 rounds fired – Range about 4000 yards. 118th Battery posted as 4th Battery of the Brigade	KGA
13/2/15	At 9.40 a.m. Observing officer reported our trenches being shelled by German battery from S.E. direction. 69th & 100th Batteries opened fire at once on the two short range hostile batteries registered by aeroplane, but fire of German battery continued intermittently. When 69th and 100th	

Army Form C. 2118.

Instructions regarding War Diaries and Intelligence Summaries are contained in F. S. Regs., Part II. and the Staff Manual respectively. Title pages will be prepared in manuscript.

WAR DIARY
or
INTELLIGENCE SUMMARY.
(Erase heading not required.)

Hour, Date, Place	Summary of Events and Information	Remarks and references to Appendices
YPRES 13/2/15	Batteries had ceased firing, they were shelled, but the enemy's fire fell short. Heavy rain fell all morning: afternoon fine.	KGL
14/2/15	11.10 a.m. orders received from G.O.C. R.A. to support attack by our infantry on trench S. of YPRES canal. 69th Battery had to switch 16 degrees to fire on this line - objective not in our zone - one gun only could be employed, and its platform was considerably damaged owing to soft nature of ground. Searching and sweeping fire employed, range 4700 to 4900 yards. Line and range taken from map - observation impossible. In the course of the afternoon several bursts of shell fire from hostile batteries fell in neighbourhood of our battery positions - range & line were inaccurate and nothing fell nearer than 100 yards to our positions.	KGL
15/2/15	All batteries opened fire at allotted points of German support trenches in brigade zone at the order of G.O.C. R.A. at 5.45 a.m.; stopped at 6.5 a.m. and reopened at 6.25 a.m. by order of G.O.C. R.A. Ceased fire at 7.15 a.m. on same authority. Searching and sweeping fire employed. 330 rounds expended.	

Instructions regarding War Diaries and Intelligence Summaries are contained in F. S. Regs., Part II. and the Staff Manual respectively. Title pages will be prepared in manuscript.

WAR DIARY
or
INTELLIGENCE SUMMARY.
(*Erase heading not required.*)

Army Form C. 2118.

Hour, Date, Place		Summary of Events and Information	Remarks and references to Appendices
YPRES	16/2/15 9.10 p.m.	83rd Infantry Brigade reported attacks on our front at the two extremes of our brigade zone. 69th and 103rd Batteries immediately opened fire on German support trenches. About 45 rounds had been expended when observing officer reported all quiet, and batteries ceased fire; infantry brigade headquarters informed.	
	17/2/15.	11.30 a.m. Infantry Brigade HQs reported attack on portion of our trenches at ZWARTELEEN – not in brigade zone – 103rd Battery opened fire on wood in rear of German trenches at this point, searching from 3600 to 3900 yards.	KG
		2pm Enemy reported active ~~just~~ north of YPRES canal. At order of G.O.C. R.A. 69th and 100th Batteries opened fire on German support trenches in this area – not in the brigade zone so observation was not possible.	
		3 p.m. 69th Battery ~~fired~~ fired on the same area ~~as~~ as above, and 103rd Battery fired at railway cutting as infantry ~~reported~~ reported ~~[illegible]~~ attacks at these points. The 69th Battery were shelled ~~with~~ with high explosive during this firing – one man wounded in leg. 5.30 p.m. 118th Battery marched into VLAMERTINGHE to join the Brigade.	
	18/2/15.	3 p.m. Observer reported our trenches were being shelled by trench mortar and shrapnel. In reply 100th Battery shelled German trenches in centre of our zone until	

Army Form C. 2118.

Instructions regarding War Diaries and Intelligence Summaries are contained in F. S. Regs., Part II. and the Staff Manual respectively. Title pages will be prepared in manuscript.

WAR DIARY
or
INTELLIGENCE SUMMARY.
(Erase heading not required.)

Hour, Date, Place	Summary of Events and Information	Remarks and references to Appendices
YPRES 18/5/15	enemy's fire was reported to have ceased. 21 Rounds were fired: observer reported one hit on parapet and others apparently in German trench. At 3.45pm. observer reported further shelling of our trenches. 100th Battery fired on short range battery registered in woods [illegible] of railway - range 3900 yds.	range 3650 yds KG
20/5/15	9 a.m. 69th Battery fired on house supposed to contain [illegible]. Range found to be 3500 yards. Six direct hits obtained, knocking down half one side of house.	
	4 30 pm 83rd Infantry Brigade asked for support in an attack by their right on German trench. 69th Battery fired on [illegible] of German trench - range taken from map - observation impossible. 69th Battery shelled while firing by battery about 5 inch calibre - firing high explosive from [illegible] direction - one man wounded. One of enemy's shell [illegible] from No. 1 Gun.	KG
21/5/15	At 2 30 a.m. 69th Battery fired on area in rear of German trenches S.W. of Brigade zone by order of G.O.C. R.A. in support of attack by our infantry in that front. Range and line from map - range 3700 yards. Fire continued for 20 minutes till stopped by order of G.O.C. R.A. Rounds expended 48.	

(73989) W4141—463. 400,000. 9/14. H.&J.Ltd. Forms/C. 2118/10.

Instructions regarding War Diaries and Intelligence Summaries are contained in F. S. Regs., Part II. and the Staff Manual respectively. Title pages will be prepared in manuscript.

WAR DIARY
or
INTELLIGENCE SUMMARY.
(Erase heading not required.)

Army Form C. 2118.

Hour, Date, Place	Summary of Events and Information	Remarks and references to Appendices
YPRES 21/2/15	At 7.30 am the 69th Battery re-opened searching and sweeping fire on the same area in support of another attack, until the 100th Battery had also opened fire on this area: 69th Battery were then ordered to stop. The 100th Battery maintained a slow rate of fire till 9.15 am. when they were stopped by order of G.O.C. R.A. A total of 110 rounds ~~was~~ fired.	
~~[illegible]~~	At 9.0 pm. the 83rd Infantry Brigade were relieved by 13th Infantry Brigade in section of trenches in the brigade zone. Orders received from G.O.C. R.A to be on the alert while the relief took place –	KG
24/2/15	Brigade zone extended to S.W. to include that previously covered by ~~[illegible]~~ Belgian battery, and section of infantry trenches in the zone named C area Left Section – Received 10.30 a.m.	Appendix I attached. Div Art.y Order BM 170 d/- 24/2/15
	Infantry reported short range hostile gun in brigade zone shelling their trenches. 100th Battery fired a few rounds at estimated position of this gun. It was arranged with Infantry Brigade Headquarters that at the signal SHORT RANGE, a battery should open fire at once on this gun.	
	At 10.30 a.m. infantry reported they were being shelled, but direction of battery was unknown. At request of G.O.C. Infantry Brigade the 100th and 103rd Battery shelled enemy trenches	

Instructions regarding War Diaries and Intelligence Summaries are contained in F. S. Regs., Part II. and the Staff Manual respectively. Title pages will be prepared in manuscript.

WAR DIARY
or
INTELLIGENCE SUMMARY.
(Erase heading not required.)

Army Form C. 2118.

Hour, Date, Place	Summary of Events and Information	Remarks and references to Appendices
YPRES 24/2/15	in C area in reply at 10.55 a.m. for 40 minutes; about 80 rounds were fired.	
	At 4.5 p.m. the infantry brigade asked for support in D area. Although outside the brigade zone on the Eastern side, the 103rd Battery opened fire on rear of German trenches	4.12 pm
	Their fire could not be observed by observing officer, and the range was lengthened accordingly for safety. At 4.25 p.m. their fire was stopped as they were being heavily shelled by 5.9 inch hostile battery from the South; for 25 minutes they were under fire. Telephonic communication to Brigade Headquarters from 103rd & 100th batteries cut by enemy's shell fire at 4.30 p.m. One gun and wagon body of 100th Battery damaged; dug-out of 100th battery Commander destroyed; acting B.S.M. Barton, 103rd battery slightly wounded.	
	At 5.5 p.m. hostile battery re-opened fire on 100th & 103rd Batteries and a 4-inch battery shelled 69th Battery position; one shell hit the corner of O.C. 69th battery's dugout. This bombardment lasted 15 minutes. One shell struck wagon body of No 4 gun, 103rd battery, setting it on fire, and destroyed the telephonists hut and Battery Commander's dug-out. Lieut. A.G. HESS, "N" Battery, R.H.A. attached 103rd Battery, and Lieut. C.E. CUMMING died of wounds about 3 hours later.	

Army Form C. 2118.

Instructions regarding War Diaries and Intelligence Summaries are contained in F. S. Regs., Part II. and the Staff Manual respectively. Title pages will be prepared in manuscript.

WAR DIARY
or
INTELLIGENCE SUMMARY.
(Erase heading not required.)

Hour, Date, Place	Summary of Events and Information	Remarks and references to Appendices
YPRES. 24/2/15	Major J.W. HOPE wounded, one gunner and one driver killed; wagon body destroyed. At 11.10 p.m. the 103rd battery were withdrawn from their position, being relieved by the 118th Battery in a new position which they had occupied before 5.45 a.m. 25/2/15.	KGl
25/2/15.	11.47 a.m. Signal SHORT RANGE received from Infantry. 100th Battery fired 3 salvoes from 3 guns at short range battery. 11.5 a.m. 69th Battery shelled with H.E. shrapnel. One wagon body pierced by bullets, destroying 2 fuzes without exploding the ammunition.	KGl
26/2/15	Signal SHORTRANGE from Infantry received at ~~[illegible]~~ 2.52 p.m. and 100th Battery fired 4 salvoes, opening fire 2.55 p.m. Received again at 4.47 p.m. 100th Battery fired 2 salvoes 4.50 p.m. No report received from Infantry as to result. 69th Battery commenced to change position at 8.30 p.m. and reported ready to open fire in new position at 10.25 p.m. 13th Infantry Brigade relieved by 83rd Infantry Brigade commenced at 8.30 p.m. Orders received from G.O.C.R.A. to be on the alert. Relief completed 10.30 p.m. in C area. Observers reported all quiet. Telephone line laid from Battalion headquarters C area	

(73989) W4141—463. 400,000. 9/14. H.&J.Ltd. Forms/C. 2118/10.

Instructions regarding War Diaries and Intelligence Summaries are contained in F. S. Regs., Part II. and the Staff Manual respectively. Title pages will be prepared in manuscript.

WAR DIARY
or
INTELLIGENCE SUMMARY.
(Erase heading not required.)

Army Form C. 2118.

Hour, Date, Place	Summary of Events and Information	Remarks and references to Appendices
YPRES 26/2/15	direct to 118th Battery. Communication not established till 7am 27/2/15. Lieut E.P. SIMPSON R.H.A. attached 69th Battery wounded by a rifle bullet in head and neck while observing from trenches	KGA
27/2/15.	1.15 pm. 100th Battery ordered to fire on short range field gun position at request of G.O.C.R.A.; position located by infantry. Battery fired a few rounds at map range viz 4000 yards. Observation not possible from our observing station.	KGA
28/2/15.	69th Battery opened fire with one section on above-mentioned field gun at request of G.O.C.R.A. 8 rounds fired in bursts with long intervals.	
	118th Battery attempted to register on German trenches but ~~[illegible]~~ communication with observer was cut by shell fire in trenches almost at once. 2 rounds fired were unobserved.	
	7.pm. 100th Battery commenced to change position. they were ready to open fire in new position at 9.40 p.m.	
	Artillery of Division divided into groups. 31st Brigade allotted to no. 2 group, commanded by Lt. Colonel E J Duffus CB. and placed under orders of G.O.C. Infantry Brigade Left Section vide attached –	Appendix II attached (Copy)
	The weather has been very variable during the past	

(73989) W4141—463. 400,000. 9/14. H.&J.Ltd. Forms/C. 2118/10.

Instructions regarding War Diaries and Intelligence Summaries are contained in F. S. Regs., Part II. and the Staff Manual respectively. Title pages will be prepared in manuscript.

Army Form C. 2118.

WAR DIARY
or
INTELLIGENCE SUMMARY.
(Erase heading not required.)

Hour, Date, Place	Summary of Events and Information	Remarks and references to Appendices
YPRES 28/2/15	fortnight. Snowy and rainy days have alternated with foggy and fine but windy, days. The ground is still very heavy and sodden.	K.G.A.
	L. S. T. Kelly Lieut. Col. R.F.A. Comdg. 31st Brigade. 1.3.15.	

Appendix I

Copy

B.M. 170 24.2.15.

1. Owing to the present shortage of ammunition with the Belgian Artillery it has been found necessary to alter somewhat the zones of fire allotted to 18 pr. Brigades.

2. The front is now divided into three areas and allotted as follows :-

From	To	Unit
I 34 C 97	Railway (inclusive)	31st Bde -
O 3 C 28	I 34 C 97	3rd -
Railway (inclusive)	I 30 (centre)	146th -

The necessary adjustments will be made to enable batteries to take on front line of German trenches.

3. The Belgian Artillery are allotted as under

A any portion of 3rd Bde Area.
Q " " " 31st " "
W + Z " " 146th

4. The Howitzers and Heavy Batteries are allotted as follows :- One howitzer & one heavy to each Infantry Brigade Section

5. For the purposes of [illegible] the sections of the Infantry defence line is divided into areas as under by 28th Divl Order No. 1. of 23rd February :-

P.T.O.

Right Section { A area   Rt. line of Canal
B area   Canal to left of trench 32 }

Left Section { C area   Left of trench 32 to railway
D area   Railway to left of line }

10.30 am

(Sd) V. M. Fergusson
Maj. B.M.R.A.

28

(4) When all arrangements are complete for bringing this redistribution into effect Group Commanders will furnish a report

(5) Acknowledge

Sd/ [illegible]
Major [illegible]
[illegible]

6-45 pm

APPENDIX II.

BM/181 — 26-2-15

In order that cooperation between the Infantry & the guns may become yet more intimate, the Brig General R.A. has decided to redistribute the Divisional Artillery as follows:-

(1) Under orders of Infantry Brigade Commanders

(a) GROUPED with the RIGHT Infantry Brigade
3rd Brigade. R.F.A.
One Howitzer Bty. R.F.A.
This right group to be commanded by Lt Col. A.L. WALKER

(b) GROUPED with the LEFT Infantry Brigade
31st Brigade R.F.A
146th " "
One howitzer battery, R.F.A
This left group to be commanded by Lt Col E.T. DUFFUS. CB

(2) Under the direct orders of the Brig Gen R.A
Heavy Brigade R.G.A.
2 groups Belgian Artillery

(3) OC 8th (Howitzer) Brigade will allot his batteries to the two sections as early as possible, informing Lt Col Walker

121/48/4

28th Division

31st Bde: R F A.

Vol III 1 – 31.3.15

Instructions regarding War Diaries and Intelligence Summaries are contained in F. S. Regs., Part II. and the Staff Manual respectively. Title pages will be prepared in manuscript.

WAR DIARY
or
INTELLIGENCE SUMMARY.
(Erase heading not required.)

Army Form C. 2118.

Hour, Date, Place	Summary of Events and Information	Remarks and references to Appendices
YPRES. 1/3/15	9.10 a.m. At request of G.O.C. R.A. 69th Battery fired at field gun located by Infantry at I 34 d 90 – Range ~~4400~~ from map – Section of 69th battery fired bursts, searching from 4300 to 4500, & sweeping. Infantry then reported through Brigade Major R.A, that this was apparently not the position of the field gun, and suggested I 35 c 77 aaa. 118th Battery fired two salvoes at this point at 9.55 a.m. 11.15 a.m. Five shell fell round position of 118th Battery. 4.20 p.m. In reply to message SHORT RANGE from the Infantry the 118th Battery fired salvoes at the supposed position of the short range field gun	Ref. Belgium map Sheet 28 – 1/20,000, N.W.
~~2/3/15~~. 2/3/15	11.20 p.m. to 11.45 p.m. A considerable number of shell fell in the neighbourhood of the ECOLE DE BIENFAISANCE and near the battery positions. At 12.30 a.m. the shelling commenced again and continued till 1 a.m. The enemy's fire appeared to sweep from the School to the moat round YPRES. Six shell burst within a few yards of 69th Battery position wounding four men, two of whom died during the night. The day was fine and windy. The 118th Battery fired registering rounds in the afternoon.	KGA.
3/3/15. →	11.46 a.m. the signal SHORTRANGE received from infantry. 118th Battery fired a salvo at 11.50 a.m. and a second one at 11.56 a.m. with an increase of 200 yards in range, as the field gun's position was reported further S.E.	KGA. KGA

Instructions regarding War Diaries and Intelligence Summaries are contained in F. S. Regs., Part II. and the Staff Manual respectively. Title pages will be prepared in manuscript.

WAR DIARY
or
INTELLIGENCE SUMMARY.
(Erase heading not required.)

Army Form C. 2118.

Hour, Date, Place	Summary of Events and Information	Remarks and references to Appendices
	12.30 p.m. 100th Battery registered on a house 50 yards in rear of German trenches. Range 4300.	
	3 p.m. 118th Battery registered on a house in their zone in rear of German trenches.	
	The following officers joined the brigade.	
	Lt Broadhurst G H, 2Lt Brink J.H, 2Lt Mollindinia W,	
	2Lt Kilkelly E C R, 2Lt Hollwey J.B,	KJA
4 3 15	9.45 am the 118th Bty fired 3 registering rounds; the telephonist with O.O slightly wounded & was replaced	
	11.0 am Observing Officer signalled "short range": the 118th Bty fired two salvos & then two more with increased range at I 35 c 7.7: the last two were unobserved.	
	11.20 am The enemy shelled the 69th & 118th Btys with 5.9" HE & 4" shrapnel till 12.8 & then four more shrapnel shell at intervals. No Casualties	

(73989) W4141—463. 400,000. 9/14. H.&J.Ltd. Forms/C. 2118/10.

Instructions regarding War Diaries and Intelligence Summaries are contained in F. S. Regs., Part II. and the Staff Manual respectively. Title pages will be prepared in manuscript.

WAR DIARY
or
INTELLIGENCE SUMMARY.
(Erase heading not required.)

Army Form C. 2118.

Hour, Date, Place	Summary of Events and Information	Remarks and references to Appendices
	2.16 pm One HE + one Shrapnell in front of 100th Bty	
	3.27 pm The 100th Bty fired two salvos at the "Short range", which stopped him firing.	KGI.
5. 3. 15	12 Rounds shrapnell were fired at intervals throughout the night at 118th Bty, the enemy presumably thinking they would be moving	
	11.15 am The enemy started shelling the supports in our zone: The 100th Bty fired 9 rounds at their trenches to retaliate before the enemy's shelling stopped.	
	11.37 am "Short range": the 100th Bty fired 2 salvos.	
	12.25 pm till 1.2 pm 18 HE + 3 Shrapnell between 100th + 118th Bty	
	1.30 pm Between 30 + 40 shell, mostly HE fell between the 100th + 118th Btys, splinters causing slight damage to equipment; 3 men of 118th Bty were wounded. Shelling stopped at 3.0 pm	
	4.15 Observer reported "Short range": 100th Bty fired two Salvoes at I.35.A.10.0	

Instructions regarding War Diaries and Intelligence Summaries are contained in F. S. Regs., Part II. and the Staff Manual respectively. Title pages will be prepared in manuscript.

WAR DIARY
or
INTELLIGENCE SUMMARY.
(Erase heading not required.)

Army Form C. 2118.

Hour, Date, Place	Summary of Events and Information	Remarks and references to Appendices
	4·20 pm 100th Bty fired one Salvo at I 35 D 37	
	4·45 pm KOSB Hq reported "short range"	
	4·47 pm 100th Bty fired two Salvos at I 35 D 37	
	The 103rd Battery started to prepare their new position.	KJ.
	~~preparatory~~	
6.3.15	A test was carried out to ascertain how quickly fire could be turned onto the German trench. At 10 12 am the KOYLI Hq asked for fire on the enemies trench at I 35 a 35	
	10·15 am the 100th Bty fired 4 Salvos	
	3·0 pm the 103rd Bty renewed the preparation of their position.	KJ.
7.3.15	11·12 am 100th Bty fired two Salvos at enemies trench	
	The 103 + 118 continued to prepare their positions and moved into them in the evening. The 69th Battery went back to the wagon line billets. On this day, by order of G.O.C.R.A, a separate observer for each battery was sent to the trenches.	

Army Form C. 2118.

Instructions regarding War Diaries and Intelligence Summaries are contained in F. S. Regs., Part II. and the Staff Manual respectively. Title pages will be prepared in manuscript.

WAR DIARY
or
INTELLIGENCE SUMMARY.
(Erase heading not required.)

Hour, Date, Place	Summary of Events and Information	Remarks and references to Appendices
8.3.15	10.24am "SHORT RANGE" was sent up and the 100th Battery fired two salvos at O.5.b.3.7 12.0 noon The 118th Battery began to register from their new position & found the range & corrector to the German trench to be cor 154 4250 1.0pm The 100th & 118th Batteries fired 4 salvos each, the 100th cor 156 4250, the 118th at cor 154 4250. 3.0pm The 100th & 118 batteries fired 5 more salvos same range & corrector; those of 118th were slightly over. 3.11pm The 100th Battery fired a salvo at SHORT RANGE The 103rd did not open fire.	K.S.
9.3.15	9.45 The 103rd started registering from their new position. They found the range to O 34 d 3 3 to be 4250 with Mk I shell & 4175 with Mk II. In accordance with orders from the left group commander, the 100th & 118th fired 4 salvos at trenches opposite 36 + 37 at 10.48 am and 2 salvos at 30 secs interval at 1.30 pm and 2 more at 1.40 pm. The observer reported the result of all these rounds as good. This was a clear day & several aeroplanes were over but no fire was opened on us.	

Instructions regarding War Diaries and Intelligence Summaries are contained in F. S. Regs., Part II. and the Staff Manual respectively. Title pages will be prepared in manuscript.

WAR DIARY
or
INTELLIGENCE SUMMARY.
(Erase heading not required.)

Army Form C. 2118.

Hour, Date, Place	Summary of Events and Information	Remarks and references to Appendices
	The reports of the infantry received by the GOC 28 Division were very complimentary to the left group on this day.	KG
10.3.15	9.30 am SHORT RANGE from the infantry. The 100th battery fired at O 5 6 37 at 4600. All three batteries fired a few registering rounds in the morning.	
	12.3 pm The brigade cooperated with the infantry in a fire attack, each battery firing 5 salvos in quick succession at the following targets: the 100th Battery fired on the trenches with a range of 4175, the 103rd battery fired on the SHORT RANGE battery with a range of from 4200 to 4400 & the 118th fired on a maxim emplacement at 4500.	
	1.30 pm The 103rd observer reported that he had located a trench mortar in a house, and fired a salvo at it	
	2.10 pm The 100th fired a salvo at SHORT RANGE.	KG

Instructions regarding War Diaries and Intelligence Summaries are contained in F. S. Regs., Part II. and the Staff Manual respectively. Title pages will be prepared in manuscript.

WAR DIARY
or
INTELLIGENCE SUMMARY.
(Erase heading not required.)

Army Form C. 2118.

Hour, Date, Place	Summary of Events and Information	Remarks and references to Appendices
11.4.15.	In the morning all the batteries fired a few rounds for registration in their zones. At 2.45 p.m. the infantry started a fire attack in which this brigade cooperated by firing 7 salvos at 2 minute intervals beginning at 2.45 pm. The 100th fired at their portion of the German trench with a range of 4175; the 103rd searched behind their trench; the 118th fired at their trench ~~searching~~ at 4200, searching 25 yards each way. At 3.20 pm the Belgian artillery reported an attack on the ZWARTELEN Salient, which actually did not take place. The 100th & 118th batteries searched behind hill 60 with several salvos. At 4.50 the infantry were opened on by a trench mortar, and the 103rd battery fired three salvos at it.	K.G.A.

Army Form C. 2118.

Instructions regarding War Diaries and Intelligence Summaries are contained in F. S. Regs., Part II. and the Staff Manual respectively. Title pages will be prepared in manuscript.

WAR DIARY
or
INTELLIGENCE SUMMARY.
(Erase heading not required.)

Hour, Date, Place	Summary of Events and Information	Remarks and references to Appendices
12. 3. 15	8.15 am. The three batteries cooperated in a fire attack with the infantry, by firing Salvos at 6 minute intervals till 9.15 am.	
	10.23 am The 103 Bty observer reported a short range gun opened on trench 31. The 100th Battery fired two rounds each at O 5 B 20 + O 5 B 18, which apparently stopped the gun firing.	
	10.52 The 103rd Bty fired 4 HE ~~rds~~ at a trench mortar at I 34 d 3 6	
	12.20. The 118th fired 8 rounds at a light German battery at I 35 b 3 6.	
	2.50 pm The three batteries repeated the same procedure as at 8.15 am ceasing fire at 3.45 pm.	
	The 103rd Battery were considered to be too close to the Lille Gate + shifted at dusk to their original position by the railway.	
	40 feet of ~~the~~ our trench were blown up this evening near ZWARTELEN, + the 118th were ready to fire on the supports if an attack came off, but all was quiet.	K.G.A.

Instructions regarding War Diaries and Intelligence Summaries are contained in F. S. Regs., Part II. and the Staff Manual respectively. Title pages will be prepared in manuscript.

WAR DIARY
or
INTELLIGENCE SUMMARY.
(Erase heading not required.)

Army Form C. 2118.

Hour, Date, Place		Summary of Events and Information	Remarks and references to Appendices
~~YRES~~	13.3.15.	Lt BROADHURST to 103rd BG.	Lack of High Explosive.
YPRES.		Periodic bombardments of enemy trenches.	Shrapnel of little use against trenches.
	14-3-15	trench 37 bombarded by bombs. 118 turned on to point where bombs thrown was supposed to be.	periscopes necessary for observation from forward battery at a scale of at least 3 per battery.
	6.15	Heavy shell fire observed to our right front at St ELOI which Germans were attacking. Telephone wires from batteries to infantry trenches continually being cut. One officer, ~~usually~~ a subaltern, observes during day for each battery and one at night for brigade. 69th relieved 100th Battery which went to billets in rear. CB	
	15-3-15. 2 a.m	batteries on the alert by order. Infantry made counter attack on St ELOI.	Difficulties arising of communication between infantry and artillery.
	11.15 a.m	118th & 69th fired a few ~~rounds~~ salvoes at enemy batteries which were troubling our infantry. These enemy batteries were located by observations from forward trenches of flashes and direction of shell holes. This location was in no way certain. CB	Telephones indistinct owing to induction produced by the number of wires running close together.
	16-3-15. 9.30 a.m	69th fired on new earthwork thrown up by enemy. In afternoon ~~firing~~ test of communication between artillery and infantry. Message sent from infantry battalion at ~~4~~ 4.34 p.m received at Art. Bde H.Q. at ~~4~~ 4.44 p.m and batteries fired at 4.46 and 4.48. Delay between infantry and artillery owing to complicated message sent I.E. Place from time date code ~~at~~ time etc. CB	

Instructions regarding War Diaries and Intelligence Summaries are contained in F. S. Regs., Part II. and the Staff Manual respectively. Title pages will be prepared in manuscript.

WAR DIARY
or
INTELLIGENCE SUMMARY.
(Erase heading not required.)

Army Form C. 2118.

Hour, Date, Place	Summary of Events and Information	Remarks and references to Appendices
YPRES 17-3-15	A quiet day. Batteries fired a few registering rounds on trenches. CB	
18-3-15	A quiet day. Batteries verified 4/118 fired at the "whizz bang" whose position cannot be truly located. General Headlam General S.D. Browne General ~~[illegible]~~ Gay and the Colonels of artillery ~~and~~ brigades ~~[illegible]~~ of 28th Div met at the 31st Bde RFA billet and discussed telephonic communication. ~~[illegible]~~ ~~[illegible]~~. CB	
19-3-15	A quiet day. 103rd made arrangements with airman for aeroplane observation on the morrow — white cross on ground to mark position for dropping messages, special electric lamp for signalling. A supplementary method of communication at night between infantry & batteries by means of rockets discussed. CB	According to F S R II ~~[illegible]~~ office should be cut down to a minimum yet office work has swollen to vast proportions. Returns, states reports, enquiries, messages clutter the room & clog the mind of the Bde Staff. It is suggested that a rubber stamp be obtained with a single appropriate word ~~[illegible]~~ which be a sufficient reply to most questions received here.
20-3-15.	103rd fired with aeroplane observation — a white letters ~~[illegible]~~ of canvas on the ground where ~~[illegible]~~ a signaller with a Special electric lamp signalled to air observer. In morning 69th fired on a new sap thrown forward by enemy. CB new targets spotted by air observer.	
21-3-15	Very clear cloudless day. Many German aeroplanes about which kept batteries quiet. Fourth battery position to be chosen and prepared. Attack expected & batteries to fire in case of heavy rifle fire in front. CB	
22-3-15	118 registered in the afternoon by aeroplane. 100th Battery relieved 69th which went to billets in rear. Recce party left to prepare new CB position for fourth battery of brigade.	

(73989) W4141—463. 400,000. 9/14. H.&J.Ltd. Forms/C. 2118/10.

Instructions regarding War Diaries and Intelligence Summaries are contained in F. S. Regs., Part II. and the Staff Manual respectively. Title pages will be prepared in manuscript.

WAR DIARY
or
INTELLIGENCE SUMMARY.
(Erase heading not required.)

Army Form C. 2118.

Hour, Date, Place		Summary of Events and Information	Remarks and references to Appendices
YPRES	23-3-15	100th Bty registered by aeroplane. Major ~~Barr~~ Hudson comdg 118 went forward and reconnoitred positions close behind (1000x about) infantry trenches where a section of guns could be placed to enfilade enemy trenches on left. General Sir H. Smith Dorrien comdg II Army arrived in afternoon and looked at 118th Bty position. CB	
	24-3-15	103rd fired Grounds.	
	25-3-15	~~Communication~~ Letter from Staff about communication with infantry. no firing other than registration. 69th ~~preparing a few the battery position in ground of which details are~~. CB	
	26-3-15 8-30	103rd fired on enemy trench mortar which was worrying our infantry. A very clear day. Two enemy observation balloons up which stopped our firing. CB	
	27-3-15 11AM	103rd fired on trench in front of 34 and 118th on hill 60. CB	informed by R.A. H.Q. that a number discs for shell to increase ∠ of descent ~~fuzes~~ will shortly be available for issue.
	28-3-15	10 A.M. 118th on hill 60. noon 103rd on trench mortar.	
29-3	3 p.m	100th battery blew in portion of German parapet with percussion. Infantry very pleased. 69th ~~in~~ went into their new position in the evening. CB	
30-3		69th registered - 118th on hills 60 & 59. Gen Gay, Divisional Art Commander, visited Brigade. CB	—
31-3		100th fired on German trenches - 118th on hill 60 & 59. Mules to be ~~issued~~ issued to batteries in the place of light draught horses. Enemy's observation balloons up. Enemy aeroplanes reconnoitre very early in the morning, they are always put to flight by our own machines, ~~[illegible]~~. CB	
	~~[illegible]~~	~~103 fired on house called Forest Lodge. 118th on German trenches.~~ CB	K G Ireland Lt. RFA Adjt 31st Bde

121/5140

28th Division

31st Bde: R. F. A.

Vol IV 1–30.4.15.

Instructions regarding War Diaries and Intelligence Summaries are contained in F. S. Regs., Part II. and the Staff Manual respectively. Title pages will be prepared in manuscript.

WAR DIARY
or
INTELLIGENCE SUMMARY.
(Erase heading not required.)

Army Form C. 2118.

Hour, Date, Place			Summary of Events and Information	Remarks and references to Appendices
YPRES	1-4-15		100th fired on German trenches 8 rounds – 103rd on house called Forest Lodge. Ammunition expended 27 rounds shrapnel in all	
	2-4-15		69th fired within two minutes of call from infantry. The message was telephoned from Battalion H.Q through Art Bde H.Q. This was a test of communication. The 69th detachments were in their dug-outs owing to their being shelled, otherwise they would have been quicker.	
	3-4-15		100th and 103rd fired on supposed positions of short range battery. In afternoon at 2pm enemy fired high explosive shrapnel on the 103rd. Major Hope returned in the morning and rejoined 103rd.	
	4-4-15	11AM	100th battery fired on miner wafer house. 69th on hill 60.	
	5-4-15	~~[illegible]~~ 11 AM	Trench 35 was heavily bombed by a battery of enemy trench mortars. The trench was blown in in many places and the infantry forced to evacuate. W. H Hawkins ~~[illegible]~~, the 100th observer was twice buried. Five points were fired on before mortars were located and then owing to ~~[illegible]~~ curtailment of ammunition effective fire could not be maintained. The enemy mortars, however, stopped for the time but commenced later at 3p.m when 69th fired 6 rounds of high explosive at the house where mortars were entrenched, stopping their fire.	

Instructions regarding War Diaries and Intelligence Summaries are contained in F. S. Regs., Part II. and the Staff Manual respectively. Title pages will be prepared in manuscript.

WAR DIARY
or
INTELLIGENCE SUMMARY.
(Erase heading not required.)

Army Form C. 2118.

Hour, Date, Place	Summary of Events and Information	Remarks and references to Appendices
YPRES 6-4-15 10A.M.	Trench mortars again started on trench 35. 100th and 69th opened on supposed position of enemy mortars, with no effective result. Permission to ~~[illegible]~~ exceed daily allowance was asked for but refused. Mortars stopped after an hour's bombing.	
1.35 p.m	Bombing recommenced batteries fired a few rounds, without appreciable effect. Bombing stopped in half an hour. Col Kelly went over to ZONNEBEKE to see French positions which we are to take over.	
7-4-15	a quiet day, 100th registered. ~~[illegible]~~. In the evening batteries stood to the guns as the infantry ~~[illegible]~~ were expecting an attack. In half an hour the scare blew over. Secret orders to move on the morrow ~~[illegible]~~ nothing definite settled as to billets in new position. Orders as to billetting area arrived late in evening.	
8-4-15	Battery wagons and transport moved from VLAMERTINGHE to billeting area two miles W of POPERINGHE. A section from each battery was withdrawn in the evening and replaced by a section of relieving ~~[illegible]~~ batteries.	

(73989) W4141—463. 400,000. 9/14. H.&J.Ltd. Forms/C. 2118/10.

Instructions regarding War Diaries and Intelligence Summaries are contained in F. S. Regs., Part II. and the Staff Manual respectively. Title pages will be prepared in manuscript.

WAR DIARY
or
INTELLIGENCE SUMMARY.
(*Erase heading not required.*)

Army Form C. 2118.

Place	Date	Summary of Events and Information	Remarks and references to Appendices
YPRES	8-4-15	relieved sections went to ~~[illegible]~~ their respective wagon lines at VLAMERTINGHE for the night.	Telephone wires were not ~~[illegible]~~ reeled up but were handed over to 28th Bde. RFA. as they lay.
ST JAN-TER-BIEZEN	9-4-15	Batteries except sections in action moved in the morning to billets at St JAN about two miles W of POPERINGHE. In the evening remaining sections were withdrawn and joined their batteries. ~~Majors of batteries [illegible] new billets and wagon lines in new positions~~. 2/Lieut J A DONNELLY to 69th Battery from Base. Lieut. J. H. BRADDICK to Brigade Ammn Coln from Base.	2/Lt Donnelly [illegible]
	10-4-15	~~Brigade Staff~~ a days rest. OC's of batteries went out by motor to inspect billets and wagon lines in new position at VLOORENHOEK.	
FREZENBURG	11-4-15	Brigade Staff moved to new billet at VLOORENHOEK in the morning. First sections of batteries went into position in the evening, relieving a French section. The reliefs were completed by 11.30 p.m. 69th, 103rd, 118th in action. The 100th remained in rest. Battery positions were about 1500x W of ZONNEBEKE. Enemy's front trenches about 3000x away.	
	12-4-15	Sections in action registered. Remaining sections came into action in the evening, completing the relief of the French batteries. A Zeppelin passed over in the night.	
	13-4-15	About 5 p.m a 21cm Howitzer shelled the area of the 69th and 103rd batteries and infantry supports along railway line. The shelling continued for one hour and a half and again later. Detachments were withdrawn from ~~[illegible]~~ guns. One serjeant of the 103rd was wounded and one gun of the 69th damaged by a shell which burst a yard from the right wheel of the gun.	
	14-4-15	The	

Instructions regarding War Diaries and Intelligence Summaries are contained in F. S. Regs., Part II. and the Staff Manual respectively. Title pages will be prepared in manuscript.

WAR DIARY
or
INTELLIGENCE SUMMARY.
(Erase heading not required.)

Army Form C. 2118.

Place	Hour, Date, Place	Summary of Events and Information	Remarks and references to Appendices
FREZENBURG	14-4-15	The three batteries in action registered targets in their zones.	
	15-4-15	[illegible] & 69 did not fire. 118 registered. In the evening 4 batteries [illegible] as an attack by the Germans all along the line was expected. Nothing unusual, however, took place.	
	16-4-15	The 103rd verified WHITE LODGE (J 6 a 3.4) and registered ground in front of trenches A and B the right trenches of 84th Inf. Bde. 69th Right Sectn changed with the 149 Battery Sectn. 118th registered to N in the zone they are taking over	
	17-4-15	Bde H.Q. moved further forward. 69th Sectn registered new zone. At 8 pm new system of grouping comes into ~~[illegible]~~ force by which 31st Bde + 37th Howz Battery come under the command of Lt Col [illegible] to support the 84th Infantry Bde; each battery having communication ~~[illegible]~~ with the Battn whose front it covers.	
	1 pm	The other sectn of 69th changes and Battery covers zone of left Battn of Bde. Lt Broadhurst was admitted to hospital sick. Lt Holloway takes over duties of Orderly Officer to O.C. Brigade. 2/Lt Thomas came from Coln to 103rd Battery	

(73989) W4141—463. 400,000. 9/14. H.&J.Ltd. Forms/C. 2118/10.

Instructions regarding War Diaries and Intelligence Summaries are contained in F. S. Regs., Part II. and the Staff Manual respectively. Title pages will be prepared in manuscript.

WAR DIARY
or
INTELLIGENCE SUMMARY.
(Erase heading not required.)

Army Form C. 2118.

Hour, Date, Place		Summary of Events and Information	Remarks and references to Appendices
FREZENBURG	18-4-15.	at 8.15 a.m. the 69th 118th & 37th Howr. commenced to fire on German trenches in front of 21 and 22 in 84 Inf. Bde Zone; firing ceased at 8.45 — Infantry report that it was accurate and effective except in the case of a few short bursts. During the afternoon the 37th Battery dealt with the German M.W. (minenwerfer) while the 69th kept up short bursts of fire on German trench D23 c 4 4 to D23 c 4.6. The 103 Battery registered their Zone from their new line of Guns. 2/Lt Kennedy rejoins Bde. and Capt. the Hon. H. G. L. Playfair is posted to the Bde. Major S. G. R. Willis took over command of 69th Battery vice Major Bedwell ~~sent on sick leave~~, admitted to Hospital	
	19-4-15	The 37th continued to take on the M.W. but their fire did not effectually silence the M.W. The 118 shelled a Machine Gun Empt. in Enemies' front trench. During the afternoon the 69th fired at intervals	

(73989) W4141—463. 400,000. 9/14. H.&J.Ltd. Forms/C. 2118/10.

Instructions regarding War Diaries and Intelligence Summaries are contained in F. S. Regs., Part II. and the Staff Manual respectively. Title pages will be prepared in manuscript.

WAR DIARY
or
INTELLIGENCE SUMMARY.
(Erase heading not required.)

Army Form C. 2118.

Hour, Date, Place	Summary of Events and Information	Remarks and references to Appendices
FREZENBURG 19-4-15	on the same portions of trench as yesterday to enable the infantry to carry on digging. The change of the 100 with 118th who go back to rest, was completed at 1130 pm.	
20-4-15	The 100th Battery registered its zone in the morning, the 69th fired at intervals on the same bit of trench in front of junction of 21+22 trench Capt The Hon. G. Playfair was killed while observing from the front line trenches. Orders received from B.M. RA to prepare position for fourth battery to be able to shoot on D.29. Wire put out connecting Bde to Batteries from advanced Infantry Bde. fighting HQ at D.27.a.9.2.	
21-4-15.	All Batteries started firing at 10.50 on German trench in D 29 with a section of 69th on trench in front of trenches 21, + 22. firing ceased at 12.30 pm. at 4.45 batteries started again and fired for half an hour. at 5.35 pm G.O.C. 84th Inf Bde. ordered all batteries to fire for five minutes rapid the 100th was not able to	By order [illegible] of G.O.C. R.A. to relieve pressure on hill 60

Instructions regarding War Diaries and Intelligence Summaries are contained in F. S. Regs., Part II. and the Staff Manual respectively. Title pages will be prepared in manuscript.

WAR DIARY
or
INTELLIGENCE SUMMARY.
(Erase heading not required.)

Army Form C. 2118.

Hour, Date, Place	Summary of Events and Information	Remarks and references to Appendices
FREZENBURG	fire as they were being shelled; during this shelling Sgt Aves of the 69th battery was wounded. Major Ramsden selected another position and began digging about 7.30 pm. Lt F.R. Barry + Lt A. Barker of the 3rd New Army joined for a period of 14 days instruction. Lt G.H. Broadhurst rejoins 2/Lt Brink is temporarily transferred to the 69th to replace 2/Lt Mackenzie who has been sent to rest for several days.	111th and 112th Brigades
22-4-15.	The 100th battery selected an alternative position. at 11.20 69th fired on trench howitzers and also at party of Germans collecting wood. at 3 pm 69th fired on German front trench at 22 and the 100 at trench opposite 20. at 7.20 pm the Brigade opened fire to cover area near at crossroad ~~[illegible]~~ at BROADSEINDE	

Instructions regarding War Diaries and Intelligence Summaries are contained in F. S. Regs., Part II. and the Staff Manual respectively. Title pages will be prepared in manuscript.

WAR DIARY
or
INTELLIGENCE SUMMARY.
(Erase heading not required.)

Army Form C. 2118.

Hour, Date, Place	Summary of Events and Information	Remarks and references to Appendices
FREZENBURG 23/4/15 2	12.20 am 69th support 22 trench in response to "SOS" message, and fired 207 rds at German trench. [illegible] rations arrived for Bde last night. sanction to use iron rations if no ration arrive today given at 8.30 a.m. — the 100th fired six rounds on gun target at E.20.a.1.6 and the 103rd fired six rds [illegible] I.30 [illegible] 22. The 69th at 12 noon ~~fired~~ ranged on M.W. and fired 5 rounds H.E. at it and at 1.30 pm fired on fleeing Germans who were scattered by 34th Howr. at 3.30 pm. the 103rd engaged battery at D.30.c.2.5 and silenced it. During the afternoon the 69th fired at intervals on M.W. emplacements and at 5.0 pm — shelled party of Germans near to M.W. emplacement.	Fire was greatly hindered by presence of German aeroplanes, ~~[illegible]~~

(73989) W4141—463. 400,000. 9/14. H.&J.Ltd. Forms/C. 2118/10.

Instructions regarding War Diaries and Intelligence Summaries are contained in F. S. Regs., Part II. and the Staff Manual respectively. Title pages will be prepared in manuscript.

WAR DIARY
or
INTELLIGENCE SUMMARY.
(Erase heading not required.)

Army Form C. 2118.

Hour, Date, Place	Summary of Events and Information	Remarks and references to Appendices
24/4/15 84. Infantry Bde. H.Qrs.	Battery while it was changing position by keeping down the fire of this battery. During the afternoon the 69th and 100th Batteries fired on German trenches opposite to 22. The situation in these trenches (20—22) was unsettled as two large Minenwerfer were bombing them all the afternoon. A 'Whizz Bang' was enfilading 22 trench from D 23 & 4.3 and was taken on by the 146th Bde. Casualties Bde H.qrs 1 man killed 1 wounded 69th {1 gunner {1 Driver } wounded 100 {2 gunners killed {1 gunner wounded 103 B.S.M. Milne wounded	

Instructions regarding War Diaries and Intelligence Summaries are contained in F. S. Regs., Part II. and the Staff Manual respectively. Title pages will be prepared in manuscript.

WAR DIARY
or
INTELLIGENCE SUMMARY.
(Erase heading not required.)

Army Form C. 2118.

Hour, Date, Place	Summary of Events and Information	Remarks and references to Appendices
FROZENBURG 24-4-15	Lt Col. Kelly ~~[illegible]~~ changes his H.Qrs. to 84th Infantry Bde H.Qrs to ensure the necessary co-operation owing to the sudden offensive movement by the Germans along the northern side of the YPRES salient. The 18th Battery came into action on the west bank of the Yser canal north of YPRES and is not under direct command of the Bde. The 89th, 100th and 103rd each kept one section on their original ~~[illegible]~~ positions and turn the other to the north to repel the German attacks, the 100th Battery moving one section into a new position to do this. The Sectn of 103rd which was on the old line engaged and kept in check a German Field Battery at D 30 c 25 which had the FREZENBURG cross roads very accurately registered and which must have had direct observation on this point. The 103rd greatly assisted the heavy	

Army Form C. 2118.

Instructions regarding War Diaries and Intelligence Summaries are contained in F. S. Regs., Part II. and the Staff Manual respectively. Title pages will be prepared in manuscript.

WAR DIARY
or
INTELLIGENCE SUMMARY.
(Erase heading not required.)

Hour, Date, Place	Summary of Events and Information	Remarks and references to Appendices
25/4/15 84th Infantry Bde Hqrs.	at 3.10 pm the 2nd Northumberlands reported Minenwerfers firing on 22 and 23 trenches, the 69th engaged these with H.E. followed by Shrapnel D23c83. at 5 pm the 69th turned on to Minenwerfer in D23a10.4 while the 100th shelled parapet in front of trench 20. at 5.25 2nd Northumberlands reported 21 trench being shelled with H.E. from front and right flank. 103rd turned on to D30c25 and the 69th on E20c12. at 5.34 pm O.C. 146th Bde reports from 366 Battery that our infantry are retiring over the CRAVEN STAFEL ~~staff~~ ridge, the 69th were informed of this at 5.41 pm.	

(73989) W4141—463. 400,000. 9/14. H.&J.Ltd. Forms/C. 2118/10.

Army Form C. 2118.

Instructions regarding War Diaries and Intelligence Summaries are contained in F. S. Regs., Part II. and the Staff Manual respectively. Title pages will be prepared in manuscript.

WAR DIARY
or
INTELLIGENCE SUMMARY.
(*Erase heading not required.*)

Hour, Date, Place	Summary of Events and Information	Remarks and references to Appendices
84 Infantry Bde. H.Qrs. 25/4/15.	At 6 p.m. the 69th turned on the German battery in E.13 C.9.1 which the 2nd Northumberlands reported was enfilading their trench.	
	7.10 p.m. 69th opened on D 23 b.4.3 to stop Minenwerfer	
	[illegible] reported all quiet	
	7.45. 1st Monmouths reported [illegible] trench being shelled [illegible] the front the 69th opened on E.20 C.11 at 10.10 pm	
12 m.n.?	During the night the 116th Battery changed position and occupied the ridge vacated by the 4.7 Battery of the 27th Division, so that it could fire North against the German advance from GRAVENSTAFEL to ST. JULIEN	

(73989) W4141—463. 400,000. 9/14. H.&J.Ltd. Forms/C. 2118/10.

Instructions regarding War Diaries and Intelligence Summaries are contained in F. S. Regs., Part II. and the Staff Manual respectively. Title pages will be prepared in manuscript.

WAR DIARY
or
INTELLIGENCE SUMMARY.
(Erase heading not required.)

Army Form C. 2118.

Hour, Date, Place	Summary of Events and Information	Remarks and references to Appendices
84th Infantry Bde H.Qrs. 26/4/15.	12.30 am. 64th Battery received S.O.S. 21 + 22 in reply to which they fired 138 rds. Shrapnel on German front and support trenches after which Batter H.Qrs reported all quiet.	
	9.15 am. 69th reports from Northumberlands that Germans are collecting Scaling ladders opposite 21 Trench and have cleared gaps in their own parapet in front of 22.	
	1.45 pm. 103rd Battery reports that they are firing at the German Trenches and asked the Infantry to report if the shells were going too far over or not.	
	4 pm. The 100th were firing left hand corner of D.F.d.	

Instructions regarding War Diaries and Intelligence Summaries are contained in F. S. Regs., Part II. and the Staff Manual respectively. Title pages will be prepared in manuscript.

WAR DIARY
or
INTELLIGENCE SUMMARY.
(Erase heading not required.)

Army Form C. 2118.

Hour, Date, Place	Summary of Events and Information	Remarks and references to Appendices
84th Infantry Bde Area 25/4/15	5.25am Germans advancing from GRAVENSTAFEL. 8.15 am 100th Battery fired at Germans advancing over crest D 7 a + b + D8 8.30 The 103rd joined the 100th in firing on the Germans advancing over crest D 7 a + D8 11 am The 100th Battery reports — fighting seems to have nearly stopped near ST JULIEN. The 100th engaged about a brigade of infantry moving from D 7 b 7 c through ST JULIEN going S.W. between 8 am and 9 am causing them to scatter — When a report from 69th observer came in stating the Germans were shelling and using fumes on 22 trench a section of the 69th + 100th opened fire on German trench opposite 22. 2/Lieut W. MALLALIEU, 100th Battery R.F.A. wounded	

Instructions regarding War Diaries and Intelligence Summaries are contained in F. S. Regs., Part II. and the Staff Manual respectively. Title pages will be prepared in manuscript.

WAR DIARY
or
INTELLIGENCE SUMMARY.
(Erase heading not required.)

Army Form C. 2118.

Hour, Date, Place	Summary of Events and Information	Remarks and references to Appendices
[illegible] Infantry Bde H.Qrs 26/4/15.	6.5 pm The 100th reports Infantry attack seems to have made some progress and appear to have reached crest of ridge running S.E. D.15a1.8. Casualties 100th Battery Cpl Cartwright wounded. During the last three days the Germans have bombarded the whole area of the ZONNEBEKE salient very heavily, Cross roads and thatched roof farms in particular receiving ~~particular~~ attention. ~~[illegible]~~ Shells filled with inflammable explosive used against farms. A very large number burnt down in consequence. Considerable casualties in horses at the wagon lines caused by shell fire drawn by batteries of Canadian Division and 146th Brigade R.F.A., which took up positions within a few hundred yards of them.	

Instructions regarding War Diaries and Intelligence Summaries are contained in F. S. Regs., Part II. and the Staff Manual respectively. Title pages will be prepared in manuscript.

WAR DIARY
or
INTELLIGENCE SUMMARY.
(*Erase heading not required.*)

Army Form C. 2118.

Hour, Date, Place	Summary of Events and Information	Remarks and references to Appendices
FREZENBURG	Nothing happened during night.	
27/4/15	The 69th Fired on M.W. + BROODSEINDE cross roads	
	~~the~~ 100th fired on Germans working at Emplacements at 9.am. The 69th engaged battery at D.23. B.3.5. at the request of the Infantry. The 100th Battery fired at what appeared to be the commencement of German advance 500 yds W. of last reported target (forwarded to BMRA) until satisfied that no further movement was in progress. The 103rd reported all quiet along their front. [illegible] [illegible] [illegible] Bde Hqrs. wounded.	
28/4/15	at 9. Am. The situation along our front was normal. The 100th Battery was in observation of enemy's [illegible] W. of HAANEBEEK. BC. observing from E of hill 37. This was done to protect our flank. The 69th + 103 are in observation of front trench line.	

(73989) W4141—463. 400,000. 9/14. H.&J.Ltd. Forms/C. 2118/10.

Instructions regarding War Diaries and Intelligence Summaries are contained in F. S. Regs., Part II. and the Staff Manual respectively. Title pages will be prepared in manuscript.

WAR DIARY
or
INTELLIGENCE SUMMARY.
(Erase heading not required.)

Army Form C. 2118.

Hour, Date, Place	Summary of Events and Information	Remarks and references to Appendices
30th continued.	The N slopes of hill 37 were heavily shelled + telephone communication with 100th + their observer was constantly cut and very difficult to repair. The late Bde H.Qrs. was burned to the ground all but G.S. wagons telephone cart and medical carts with stores were destroyed. The staff which was in the dugout near the farm moved to Bde First aid post at D25. b. 6.2. the first aid post being moved to Farm D25 b. 1.5 German aeroplane was brought down near dugout at 1 p.m.	
	Casualties. 12822 Dr Richardson W. 69th wounded. 103rd 42316 Gr Marshall H. killed. 64554 S.S. Clark 23231 Dr Mitchell R. 61642 Dr Ellicott C. 660983 Baddle J. 413 Dr Cunningham J 71579 Dr Bunyan 65501 Dr Ross W. 89562 Dr Tingall B.H. wounded. 103rd Battery	

Instructions regarding War Diaries and Intelligence Summaries are contained in F. S. Regs., Part II. and the Staff Manual respectively. Title pages will be prepared in manuscript.

WAR DIARY
or
INTELLIGENCE SUMMARY.
(Erase heading not required.)

Army Form C. 2118.

Hour, Date, Place	Summary of Events and Information	Remarks and references to Appendices
Sheet 28 1/40000 D25.b.6.2		
29-11-15	During the night the 100th Battery fired a few rounds at house D.8.c.5.8. where movement had been observed at 5.50 am. The 103rd Battery reported that they fired at German Transport moving westward from KEIBERG last night between 10 and 11 pm. in response to similar action by the enemy.	
	7.56 am 2nd Northumberlands reported Minenwerfer firing on 21 trench and asked for artillery fire. 69th battery informed of this at 8 am.	
	11 am 69th Battery registered various points in German lines but was greatly hindered by constant presence of German aeroplanes.	
	12 noon to 1 pm 69th Battery fired at "Sausage" balloon and forced it to descend – it reappeared for a short while at a longer range.	

(73989) W4141—463. 400,000. 9/14. H.&J.Ltd. Forms/C. 2118/10.

Instructions regarding War Diaries and Intelligence Summaries are contained in F. S. Regs., Part II. and the Staff Manual respectively. Title pages will be prepared in manuscript.

WAR DIARY
or
INTELLIGENCE SUMMARY.
(Erase heading not required.)

Army Form C. 2118.

Hour, Date, Place	Summary of Events and Information	Remarks and references to Appendices
Sheet 20 D25.662 29/4/15	3.30pm 69th Battery opened fire alternately on two batteries one of which was shelling 21 trench and finally silenced the battery which was firing on 21 about 4 pm.	
	5 pm 100th Battery registered ground near GRAVENSTAFEL village ceased firing at 5.30pm.	
	5.24 pm 103rd Battery opened fire on cross roads at KEIBERG and at E 19 d.7.4. then turned on E battery at J.6.b.8.7. and at K.1.a.3.1. ceased firing at 6.10 pm.	
	9 pm 103rd Battery opened fire on cross roads D.30.d.2.6. and D 29. b.6.0. fired 32 rds shrapnel	
	11 pm reports from 100th state Germans still improving their trenches in rear of the HANNEBEKE also state German aeroplanes very active.	

(73989) W4141—463. 400,000. 9/14. H.&J.Ltd. Forms/C. 2118/10.

Instructions regarding War Diaries and Intelligence Summaries are contained in F. S. Regs., Part II. and the Staff Manual respectively. Title pages will be prepared in manuscript.

WAR DIARY
or
INTELLIGENCE SUMMARY.
(Erase heading not required.)

Army Form C. 2118.

Hour, Date, Place	Summary of Events and Information	Remarks and references to Appendices
D25 b. 6.2 29/4/15	11.40 pm — 69th Fired 8 rds at trench Mortar and 6 rds at German front trench opposite 21 trench to stop rifle grenade bombing. Casualties. 69th No. 76436 Dr J Markly wounded 30490 Dr J Maginnis 12822 Dr W. Richardson 11 horses killed 103rd No 42316 Gr H Marshall Killed	
D25 b. 6.2. 30/4/15	1.30 am — 69th Battery searched up road from cross roads at 22 trench. 11.35 — 100th Battery registered trenches in front of ST JULIEN Church also dugout in support trenches South east of ST JULIEN wood.	

(73989) W4141—463. 400,000. 9/14. H.&J.Ltd. Forms/C. 2118/10.

Instructions regarding War Diaries and Intelligence Summaries are contained in F. S. Regs., Part II. and the Staff Manual respectively. Title pages will be prepared in manuscript.

WAR DIARY
or
INTELLIGENCE SUMMARY.
(Erase heading not required.)

Army Form C. 2118.

Hour, Date, Place	Summary of Events and Information	Remarks and references to Appendices
D 25 b. 6.2 30/4/15	12 0.p.m. 69th Battery observer reports that it is a long range 5.9" How which is shelling 22 Trench. The 69th shelled German Trench in front of 22 and did considerable damage. Germans shelled 69th Farm causing it to burn very rapidly and although every effort was made to save the limbers which were in the barns they were not saved. Two wounded infantry in the barns were rescued in a serious condition. Gunner Wilson. 69th Battery was killed in the farm.	
	10 p.m – 10.30 p.m. 103rd fired at cross roads at E.26.A.1.5. — F.19.d.8.4. — D.30.d.2.6.	
	The 69th Battery who were unable to locate a large Minenwerfer searched the area from where it was firing also wood in D 23 a + b. later it was reported to be firing from front trench – ranging postponed till morning	
		Jas. S. Kelly Lieut. Col. R.F.A. Comdg. 31st Bde. 30.4.15.

(73989) W4141—463. 400,000. 9/14. H.&J.Ltd. Forms/C. 2118/10.

28th Division

121/5556

31st Bde: R.F.A.

Vol V: 1 — 31.5.15

Instructions regarding War Diaries and Intelligence Summaries are contained in F. S. Regs., Part II. and the Staff Manual respectively. Title pages will be prepared in manuscript.

WAR DIARY
or
INTELLIGENCE SUMMARY.
(Erase heading not required.)

Army Form C. 2118.

Hour, Date, Place	Summary of Events and Information	Remarks and references to Appendices
1-5-15 D.25 b.6.2.	at 8.30 The 100th Battery fired 14 rounds at various targets on the right of their zone. The 69th Battery started to search for Minenwerfer which was firing on left half of 22 trench. Sparks could be seen coming from supposed direction of the MW and after 24 rds were fired the O.C. trench reported that the MW had ceased firing. The 103rd successfully registered enemy's front trench opposite 18.	

Army Form C. 2118.

Instructions regarding War Diaries and Intelligence Summaries are contained in F. S. Regs., Part II. and the Staff Manual respectively. Title pages will be prepared in manuscript.

WAR DIARY
or
INTELLIGENCE SUMMARY.

(Erase heading not required.)

Hour, Date, Place	Summary of Events and Information	Remarks and references to Appendices
D25. b. 6.2 2/5/15	Orders received stating that 1 section per battery would probably be withdrawn to a line running just north of YPRES. The 69th fired at "sausage" observation ballon but the range was too long. The 110th fired at a German earth work which was made under cover of dark. The 103rd took on a German battery which was located by infantry. The infantry in left zone reported that Germans were bringing up guns and massing them to the N.E. of their trenches. Assistance could only be given with 1 gun of 110th Bty. At 9 P.M. the sections started withdrawing delay in getting away was caused by shells falling among the teams in the wagon line All sections arrived at their new positions by 2.30 and commenced digging	

(73989) W4141—463. 400,000. 9/14. H.&J.Ltd. Forms/C. 2118/10.

Instructions regarding War Diaries and Intelligence Summaries are contained in F. S. Regs., Part II. and the Staff Manual respectively. Title pages will be prepared in manuscript.

WAR DIARY
or
INTELLIGENCE SUMMARY.
(Erase heading not required.)

Army Form C. 2118.

Hour, Date, Place	Summary of Events and Information	Remarks and references to Appendices
2/5/15	The portion of Bde staff which was at the dressing station moved off at 10 p.m. and took up new H.Qrs. in the Wall of YPRES. Telephone lines laid out to new battery positions, which sections occupied after withdrawal	
	Casualties	
	Bde Staff	
	No Gr Hope	
	No Gr Rolph	
	at 7.25 p.m. The Buffs in left sector report that Germans were advancing in D.11a since 5 p.m. Also two German batteries taking up positions near ~~[illegible]~~ D10.d 40. Although these movements were not in zone of the Brigade and no observing officers were out to control fire in this direction assistance of single guns of 69th and 108th Batteries and a section of 37th Battery was lent shooting being done by map onto roads and likely points in this area	

(73989) W4141—463. 400,000. 9/14. H.&J.Ltd. Forms/C. 2118/10.

Instructions regarding War Diaries and Intelligence Summaries are contained in F. S. Regs., Part II. and the Staff Manual respectively. Title pages will be prepared in manuscript.

WAR DIARY
or
INTELLIGENCE SUMMARY.
(Erase heading not required.)

Army Form C. 2118.

Hour, Date, Place	Summary of Events and Information	Remarks and references to Appendices
YPRES. 3/5/15	The sections of each Battery withdrawn to positions W and S. of LA BRIQUE were reported in action by 2.30 am. Wires were laid out to observing stations and Battalion Headquarters by batteries these sections, and the positions prepared where necessary. While coming into Head qrs. Lt. Col. Kelly was wounded in the leg.	
12 m.n.	Casualties Dr Lyons killed Bdr Midwinter wounded 2 Lt Benham wounded.	
4/5/15	Shelled heavily all the morning communication with batteries impossible Major Ramsden takes over command of Bde. Batteries gave all support they were able by firing by map. During afternoon a wire was laid from Batteries to Q.H.Q line just east of POTIJZE which had direct wires to Battns, from this place Major Ramsden worked the Bde. In the evening Lt. Ireland with Bde Staff moved to dugouts in POTIJZE wood and joined Major Ramsden	

Instructions regarding War Diaries and Intelligence Summaries are contained in F. S. Regs., Part II. and the Staff Manual respectively. Title pages will be prepared in manuscript.

WAR DIARY
or
INTELLIGENCE SUMMARY.
(*Erase heading not required.*)

Army Form C. 2118.

Hour, Date, Place	Summary of Events and Information	Remarks and references to Appendices
5/5/15 POTIJZE	69th + 103rd did considerable registration with observers and dealt with machine guns and men in the open with good effect. The Rangers were being badly shelled and batteries shelled the northern side of hill 37 just East of FORTUIN. During the afternoon all batteries shot by map at roads near ST JULIEN. 100th Battery was not in proper working order probably due to the absence of telephone communication. 9.30 – 10 pm. Batteries turned on to road at FORTUIN 9 pm. 69th put some HE into VAN HEULE farm.	Casualties Lt Swain wounded.
6/5/15 POTIJZE	At the request of Gen Bols 1 section per battery was detailed to shell the German front and support trenches at intervals throughout the day while the other Section dealt with special targets. 103rd did good registration conducted by Lt Broadhurst. 100th ~~[illegible]~~ registered with all four guns during morning.	

(73989) W4141—463. 400,000. 9/14. H.&J.Ltd. Forms/C. 2118/10.

Instructions regarding War Diaries and Intelligence Summaries are contained in F. S. Regs., Part II. and the Staff Manual respectively. Title pages will be prepared in manuscript.

WAR DIARY
or
~~INTELLIGENCE SUMMARY.~~
(*Erase heading not required.*)

Army Form C. 2118.

Hour, Date, Place	Summary of Events and Information	Remarks and references to Appendices
7/5/15	69th battery successfully dealt with German attack during night. at 9am Lt Col G.H.A. White arrived at Headqrs. and took over command of Brigade. The 5th Durhams Howr T. Battery got into position and registered the German trenches near the HANNEBEKE. 103rd Battery manage to keep communication with the observer all day and did some very useful shooting. 69th and 100th had no communication with observers except through Inf. Bde. From 11.30 am to 3/pm everything was quiet after which all batteries engaged whizz bangs and front trenches. 2Lt Benham died of wounds received in action. 2/Lt Kennedy was wounded while repairing telephone wires. gun No (76) 103rd was replaced.	

Instructions regarding War Diaries and Intelligence Summaries are contained in F. S. Regs., Part II. and the Staff Manual respectively. Title pages will be prepared in manuscript.

WAR DIARY
or
INTELLIGENCE SUMMARY.
(*Erase heading not required.*)

Army Form C. 2118.

Hour, Date, Place	Summary of Events and Information	Remarks and references to Appendices
8/5/15	German started heavy bombardment of our trenches at 7 am 69th 100th 103rd turned on to German trenches and kept up a steady rate of fire. At 9.30 am the 37th and 108th Heavy Battery connected up and joined in the bombarding of the German Trenches. 9.35 am 103rd observer reported that German now were shelling our support trenches and rifle fire was heavier. 9.55 all wires to observers cut. The attack broke our line in two places but 84th Bde held until they were taken in the rear. Heavy fighting continued up till about 8.30 pm. batteries firing continuously.	Buffers caused considerable trouble
	Lt G. H. Broadhurst, 2/Lt A. Donelly } missing	
9/5/15	Quiet during the night and up to noon guns out of action replaced or repaired. attack began again against our new line with artillery bombardment	

Instructions regarding War Diaries and Intelligence Summaries are contained in F. S. Regs., Part II. and the Staff Manual respectively. Title pages will be prepared in manuscript.

WAR DIARY
or
INTELLIGENCE SUMMARY.
(Erase heading not required.)

Army Form C. 2118.

Hour, Date, Place	Summary of Events and Information	Remarks and references to Appendices
9/5/15	which knocked out a great many of our infantry and the line was broken severals times all batteries fired hard and gave valuable assistance. When reports came in that the supports which were sent up were badly knocked the 84th Bde moved head quarters to dugouts further back and conducted fire from there. At 3.p.m Head Qrs moved to Dugouts on stream to West of Canal in and then moved to Chateau near VLAMATINGHE where they spent the night	
10/5/15	Returned to dugouts on stream and prepared them for Head Quarters, batteries fired at intervals directed by observers on the whole the front was quiet Bl Gen Gay left the Division. 103rd Battery moved to old position near LA BRIQUE	

(73989) W4141—463. 400,000. 9/14. H.&J.Ltd. Forms/C. 2118/10.

Instructions regarding War Diaries and Intelligence Summaries are contained in F. S. Regs., Part II. and the Staff Manual respectively. Title pages will be prepared in manuscript.

WAR DIARY
or
INTELLIGENCE SUMMARY.
(*Erase heading not required.*)

Army Form C. 2118.

Hour, Date, Place	Summary of Events and Information	Remarks and references to Appendices
11/5/15 Dug Outs on Stream.	All guns except 1 in 103rd were fit for action this morning The 103rd took on Germans on FREZENBURG while the 100 enfilade trenches on the same ridge most of the day was spent in selection of observing stations suitable to carry out the new system (ie shelling Germans trenches not guns)	
	2/Lt Short R. 2/Lt Dalby C. 2/Lt Smith J.T. } joined the Bde	
	During the night the 69th fired on roads which the Germans used for transport.	

(73989) W4141—463. 400,000. 9/14. H.&J.Ltd. Forms/C. 2118/10.

Army Form C. 2118.

WAR DIARY
or
INTELLIGENCE SUMMARY.
(Erase heading not required.)

Instructions regarding War Diaries and Intelligence Summaries are contained in F. S. Regs., Part II. and the Staff Manual respectively. Title pages will be prepared in manuscript.

Hour, Date, Place	Summary of Events and Information	Remarks and references to Appendices
12/5/15.	Preparations were made with the two batteries RHA which are going to take over the zone of the 69th 100th and 103rd and sections of 69th + 100th warned to withdraw at 8.30 pm. Great confusion was caused by absence of orders from [illegible] H. Qrs. Time of withdrawal, Rest area or any other written orders were not received until sent for. During the morning the 103rd gave the front trenches a heavy shelling for about ten minutes, the German replied but ceased when 103rd opened again. Rest area given to Bde square 32 just South of ABELLE [illegible] no room in houses as [illegible] part of 5th Corps H. Qrs. At 8.30 pm sections were withdrawn to wagon lines where they stayed the night.	

(73989) W4141—463. 400,000. 9/14. H.&J.Ltd. Forms/C. 2118/10.

Instructions regarding War Diaries and Intelligence Summaries are contained in F. S. Regs., Part II. and the Staff Manual respectively. Title pages will be prepared in manuscript.

WAR DIARY
or
INTELLIGENCE SUMMARY.
(Erase heading not required.)

Army Form C. 2118.

Hour, Date, Place	Summary of Events and Information	Remarks and references to Appendices
13/5/15.	at 5.0 am the Germans bombarded the front trenches, and as the request of the Cav Gen our batteries bombarded their trenches. in Zone B	
	7.0 am. Observers report no movement visible but trenches still heavily shelled	
	8.50 Batteries shelled houses in C.29 centre	
	9.45 103rd turned on with rapid fire to I.6.A where germans were seen in the valley	
	9.55 69th + 100th onto I 6 abc	
	10.15 1 gun of 103rd withdrawn out of action. Cav reported our line S. VERLORENHOEK pushed back. Counter arranged for 10.30	
	11.10 Fire on I 6 abc reported effective	
	12.50 103rd turned onto farm I 5 B. reported full of Germans several direct hits obtained	

(73989) W4141—463. 400,000. 9/14. H.&J.Ltd. Forms/C. 2118/10.

Instructions regarding War Diaries and Intelligence Summaries are contained in F. S. Regs., Part II. and the Staff Manual respectively. Title pages will be prepared in manuscript.

WAR DIARY
or
INTELLIGENCE SUMMARY.
(Erase heading not required.)

Army Form C. 2118.

Hour, Date, Place	Summary of Events and Information	Remarks and references to Appendices
13/5/15	1pm 69th turned on to farms C 23 d 1.6 & C 29 b 5.8 Germans digging between them	
	3pm 100 + 103 on I 6 a [illegible]. for 3/4 hrs.	
	5pm 103rd observer reported enemy attacking at C 29 b 5.5 [illegible]	
	[illegible] batteries [illegible] turned [illegible] German [illegible]	
	[illegible] 103rd [illegible]	
	[illegible] orders from [illegible] to concentrate fire on farms C 29 [illegible] to knock out M.G.	
	[illegible] 100th turned on to C 29 b [illegible]	

(5132) Wt. W 2384-583. 8/14. 15,000 Pads. Wy. & S., Ltd.

"B" Form.

Army Form C 2122.

MESSAGES AND SIGNALS.

No. of Message

Prefix .... Code .... m.	Received	Sent	Office Stamp.
Office of Origin and Service Instructions. / Words.	At .... m.	At .... m.	69
	From CRA.	To	
	By [illegible]	By	

TO G O C 31st Bde

Sender's Number.	Day of Month	In reply to Number	AAA
* BM/851	14		

G O C Canada Cav force wire begins aaa Please convey to the artillery under your command my compliments on the effective support it has afforded the Cav. force during the recent operations aaa The rapidity of its response and the volume of fire has greatly assisted my Cav. aaa ends

From B M R A Cav force

Place

Time 9.45 PM

* This line should be erased if not required.

Instructions regarding War Diaries and Intelligence Summaries are contained in F. S. Regs., Part II. and the Staff Manual respectively. Title pages will be prepared in manuscript.

WAR DIARY
or
INTELLIGENCE SUMMARY.
(Erase heading not required.)

Army Form C. 2118.

Hour, Date, Place	Summary of Events and Information	Remarks and references to Appendices
14/[illegible]/15	A quiet day very little happened along our front. At 3.15 pm the 103 + 69th at request of 3rd Cav. Div. turned on to supposed concentration of Germans in I 6 a + c but after consultation with G.O.C. 1st Cav. Div. their fire was stopped and it was arranged that assistance from zones outside our own would not be asked for unless urgently required.	
	2/Lt Poer joined Bde and was posted to 103rd Batty.	
14/[illegible]	Nothing special to record today. 100th Battery did not fire, 69th [illegible] registered. 103rd Observer reported farm C 29 b 6/4 to be used as observing station and put several rounds HE into farm causing a lot of smoke after which no movement was seen.	
	Troops [illegible] observed at ZONNEBEKE and FREZENBURG	

 2/Lt. L. H. Poer joined 103rd Batty. on posting to Brigade. [illegible]

Instructions regarding War Diaries and Intelligence Summaries are contained in F. S. Regs., Part II. and the Staff Manual respectively. Title pages will be prepared in manuscript.

WAR DIARY
or
INTELLIGENCE SUMMARY.
(Erase heading not required.)

Army Form C. 2118.

Hour, Date, Place	Summary of Events and Information	Remarks and references to Appendices
16/5/15	very quiet all day 103rd fired at some houses, 69th registered, 400th did not fire.	
17/5/15	nothing to report.	
18/5/15	103rd battery registered FREZENBURG cross roads 69th verified their zone. all quiet along our front	
CHATEAU 19/5/15	still quiet along our front. 103rd Battery killed some Germans walking in the open. 69th Battery fired on roads during night	
CHATEAU 20/5/15	103rd at the request of cavalry tried to burn down the horse shelters in C29d43 and used incendiary shells, but owing to the slight structure and damp nature of the shelters, they were not set on fire. The 69th fired 8 observed rounds on German trenches at request from Warwicks. ammunition now allowed at rate of 3 rds per gun. no H.E.	

(73989) W4141—463. 400,000. 9/14. H.&J.Ltd. Forms/C. 2118/10.

Army Form C. 2118.

Instructions regarding War Diaries and Intelligence Summaries are contained in F. S. Regs., Part II. and the Staff Manual respectively. Title pages will be prepared in manuscript.

WAR DIARY
or
INTELLIGENCE SUMMARY.
(Erase heading not required.)

Hour, Date, Place	Summary of Events and Information	Remarks and references to Appendices
CHATEAU. 21/5/15	Still quiet along our front 69th registered and checked lines also fired at farm which appeared to be H Qrs. ~~[illegible]~~ C.30.b.8.8	
22/5/15	103rd took on H Qrs, fired at yesterday by 69th, and after the 69 How Battery had put some Lyddite they fired at a spot where the Germans halted yesterday	
23/5/15	105th Battery fired a few rounds at Germans [illegible] in their front line trench and dispersed them [illegible] the road [illegible] at farm [illegible] ZONNEBEKE [illegible] 105th Battery [illegible] Germans [illegible] D [illegible] C [illegible] field South of it (D.26.A) [illegible] R.A.	
24/5/15	[illegible] and [illegible] attacks by Germans [illegible] East of YPRES [illegible] opened fire at once on Germans [illegible]	KG1

(73989) W4141—463. 400,000. 9/14. H.&J.Ltd. Forms/C. 2118/10.

Instructions regarding War Diaries and Intelligence Summaries are contained in F. S. Regs., Part II. and the Staff Manual respectively. Title pages will be prepared in manuscript.

WAR DIARY
or
INTELLIGENCE SUMMARY.
(Erase heading not required.)

Army Form C. 2118.

Hour, Date, Place	Summary of Events and Information	Remarks and references to Appendices
	trenches in their zones and maintained rapid fire until information was received at 4.0 a.m. ~~[illegible]~~ from the infantry that attacks in our zone had been driven off; rate of fire was reduced until 5.0 a.m. when Royal Irish Fusiliers reported artillery assistance no longer required - fire of batteries stopped.	
	5.30 a.m. Orders received from Brigade Major R.A. to assist 4th Division on St JULIEN road (north of Brigade zone) - 69th Battery ordered to fire on WIELTJE - St JULIEN road; 100th Battery ordered to fire between ~~[illegible]~~ this road and WIELTJE - St. JULIEN road. Steady rate of fire ordered.	
	6.00 a.m. Observer 69th Battery, who had obtained touch with O.C. R. WARWICK regt. (holding the left of our zone) reported their front all quiet.	
	6.15 a.m. 10th Brigade (4th Division) reported our front [illegible] on WIELTJE - FORTUIN road. Rate of fire of 69th and 100th Batteries increased.	
	7.0 a.m. message from Brigade Major R.A. 28th Division received thanking brigade for its support of 4th Division and stating that ~~their fire~~ our support was no longer required - 69th and 100th Btys ordered to stop firing.	KGL

Instructions regarding War Diaries and Intelligence Summaries are contained in F. S. Regs., Part II. and the Staff Manual respectively. Title pages will be prepared in manuscript.

WAR DIARY
or
INTELLIGENCE SUMMARY.

(Erase heading not required.)

Army Form C. 2118.

Hour, Date, Place	Summary of Events and Information	Remarks and references to Appendices
	7.40 am. At request of G.O.C 85th Infy Bde. 100th & 103rd Batteries [illegible] to place belt of fire across railway in I 6 C in support of local counter-attack.	
	8.15 am. G.O.C 85th Infy Bde reported his line intact [illegible] I 6 C. Fire of 103rd and 100th Batteries stopped.	
	8.38 am. Report received from observer 65th Battery that enemy were advancing [illegible] railway I 6 C. 103rd Battery ordered to open fire [illegible] searching and sweeping at steady rate. [illegible] stopped [illegible]	
	9 am [illegible] 69th and 100th Batteries shelled [illegible] to their [illegible] [illegible] N. of NEWERKHUEK [illegible] [illegible] 100th Battery also fired at [illegible] in enemy's [illegible]	
	From 12 [illegible] to 2.55 am 25/5/15 the 69th, 100th and 103rd Batteries fired [illegible] of G.O.C R.A. searching and sweeping from railway [illegible] I 11 [illegible] to [illegible] northern slopes of hill [illegible] up to wood in I 12 [illegible] in support of counter-attack of 84th Infantry brigade, [illegible]	

(73989) W4141—463. 400,000. 9/14. H.&J.Ltd. Forms/C. 2118/10.

Instructions regarding War Diaries and Intelligence Summaries are contained in F. S. Regs., Part II. and the Staff Manual respectively. Title pages will be prepared in manuscript.

WAR DIARY
or
INTELLIGENCE SUMMARY.
(*Erase heading not required.*)

Army Form C. 2118.

Hour, Date, Place	Summary of Events and Information	Remarks and references to Appendices
	Germans had driven a wedge into British line South of Roulers railway and this brigade had been ordered to drive the enemy out of it. About 1600 rounds per battery were expended, and the fire was all unobserved as opportunity was not given to arrange observing stations and communications, and battery observers had still to watch our own front	Royal Irish Fusiliers report fire of our artillery during gas attack most effective ~~[illegible]~~ turning off the German attack completely and causing them considerable casualties. Our front is a result very quiet all day. KGI
25/5/16	From 9.0 a.m. to 11.25 a.m. by order of G.O.C. R.A. the 69th & 103rd batteries again shelled wood in I.12.a, with continuous slow rate of fire to prevent Germans massing there.	
	By 10.30 a.m. observing stations for 69th & 103rd batteries had been established for this zone & communications in working order.	
	Zone of brigade was changed from area previously covered North of VERLORENHOEK to area South of Roulers railway. Batteries all registered German trenches in this zone and other points of importance	KGI

(73989) W4141—463. 400,000. 9/14. H.&J.Ltd. Forms/C. 2118/10.

Instructions regarding War Diaries and Intelligence Summaries are contained in F. S. Regs., Part II. and the Staff Manual respectively. Title pages will be prepared in manuscript.

WAR DIARY
or
INTELLIGENCE SUMMARY.
(*Erase heading not required.*)

Army Form C. 2118.

Hour, Date, Place	Summary of Events and Information	Remarks and references to Appendices
26/5/15	At various times batteries fired a few rounds at German working parties seen in zone, dispersing them. At 4.0 pm. 100th Battery co-operated with 9.2" How. which was shelling BELLEWAARDE farm, by firing shrapnel in rear of it to catch any of the enemy evacuating it. This farm was known to contain machine guns.	KJB
28/5/15	Relief of 31st Brigade R.F.A. by 2nd Brigade R.F.A. 6th Division arranged. Battery commanders of new brigade arrived at 2 p.m. to make arrangements for taking over. 10.0 p.m. 1st Sections of the brigade relieved by first sections of 2nd Brigade R.F.A. and withdrawn to [illegible]. 2Lt. C. Brown joined 100th Batty. on posting to Brigade, & Temp. Lt. J. R. [illegible]-Smith joined 118th Batty. on posting to Brigade.	KJB [illegible]
29/5/15	Sections of 2nd Brigade in action were registered on new zones. Remaining sections of 31st brigade relieved at 10.50 p.m. and withdrew to ABEELE. At 11.0 p.m. command of R.F.A. in this sector passed to O.C. 2nd Brigade R.F.A.	KJB

(73989) W4141—463. 400,000. 9/14. H.&J.Ltd. Forms/C. 2118/10.

Instructions regarding War Diaries and Intelligence Summaries are contained in F. S. Regs., Part II. and the Staff Manual respectively. Title pages will be prepared in manuscript.

WAR DIARY
or
INTELLIGENCE SUMMARY.
(Erase heading not required.)

Army Form C. 2118.

Hour, Date, Place	Summary of Events and Information	Remarks and references to Appendices
ABEELE 29/5/15	Orders received that 27th Division were to form part of Army Reserve – O.C. 31st Brigade to get in touch with G.O.C. 84th Brigade as soon as possible in rest area at HERZEELE.	Kgl
	G.O.C. Vth Corps paid a visit to Brigade Headquarters 69th Battery and Ammunition Column.	
30/5/15	10.0 a.m. Billetting parties sent on to HERZEELE area.	Kgl
	2 pm Brigade left ABEELE and reached new billets in HERZEELE area at 5.0 pm.	
31/5/15	Refitting of brigade commenced	
	Temp 2nd Lieut. E. A. Rodin joined Headquarters Staff on attachment to the Brigade.	Kgl

28th Division

181/58½

31st Bde: R.F.A.

Vol VI 1 — 30.6.15

Instructions regarding War Diaries and Intelligence Summaries are contained in F. S. Regs., Part II. and the Staff Manual respectively. Title pages will be prepared in manuscript.

WAR DIARY
or
INTELLIGENCE SUMMARY.
(Erase heading not required.)

Army Form C. 2118.

Hour, Date, Place	Summary of Events and Information	Remarks and references to Appendices
1st – 16th June	Bde at rest HERZEELE 5 days leave granted to all officers. Lt E.W. GRIFFITH RAMC. joined Bde on 15th to replace Lt MacConaghie. Major Mortimore RFA was posted to 103rd Battery on 15th to replace Major Hope who was posted to Div Staff.	On the Gen Bulfin inspected the Bde
17th	First Sectns. of 69th 100th + 118th go into action near DICKEBUSCH to relieve the Sections of the 48th Bde coming out.	
DICKEBUSCH H.34.a.6.10. 18th	Bde H.qrs and 103rd Battery leave rest area – Bde Head Qrs to DICKEBUSCH and 103rd Battery to N5 d.8.6. where they are in rest. At 12 noon O.C. 31st Bde takes over command of guns in action. remaining sectns of 48th Bde will be relieved tonight. Batteries carried out registration of their zones this morning	
19th	Second Sections in action – registration of zones continued 100th B.C. selected new observing stations in the trenches which with the assistance of 118 O.B. enabled him to see the whole of his zone	

J.B. Holloway [illegible] RFA

(73989) W4141—463. 400,000. 9/14. H.&J.Ltd. Forms/C. 2118/10.

Instructions regarding War Diaries and Intelligence Summaries are contained in F. S. Regs., Part II. and the Staff Manual respectively. Title pages will be prepared in manuscript.

WAR DIARY
or
INTELLIGENCE SUMMARY.
(Erase heading not required.)

Army Form C. 2118.

Hour, Date, Place	Summary of Events and Information	Remarks and references to Appendices
June DICKEBUSCH 20th	Bde Comdr and O.C. 103rd Battery selected position for 103rd Battery to right rear of 118th Battery. 100 Battery prepared new observing stations and improved communications to these.	
21st	69th fired 5 rounds at Piccadilly farm to stop sniping. other batteries did not fire.	100th continued preparat of observing stations.
22nd	all quiet along our front batteries registered.	
23rd	100th Observing stations completed and registration carried out	
24th	69th received two request from the infantry to open fire during the night on bombing parties During the day a communication test was carried out by 100th. Zone extended to the left and covered by the 118th Battery	J.B. Hollway Adjt RFA

Army Form C. 2118.

Instructions regarding War Diaries and Intelligence Summaries are contained in F. S. Regs., Part II. and the Staff Manual respectively. Title pages will be prepared in manuscript.

WAR DIARY
or
INTELLIGENCE SUMMARY.
(Erase heading not required.)

Hour, Date, Place	Summary of Events and Information	Remarks and references to Appendices
25th June DICKEBUSCH	at 12.12 am. 69th battery fired in reply to German trench mortar. all batteries registered in the afternoon situation along our front quiet 4.30. 118th Battery fired on trenches near BOIS. QUARANTE at request from the infantry who were being shelled in N.6.	
26th	69th & 118th Batteries had a few light shrapnel over their positions early in the morning one man the 118 was slightly wounded.	
27th	~~Nothing to report own~~ 69th Battery fired 24rds in reply to a German Whizz Bang which was firing with considerable effect on our trenches. During afternoon situation along our front, normal.	
28th	100th Battery again failed to hit house on hill 57 at 0.9c.4.2. all batteries registered more points in their zones.	

J. B. Holloway
4 F R.F.A.

(9 29 6) W4141—463 100,000 9/14 H W V Forms/C. 2118/10

Instructions regarding War Diaries and Intelligence Summaries are contained in F. S. Regs., Part II. and the Staff Manual respectively. Title pages will be prepared in manuscript.

WAR DIARY
or
INTELLIGENCE SUMMARY.
(*Erase heading not required.*)

Army Form C. 2118.

Hour, Date, Place	Summary of Events and Information	Remarks and references to Appendices
29th DICKEBUSCH	Bde. Comdr. with C.R.A. made a tour of trenches to test visual communication between trenches + observing station and decided that lamps were not to be used by day.	
30th	100th Battery obtained two hits on house on hill 57. 69th 110th fired a various targets. Gen. Bulfin 28th Div. went round 69th + 110th batteries. Consultation on communications at 110th battery.	DICKEBUSCH was shelled at intervals during day very slight damage. German aeroplanes active during afternoon
	Guns positions for subsidiary lines were inspected and reports rendered.	
	On the 4th June the Brigade was paraded for the Divl Comdr. (Gen Bulfin) who in a speech of some length complimented the Brigade highly on the work it had done + the assistance it had given the Infantry during the time when the Div. had been in the YPRES Salient	

F. B. Holloway
a/Lt. RFA.

28th Division

121/6344

31st Bde R.F.A.

Vol VII

1 - 31 - 7 - 15

Army Form C. 2118.

Instructions regarding War Diaries and Intelligence Summaries are contained in F. S. Regs., Part II. and the Staff Manual respectively. Title pages will be prepared in manuscript.

WAR DIARY
or
INTELLIGENCE SUMMARY.
(Erase heading not required.)

Hour, Date, Place	Summary of Events and Information	Remarks and references to Appendices
July DICKEBUSCH 1st	100th + 118th Batteries took on working parties of the Germans in their zones and dispersed them. Positions selected for single guns to enfilade zone on our right.	
2nd	Retaliation on German trenches by 69th + 118th Position for single gun fixed also that for dummy battery	D.D.R. II army inspected 5 remounts and said that were unsuitable for the purpose for which they were intended
3rd	Retaliation on front + support trenches by 69th. 100th fired salvo at 67 trench which was firing at one of our aeroplanes 100 + 118 fired at working parties. At 5 pm a display was given by 100 + 118 in conjunction with 4.5 How battery at BOIS QUARANTE and also at working party at O.19.6.67.	

J B [illegible]

(9 29 6) W 4141—463 100,000 9/14 H W V Forms/C. 2118/10

Instructions regarding War Diaries and Intelligence Summaries are contained in F. S. Regs., Part II. and the Staff Manual respectively. Title pages will be prepared in manuscript.

WAR DIARY
or
INTELLIGENCE SUMMARY.
(*Erase heading not required.*)

Army Form C. 2118.

Hour, Date, Place	Summary of Events and Information	Remarks and references to Appendices
DICKEBUSCH 4th	Considerable activity of German aeroplanes in the morning - 103rd single guns in position. 100th + 118th fired in reply to Germans guns which were shelling infantry in their zones.	Several tests were carried out by 69th Battery which on one occasion fired the gun 15 secs after the "test" —
5th	During the morning 69th + 100th registered points in their zones at 12.5 pm and 1.10pm 69 successfully engaged a working party of Germans who scattered in all directions In the afternoon the 118 fired at Hollands fm. and Bois QUARANTE	German artillery active during morning
6th	all quiet along our front. nothing of importance to record.	

J B Holloway [illegible]

Army Form C. 2118.

Instructions regarding War Diaries and Intelligence Summaries are contained in F. S. Regs., Part II. and the Staff Manual respectively. Title pages will be prepared in manuscript.

WAR DIARY
or
INTELLIGENCE SUMMARY.
(*Erase heading not required.*)

Hour, Date, Place	Summary of Events and Information	Remarks and references to Appendices
DICKEBUSCH		
7th	69th + 118th fired in retaliation. At 3.40 pm the 100th fired at Germans in communication trench in O7a8.1	
8th	During the morning the 69th fired at intervals at German support trenches where fires were observed. The 100th fired 10 rds at House in O.9C.4.2. but obtained no hits. 118th fired in retaliation on support trenches and registered communication trench in O.13.a.	
9th	118th Battery fired at supposed position of trench howr at 4.30 pm. Later it was located in HOLLANDSCHESCHUR farm and two rds were put into the building. 100th + 118th fired several test rounds which will be reported on later.	
10th	At 9.40 am 69th fired on front trenches in reply to German fire on ridge wood, hostile fire ceased almost instantly. 100th Battery dispersed a working party at 2.30 pm in O8d.6.0	at points where enfilade gun registered, the enemy have erected strong traverses

[signature]

(9 29 6) W4141—463 100,000 9/14 H W V Forms/C. 2118/10

Instructions regarding War Diaries and Intelligence Summaries are contained in F. S. Regs., Part II. and the Staff Manual respectively. Title pages will be prepared in manuscript.

WAR DIARY
or
INTELLIGENCE SUMMARY.
(Erase heading not required.)

Army. Form C. 2118.

Hour, Date, Place	Summary of Events and Information	Remarks and references to Appendices
July DICKEBUSCH		
11.	Nothing to report all quiet along our front.	
12th	Nothing to report. aeroplanes active. DICKEBUSCH shelled.	103rd began registration of zone.
13th	69th engaged a trench mortar last night also fired at dug outs behind BOIS QUARANTE early this morning 118th expended their 12 rds on various small targets Two more points were registered by the 103rd During the evening 103rd fired at Piccadilly Farm, and 118th took on group of men in O14B7.10. at 10.25pm the 69th shelled a bombing party in front of P1.	a British aeroplane was reported to have descended in flames this morning
14.	The Batteries did not fire during the morning.	Orders received about change of positions to KEMMEL.

[signature] 9th R.F.A.

Instructions regarding War Diaries and Intelligence Summaries are contained in F. S. Regs., Part II. and the Staff Manual respectively. Title pages will be prepared in manuscript.

WAR DIARY
or
INTELLIGENCE SUMMARY.
(Erase heading not required.)

Army Form C. 2118.

Hour, Date, Place	Summary of Events and Information	Remarks and references to Appendices
DICKEBUSCH 15.	Situation normal. O.C. 28th Bde came to DICKEBUSCH to see Battery positions. O.C. 31st Bde went to Kemmel to inspect new area	New positions inspected & B.C.s shown round them. 118th not yet fixed. First sections to go out night of 16/17 second sections to go out night of 17/18
16.	118th fired at German front trench in reply to German shelling other batteries did not fire. 1st sectns of all Batteries went out of action at DICKEBUSCH, on being relieved by sectns of 28th Bde, and went into new positions	ammn. being saved for registration of new zones. 1st sectn. 118th spent night 16/17th in wagon line
17th KEMMEL	Registration of 1st sectns carried out by 12 noon. O.C. 28th Bde took over at 12 noon. Bde H.Qrs moved to Kemmel at 2.30 pm and took over new area at 6 pm. At 9.30 pm 2nd sectns came out of action and went to new positions. Ammn. col moved to new area.	

J B Hollway
[illegible]

(9 29 6) W4141—463 100,000 9/14 H W V Forms/C. 2118/10

Army Form C. 2118.

Instructions regarding War Diaries and Intelligence Summaries are contained in F. S. Regs., Part II. and the Staff Manual respectively. Title pages will be prepared in manuscript.

WAR DIARY
or
INTELLIGENCE SUMMARY.
(Erase heading not required.)

Hour, Date, Place	Summary of Events and Information	Remarks and references to Appendices
18	Registration of 2nd Section carried out.	
19th	Registration continued	
20th	Registration – activity noticed on SPANBROOK MOLEN where Germans worked all night regardless of casualties.	
21st	All quiet – Germans working by day at SPANBROOK MOLEN were observed to carry planks into the front trenches, 103rd fired at these during the day & twice during night 21st/22nd	
22nd.	Major H.H. Bond posted to command 31st Brigade. Working parties busy at SPANBROEKMOLEN and S.W. of WYTSCHAETE were fired at and dispersed by 69th & 103rd Batteries and 100th Battery.	vice Lt. Col. G.H.A. White to R.H.A. – 1st Cav. Division joined the Brigade. Lieut A.G. Chase joined the Brigade – Posted to 118th Battery R.F.A.

KG

Instructions regarding War Diaries and Intelligence Summaries are contained in F. S. Regs., Part II. and the Staff Manual respectively. Title pages will be prepared in manuscript.

WAR DIARY
or
INTELLIGENCE SUMMARY.
(*Erase heading not required.*)

Army Form C. 2118.

Hour, Date, Place	Summary of Events and Information	Remarks and references to Appendices
23rd	Heavy showers and sunshine at intervals. Relaying and burying of telephone lines continued. 69th Battery registered machine gun emplacement and new communication trench on WYTSCHAETE ridge and with the 100th Battery fired on working parties in trenches behind enemies front line. 5 points were selected along the front of the Brigade zone for all Batteries to register, lettered A, B, C, D & E.	K.J.
24th	Batteries completed registration of Brigade points. Improvement of communications continued. 100th Battery continued preparation of a new position further forward, reducing their range from 3800 to 2500 yards to enemy's front line. Headquarter communications by buried lines from Battle station ~~now~~ in working order.	Lt-Colonel G.H.A. White departed to join 1st Cavalry Division. Weather changeable
25th	G.O.C.R.A. visited Battery positions. Further registration carried out by Batteries. Weather still changeable. Telephone communication with 118th Battery	K.J.

(9 29 6) W4141—463 100,000 9/14 H W V Forms/C. 2118/10

Instructions regarding War Diaries and Intelligence Summaries are contained in F. S. Regs., Part II. and the Staff Manual respectively. Title pages will be prepared in manuscript.

WAR DIARY
or
INTELLIGENCE SUMMARY.
(Erase heading not required.)

Army Form C. 2118.

Hour, Date, Place	Summary of Events and Information	Remarks and references to Appendices
	~~established~~ observing station established	KGI
26th	2.30 pm. Test of communications from Brigade Headquarters Battle station. Communications established with all Batteries and observing stations in 20 minutes from the time of leaving billet.	
	One section of 100th Battery moved into new position in closer support under cover of darkness.	
	Weather stormy with heavy showers.	KGI
27th	G.O.C. R.A. accompanied Brigade Commander in reconnaissance of positions of Batteries selected for subsidiary lines in the morning	
	At 2.30 pm the Brigade Commander carried out a test of concentrating the fire of Batteries on certain points in the Brigade zones. This brought out several weaknesses in telephone communication which must be rectified. The results of each concentration were satisfactory both in speed and accuracy for a first attempt. 2nd Section of 100th Battery occupied new position.	KGI
28th	Reconnaissance of positions for mountain guns to fire direct at short range on SPANBROEKMOLEN carried	

Instructions regarding War Diaries and Intelligence Summaries are contained in F. S. Regs., Part II. and the Staff Manual respectively. Title pages will be prepared in manuscript.

WAR DIARY
or
INTELLIGENCE SUMMARY.
(*Erase heading not required.*)

Army Form C. 2118.

Hour, Date, Place	Summary of Events and Information	Remarks and references to Appendices
	-out – O.C. Mountain Battery however selects his own position in trenches.	
	Inspection of various battery positions carried out by G.O.C.R.A. with Brigade Commander and C.R.E. to discuss preparation of dug-outs etc. for winter campaign.	
[illegible]	About 10 or 12 salvoes of 6" Shrapnel fired near 103rd Battery position – Probably intended for road or working parties digging trenches – No damage.	
	100th Battery completed registration from new position	K91
29th	Brigade Commander visited trenches in brigade zone accompanied by Brigade Major 84th Brigade, during the afternoon. Test messages to Batteries sent through from trenches produced following results:–	
	69th Battery responded to call ~~from~~ from F5 trench 3½ minutes after message was handed to operator in trench – this had to be transmitted through Battalion H.Q.s.	
	69th Battery responded to call from G2 trench sent on direct wire 1½ mins after message was given to trench operator.	
	118th Battery communication broken – When communication was established response	

Instructions regarding War Diaries and Intelligence Summaries are contained in F. S. Regs., Part II. and the Staff Manual respectively. Title pages will be prepared in manuscript.

WAR DIARY
or
INTELLIGENCE SUMMARY.
(Erase heading not required.)

Army Form C. 2118.

Hour, Date, Place	Summary of Events and Information	Remarks and references to Appendices
	did not come off till 6 minutes had elapsed. In response to registration of WYTSCHAETE Hospice by 9.2 Howitzers, the enemy shelled KEMMEL Chateau and village with 6 inch high explosive and shrapnel - Two batteries were engaged in this - The fire of our 9.2 howitzers had to be stopped to enable the Army Commander to escape from the chateau -	Lieut T Cunliffe RFA on joining is posted to Brigade Ammⁿ Colⁿ. K.S.A.
30th	At 3.30 am a heavy bombardment was heard in the neighbourhood of HOOGE and hill 60, lasting till about ~~6 am~~ 6.30 am. German attack - Batteries engaged in improving telephone communication to trenches. Reconnaissance carried out by brigade Commander in the afternoon to select positions for single guns in close support against any operations against or coming from WYTSCHAETE. Two suitable places found from which the whole area West of WYTSCHAETE could be swept with direct fire. Task of preparing these given to 118th Battery. Spell of fine weather set in.	K.S.A.

Instructions regarding War Diaries and Intelligence Summaries are contained in F. S. Regs., Part II. and the Staff Manual respectively. Title pages will be prepared in manuscript.

WAR DIARY
or
INTELLIGENCE SUMMARY.
(Erase heading not required.)

Army Form C. 2118.

Hour, Date, Place	Summary of Events and Information	Remarks and references to Appendices
31st	103rd Battery dispersed a working party at SPANBROEKMOLEN and silenced a trench mortar opposite F2 trench – 4 rounds required for each task. 69th Battery dispersed a working party N. of SPANBROEKMOLEN	K.J.I.
3rd	2.30 am. Renewed heavy firing heard E. of Ypres. Sounded like an attack by British troops. Brigade tasks for concentrating fire on various points in zone carried out at about 10.30 am. Results attached. At about 1.30 pm. small field guns shelled infantry support dug-outs in wood 200 yards ~~north~~ South of Brigade Headquarters. About 50 rounds were fired ~~by~~ for which two guns were employed. No damage was done beyond setting a small cottage on fire and slightly wounding about 5 men. 69th Battery were ordered to fire 20 rounds into L'Enfer wood in reply.	K.J.I.

K. J. Ireland, Lt. RFA
Adjt. 31st Bde

(9 29 6) W4141—463 100,000 9/14 H W V Forms/C. 2118/10

G/66

Brigade Major RA

Forwarded for information of C.R.A. Perhaps you would kindly return it.

J H R White
Lt Col
Comd 31st Bde RFA
10.7.15

I have heard of the prompt and substantial support given by the guns of the 31st Brigade to the infantry in the zone these guns are covering. I am very glad to read the message from GOC 85th Brigade

E S Bulfin

11/7/15 P.T.O.

31 2/13th

Forwarded

W Ferguson

11/7/15.

Maj [illegible]

Date	Summary of Events and Information	Remarks
1st Feby 1915	Battery moved out of action upon being relieved by a Battery under Major Woodside consisting of one Section each from 43rd and 87th Batteries	CB
2nd Feby	Bty with Transport and 6 Amm wagons from Bde Amm Col marched at 6.30am via ERQUINGHEM – BAILLEUL – LOCRE – ZEVECOLEN – OUDERDOM to road junction ¾ mile S of VLAMERTINGHE (16 miles) The Battery there came under Command of 28th Division Roads very bad condition Rained all day Billetted in small farm bad accomodation	CB.
3rd Feby	Left Section came into action at Chateau just S of KRUISTRAAL LOCK 1 mile S.E. Position on front edge of Shrubbery. Two French mortars in action just on out	

Date	Summary of Events and Information	Remarks
3rd Feby Contd	right from German Aeroplane above and General Shelling of Countryside by Germans. Zone allotted to Battery was the front of the ridge KLIEN ZILLEBEKE to ST ELOI being the only howitzers in the Division which had first taken out from the French	B
4th Feby	Arrangements made to shoot with aeroplane observation but observers camp failed. 3.30pm fired 6 lyddite on houses 1¼ miles S of YPRES near Canal at request of Infantry Centre Section brought into action at 5.30pm. Beside Left Section found wagon lines just S of HAZEBROUCK fired 6 rounds	B
5th Feby	Wireless expert with instruments attached to Battery. 3pm fired 10 rounds at HOLLEBEKE	

Date	Summary of Events and information	Remarks
5th Feby Contd	Chateau for registration obtaining several direct hits. Very cold. German aeroplanes very active flying very low. Fired 10 rounds	AB
6th Feby	1pm to 1.45pm Billet shelled by field Gun Battery. One round entering Chateau. Fired 5 rounds of Lyddite at HOLLEBEKE Chateau and village in retaliation. Considerable amount of shelling by Germans all day. Rained all day. Fired 5 rounds	AB
7th Feby	4pm Fired 5 rounds with aeroplane observation and wireless communication. – Light failed – stopped firing. Fired 5 rounds.	AB
8th Feby	8.am to 8.30am Fired with aeroplane observation. Aeroplane then disappeared. 11.30 am Fired	

Date	Summary of Events and information	Remarks
8th Feby Contd	by map on a before reported gun position in retaliation for shelling of our Billet. 12 to 12 30pm fired with Aeroplane observation at a gun position. Having Completed registration. A German 8 inch Battery opened on us with high explosive, commencing near Chateau and eventually obtaining range to Battery exactly from 1pm to 2pm German Battery stopped firing. 2.15pm German Battery opened again also a Field Battery and Light Field Howitzer. German shooting very accurate round Battery and Billet this continued up to about 4 pm Casualties:- Aeroplane wireless expert slightly wounded in head by splinter whilst in dug-out Sgt [illegible] bruised by splinter Guns buried under broken trees Shield and Gun Sight badly	

Date	Summary of Events and information	Remarks.
8th Feby Contd	bent, a pole cut in half, limber damaged by splinters 4 cartridges exploded, primers remaining intact; besides minor breakages. A French limber lifted bodily about 30 yards. Fired 36 rounds	PB.
9th Feby	Very wet and windy. Billet shelled by Field Gun Battery at intervals during day. Left and Centre Sections moved out of action, Right Section moved up to new position 500 yds in rear of former position. Fired 1 round	PB.
10th Feby	7 am Germans opened rapid fire on former position and Billet with 8 inch high explosive for 20 minutes, probably in retaliation for continual firing by "A" Battery RHA. Just on our	

Date	Summary of Events and information	Remarks
10th Feby Contd	Cpt. 1030 am to 1130 am Registered a Gun position and cross roads at HOLLEBEKE by means of aeroplane and wireless. At 1130 am to 7 pm German aeroplanes held the air. 130 pm fired on trench close to our trenches N.W of HOLLEBEKE Chateau at request of Infantry fire reported very effective by F.O.O of "A" Bty RHA and Infantry. During day fired 27 rounds	PB
11th Feby	Light too bad for aeroplane observation. Much German shelling during day	PB
12th Feby	Very cold day. During morning fired a few rounds by map at guns reported near HOLLEBEKE Chateau which promptly stopped firing. Belgium Battery relieved "A" Battery RHA. Fired 10 rounds	PB

Date	Summary of Events and information	Remarks
13th Feby	Very wet and Cold all day. Brought up "E" Sub Section Gun into action, and put in a shed wide on Right flank of position to deceive enemy as to position. No firing	PB
14th Feby	Germans shelled Billet practically all day commencing at 8.30 am Very wet all day and strong wind. Heavy firing by Belgians and 8th Brigade RFA 11.30 am fired on EIKHOF Farm and ridge to East. In the evening fired at guns near HOLLEBEKE Chateau, which stopped firing. 1.30 am in night brought another gun into action. Fired 18 rounds. The two French mortars left during night	PB

Date	Summary of Events and Information	Remarks
15th Feby	5.15 am Stood to Guns 7.30 am Fired a few rounds by map at various Gun Positions 8 am Registered EIKHOF Farm (Time Fuzes very unreliable at Long Ranges) 4 pm Registered a trench to be attacked tonight 8.40 pm Information received that trench had been taken without opposition 8.50 pm to 9.5 pm Fired rapidly on Rear of trench which was being attacked. Considerable difficulty with Gun platforms owing to continual firing with 5th Charge at Long Ranges Telephone run out to a point on Canal Bank to be used by F.O.O. No telephones or wire available before this date. Fired 73 rounds	JR
16th Feby	Commenced to register with	

Date	Summary of Events and information	Remarks
16th Feby Contd	Aeroplane Observation, but had to stop firing owing to arrival of many German aeroplanes over our position. Fired a few rounds at German Battery N of HOLLEBEKE Chateau. Billet shelled continually during day by Field Battery. One round exploded on percussion in a room of Chateau where 3 men were sitting. No one was however hurt. Impossible to locate enemies guns as they are all on opposite side of Ridge. Flashes at night only like flares. Very fine day. German aeroplanes very active. Fired 16 rounds	PB
17th Feby	Much firing from our side all night. 3.30 am Received orders to engage trench N of HOLLEBEKE Chateau. Fired on trench from	

Date	Summary of Events and Information	Remarks
17th Feby Contd	9.15 am to 5 pm. Rain & very strong wind all day which made shooting very erratic. Stood to guns from 11 pm to 2 am and from 5 am to daylight while Infantry were constructing new trench. Fired 60 rounds. (60)	PB
18th Feby	Fired on trench as yesterday from 12.30 pm to 1.45 pm. Billet shelled by Field Battery continually during morning. Stood to guns as on previous night. Fired 17 rounds	PB
19th Feby	No firing. 2nd Lieut R.L. Thompson as F.O.O. located trenches in conjunction with Infantry. The two lines being very irregular.	PB
20th Feby	Very quiet up to 4 pm. Heavy rain & thunder during morning. Heavy firing to	

Date	Summary of Events and information	Remarks
20th Feby Contd	North from 4 pm till dark. Orders received to return to 3rd Corps on relief by 65th Battery R.F.A. Fired 10 rounds	RB
21st Feby	Heavy firing last night along line. Thick fog up to 2 pm 3 pm to 4.15 pm registered German main trench. Germans retaliated by general shelling of countryside with various kinds of shell. Several German snipers apparently right behind our lines 5 pm Major Blois and Advance Party 65th Bty RFA came in relief 5.30 pm commenced to change guns. Relief completed 6.30 pm. Very cold night and hard frost. Fired 42 rounds	RB
22nd Feby	9.15 am Whole Battery and Ammunition Column less 4 guns & 4 wagons marched from back	

Date	Summary of Events and Information	Remarks
22nd Feby Contd	Billet by same route as on 2nd. Remaining 4 guns and 4 wagons started at 11 am and occupied same position in RUE DE BOITIEUX. 4 guns in action at 5.30pm. Back Billet at Farm ½ mile W of ERQUINGHEM	RB
23rd Feby	Thick fog all day. No firing	RB
24th Feby	Very Cold Rain most of day No firing.	RB
25th Feby	2pm fired a few rounds at a trench opposite BOIS BLANCS at request of Infantry who stated Rifle Grenades were fired from there. F.O.O. 72nd Battery R.F.A. reported fire effective. Several shell falling in trench and two dug outs reported destroyed. Fired 10 rounds	RB

Date	Summary of Events and Information	Remarks
26th Feby	No firing	AB
27th Feby	No firing	AB
28th Feby	No firing. Left Section relieved. Right Section in action at dusk. Right Section guns to A.O.C travelling workshops for general overhaul	AB

"C" Form (Original). Army Form C. 2123.

MESSAGES AND SIGNALS. No. of Message

Prefix SM Code [illegible] Words 19 £ s. d. Charges to collect	Received From ZHE By [illegible]	Sent, or sent out At 7.45 P. m. To EF1. By	Office Stamp. FCA. 10-7-15
Service Instructions. ZHE			

Handed in at Office m. Received 7.2P m.

TO 31st Bde RFA.
 OC 69 Bty.

*Sender's Number	Day of Month	In reply to Number	AAA
BM 623	10th		

P1 Reports [illegible] guns making splendid practice to-day

FROM
PLACE & TIME 85th [illegible]
 6.50 PM.

* This line should be erased if not required.

[illegible] 50,000 Pads. 1584—1/15. S. B. Ltd.- Forms C.2123.

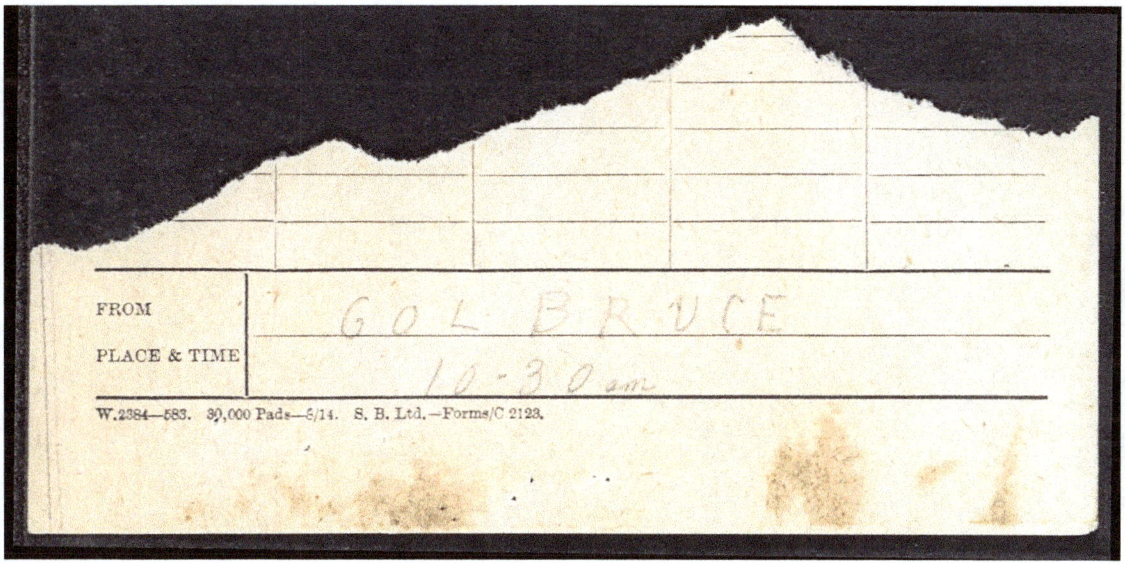

FROM GOL BRUCE

PLACE & TIME 10-30 am

W.2384—583. 30,000 Pads—5/14. S. B. Ltd.—Forms/C 2123.

"C" Form (Original).

Army Form C. 2123.

MESSAGES AND SIGNALS.

No. of Message

Prefix SM Code G/PM Words 53	Received	Sent, or sent out	Office Stamp.
Charges to collect £ s. d.	From ZHE By [illegible]	At ... m. To By	FCA 10/4/15
Service Instructions. ZHE			

Handed in at ... Office ... m. Received 3.40 P m.

TO: O.C. 31st Bde. R.F.A.

*Sender's Number	Day of Month	In reply to Number	AAA
BM617	10th		

G.O.C hopes that you will express to the 69th Battery the appreciation of their fire felt by men in the trenches AAA Their fire at once stops the enemy trench mortar when it attempts to trouble us at night and the excellent results obtained encourage our men very considerably AAA From personal observation G.O.C can testify to the interest taken in the firing of the Battery by the infantry in the trenches

FROM: 85th Inf Bde

PLACE & TIME:

* This line should be erased if not required.

Wt. W.9668—1672. 50,000 Pads. 1584—1/15. S. B. Ltd.- Forms C.2123.

Instructions regarding War Diaries and Intelligence Summaries are contained in F. S. Regs., Part II. and the Staff Manual respectively. Title pages will be prepared in manuscript.

WAR DIARY
or
INTELLIGENCE SUMMARY.
(Erase heading not required.)

XVI Bde R.F.A.

Army Form C. 2118.

851

Hour, Date, Place	Summary of Events and Information (31st Bde R.F.A.)	Remarks and references to Appendices
KEMMEL August 1st 1915	Orders received that 83rd Brigade would not be relieved by infantry of 17th Division in J to L trenches G trenches and H trenches except H1 to be handed over by 84th Brigade to 83rd Brigade on night 3rd/4th. 84th Brigade to take over all E trenches and 14 and 15 trenches from 85th Brigade on night 4th/5th. Artillery arrangements to meet this change – 365th Battery which had been placed under the orders of O.C. 31st Brigade rejoins the 8th Brigade – 367th Battery (14th Bde.) comes under the orders of O.C. 31st Brigade – At 1.20 am 100th Battery fired four rounds opposite G2 trench at infantry's request with desired effect. Large party of Germany officers wandering on KEMMEL Hill caused much excitement amongst observers – O.C. 69th Battery sent in long report on their doings. O.C. 69th reports more work done by enemy on their front trenches opposite F5 and G1. 3 small works noticed about 20 yards apart in this area – probably machine gun emplacements –	
August 2nd 1915	A stormy day. Bad light for observation and very little firing done of any consequence – Improvement of communications continued and P[illegible] of trench lines ~~[illegible]~~ along communication from batteries	

Instructions regarding War Diaries and Intelligence Summaries are contained in F. S. Regs., Part II. and the Staff Manual respectively. Title pages will be prepared in manuscript.

WAR DIARY
or
INTELLIGENCE SUMMARY.
(Erase heading not required.)

Army Form C. 2118.

852

Hour, Date, Place	Summary of Events and Information	Remarks and references to Appendices
	trenches completed – New Brigade OP selected and preparation	commenced
3.8.16	After 11 am a brigade test for ~~[illegible]~~ concentrating fire on various objectives was carried out – Results satisfactory and times quick with the exception of 100th Battery whose communications worked badly and fire was slow.	KGA
	Weather again squally and light bad.	
~~[illegible]~~	Germans blew up a mine at F4 trench at about 9.0 pm. About 7 men were buried by the collapse of the trench. The mine was not sufficiently heavily charged however and it is believed none of those buried are seriously hurt. The 103rd fired 4 rounds to encourage our infantry and subdue some of the enemy's rifle fire. Infantry however did not call for special assistance and 4 rounds were sufficient.	
	No call came from the trench to the artillery – It was not realised till next day that ~~the~~ a mine had been blown up by the battery covering the trench, although they spoke to the Battalion Headquarters.	KGA

(B 39 6) W4141—463 100,000 8/14 H W V Forms/C. 2118/10

Hour, Date, Place	Summary of Events and Information	Remarks and references to Appendices
4 8 15	Nothing to report – Another dull day, bad light. Many reports on hand viz. alternative positions for various lines of defence, positions for guns in close support, barbed wire in front of enemy's trenches etc.	L.G.A.
5. 8. 15.	Weather improving steadily.	
	Orders received that one Howitzer Battery would be affiliated to 31st Brigade R.F.A. in a few days' time.	
	Brigade Commander accompanied G.O.C. R.A. round the trenches in the morning.	
	In the afternoon positions for the new howitzer battery were reconnoitred.	
	A good deal of fresh registration carried out by the 69th and 100th Batteries, and the 103rd dispersed two working parties South of SPANBROEKMOLEN	
	69th Battery report much work done behind enemy's position, located and fired on what looked like a military wheeled carriage at O.25.a.9.10 – effective shrapnel but no direct hits with percussion. In the same work was a trestle bridge. Attention of Howitzers called to this. At 6.30 pm an erection like a mining frame	

Instructions regarding War Diaries and Intelligence Summaries are contained in F. S. Regs., Part II, and the Staff Manual respectively. Title pages will be prepared in manuscript.

WAR DIARY
or
INTELLIGENCE SUMMARY.
(Erase heading not required.)

Army Form C. 2118.

854

Hour, Date, Place	Summary of Events and Information	Remarks and references to Appendices
	appeared at N 30 a 18 near a suspected new sap-head. Two flags fluttered from it. 64th Battery fired 6 rounds at it 3 being very effective, & one reported to have carried away a flag.	
	Left Section No 2 Mountain Battery having prepared 3 emplacements in trenches F4, F3 & E2, reconnoitred a further position in E15 which is being taken in hand.	
	Movement by OC 100th Battery of lamps used by 118th from trench H1 to G4 caused some trouble to OC 118th Battery. A lamp however was moved from G3 to H1 to communicate with 118th OP if their wire broke.	KGI
6th	Bad light. Brigade Tests carried out at about 3.0 pm for concentration of fire. All Batteries responded quickly on each occasion. The 100th Battery were the slowest in taking orders.	
	103rd Battery fired at a working party on a sap-head opposite F2 at request of infantry and stopped their work.	
	Orders received from CRA that no more ammunition was to be fired during the week except in response to urgent call for help from the	

Instructions regarding War Diaries and Intelligence Summaries are contained in F. S. Regs., Part II. and the Staff Manual respectively. Title pages will be prepared in manuscript.

WAR DIARY
or
INTELLIGENCE SUMMARY.
(Erase heading not required.)

Army Form C. 2118.

855

Hour, Date, Place	Summary of Events and Information	Remarks and references to Appendices
	infantry or under direct orders from C.R.A.	
	69th Battery report much work done by enemy at O.25.a.91. - Screens near trestle bridge referred to yesterday were removed, showing earthworks in their places, with sandbags arranged on them in peculiar formation - Communications to an alternative O.P. laid	B/89 Howitzer Battery arrived at 4.30 pm from 1st Division ~~and~~ comes under the orders of O.C. 31st Brig.
	100th report much work on front trench (enemy) at N.30.c.27 transforming it into a redoubt - Position for a gun suspected.	
	Platform in E 15 post 12 completed by No. 2 Mountain Battery -	[illegible]
7th	~~No.~~ O.C. Left Section No. 2 Mountain Battery selected another gun platform in D 4. - Targets - machine gun emplacement, trench in enfilade, & 30 yards of wire. Range about 35 yards.	
	Orders received from 25th Divisional Artillery with reference to a demonstration on SPANBROEKMOLEN to distract attention from attack on HOOGE and draw fire of hostile guns. To take place at 3.0 am to 3.50 am on 8th.	
	All Batteries of 31st Brigade also 367th Battery, to fire from 3.0 am till 3.10 am, & from 3.20 am to 3.50 am. Rounds allotted to 18 pr. Battery 48 shrapnel - 9.2" How	

(9 29 6) W4141—463 100,000 9/14 H W V Forms/C. 2118/10

Instructions regarding War Diaries and Intelligence Summaries are contained in F.S. Regs., Part II. and the Staff Manual respectively. Title pages will be prepared in manuscript.

WAR DIARY
or
INTELLIGENCE SUMMARY.
(Erase heading not required.)

Army Form C. 2118.

856

Hour, Date, Place	Summary of Events and Information	Remarks and references to Appendices
	to fire 6 rounds – A/149 Hows. (4.5") to fire 56 Lyddite and 148 Shrapnel. 8 Batteries in all of RA guns concentrated on the area.	
	5.0 pm Demonstration postponed for 24 hours.	KM.
8th	69th and 103rd Batteries registered KRUISSTRAAT CABARET in 146th Bde. Zone.	Details of Brigade Headquarters and one Battery – 6 officers and 36 other ranks – of 123rd Brigade, 37th Division attached for a week's instruction, arrived at 4.0 pm
	B/89 Howitzer Battery commenced preparation ~~registration~~ of Battery position.	
	No 2 Mountain Battery selected 2 more sites for emplacements in D3 and D2 trenches. Targets – machine gun emplacement at 120 yards and a kind of Saphead at 130 yards range.	
9th	B/89 put one section in action during the night. Bombardment of Spanbroekmolen carried out as ordered. Enemy replied feebly. Attack at HOOGE lasted till about 8.30 am. from sound of firing – firing died down considerably at about 4.30 am.	
	At 3.20 pm. 69th Battery put 2 rounds into a German working party on SPANBROEKMOLEN, causing some casualties – one man seen to fall –	KM
10th	Remaining Section of B/89 brought into action during the night –	
	Dull day nothing to be observed – Both	

Instructions regarding War Diaries and Intelligence Summaries are contained in F. S. Regs., Part II. and the Staff Manual respectively. Title pages will be prepared in manuscript.

WAR DIARY
or
INTELLIGENCE SUMMARY.
(Erase heading not required.)

Army Form C. 2118.

85/

Hour, Date, Place	Summary of Events and Information	Remarks and references to Appendices
	Black Redoubt and Spanbroekmolen reported to be considerably damaged by bombardment.	K.f.1.
11th	B/89 Battery continued registration	
	Other Batteries carried out tests for burning of 85 fuze - Bar indicator did not give proportionate results.	K.f.1.
	Weather still stormy and light very poor.	
12th	Further tests of 85 fuze carried out. General results, burning of fuze very regular once found, but corrector not proportionate.	K.f.1.
	B/89 Hows continued registration.	
13th	2.45 p. G.O.C. R.A. held a test of concentration of fire and communications. Times taken by Batteries to respond (from time order was given) are attached	
	5.0 pm. Enemy fired 5 rounds 5.9" H.E. into KEMMEL 3 fell round Brigade Headquarters, the nearest being 30 yards away.	
	5.25 pm. 10?th Battery obtained 2 very effective rounds amongst German working party at SPANBROEKMOLEN and dispersed them	K.f.1.

(9 29 6) W 4141—463 100,000 9/14 H W V Forms/C. 2118/10

Instructions regarding War Diaries and Intelligence Summaries are contained in F. S. Regs., Part II. and the Staff Manual respectively. Title pages will be prepared in manuscript.

WAR DIARY
or
INTELLIGENCE SUMMARY.
(Erase heading not required.)

Army Form C. 2118.

858

Hour, Date, Place	Summary of Events and Information	Remarks and references to Appendices
14th	Brigade laid fresh wire to B/89th Observing station. B/89 registered 3 more points in Brigade zone. 69th Battery dispersed a working party near Spanbroekmolen at 3.30 pm. with their first round. Positions prepared up to date by O.C. Left Section No. 2 Mountain Battery shown in attached list.	KS!
15th	Orders received from Divisional Artillery to occupy Battle Headquarters at 3.0 p.m. At 3.0 pm. Brigade Headquarters were in communication with all Batteries, observing stations and C.R.A., from Battle Station. 84th Brigade opened their Battle station at 3.10 pm. Division then carried out test of concentration of Artillery fire. First order received at 3.26 pm to fire on PECKHAM Farm, which is only 60 yards from my own trenches, was complied with 20 mins before the trench had been cleared. Results of test attached	KS!

Instructions regarding War Diaries and Intelligence Summaries are contained in F. S. Regs., Part II. and the Staff Manual respectively. Title pages will be prepared in manuscript.

WAR DIARY
or
INTELLIGENCE SUMMARY.
(Erase heading not required.)

Army Form C. 2118.

659

Hour, Date, Place	Summary of Events and Information	Remarks and references to Appendices
16th.	Some curious loopholes in German trench opposite 14 trench having been reported, orders were issued to D/59 How. Battery to shell them as early as possible this morning, observing from the trench. Battery opened fire, when trench 14 had been cleared, at about 8.30 am. Communication then broke down and the bombardment was put off till the afternoon when D/59 obtained 7 direct hits on the trench but owing to strength of its construction were unable to destroy the redoubt or loopholes. A certain amount of damage was done for which enemy retaliated with rifle grenades all night.	
17th.	Brigade Commander went to 14 trench at 6.30 am to inspect damage done by D/59 battery's bombardment. The enemy had done a good deal of repair work during the night [illegible] rather, firing rifle [illegible]	
	[illegible] the Germans exploded a mine [illegible] very little damage. No [illegible] trench	

[illegible]

Army Form C. 2118.

860

Instructions regarding War Diaries and Intelligence Summaries are contained in F.S. Regs., Part II. and the Staff Manual respectively. Title pages will be prepared in manuscript.

WAR DIARY
or
INTELLIGENCE SUMMARY.
(Erase heading not required.)

Hour, Date, Place	Summary of Events and Information	Remarks and references to Appendices
	Considerable artillery and a good deal of shelling during the night, in the area North of the Division of Dickebusch.	
	Enemy's guns also active round the trench during the day.	
	Weather stormy — fine at intervals.	
17th	115th Battery was successfully ranged onto a working party near MAEDELSTEDE Farm by an infantry officer in the trenches.	KM
18th	Visit by Lord Kitchener and French Minister of War to Scherpenberg. Brigade Commander, Adjutant, 1 officer and 30 men detailed to parade for them at 11 a.m. The inspection of the A units took place, the 2 Battalions of Infantry were accorded a cursory glance. Parade dismissed 11.45 a.m. A quiet day.	KM
19th	The Officers from 51st Divisional Artillery reported & 6 did not arrive with the guns — 2 attached B/57 battery and 1 to 100th Battery for instruction. A quiet day.	KM
20th	Registration carried out by 67th and 115th Batteries. The 67th Battery registered a trench opposite G2 assisted by and at request of an infantry —	

Instructions regarding War Diaries and Intelligence Summaries are contained in F. S. Regs., Part II. and the Staff Manual respectively. Title pages will be prepared in manuscript.

WAR DIARY
or
INTELLIGENCE SUMMARY.
(Erase heading not required.)

Army Form C. 2118.

861

Hour, Date, Place	Summary of Events and Information	Remarks and references to Appendices
	2 pollards had been blown up at this point by the enemy, and it was expected that they were mining from there under G2 trench.	
	The Brigade Commander accompanied G.O.C. R.A. visiting emplacements prepared by Mountain Battery in K ~~and~~ H trenches, also visiting G and F trenches.	
21st	A very wet and stormy morning; weather improved in the afternoon.	
	G.O.C. 84th Brigade accompanied Brigade Commander to observing Station from which a test of fire concentration was held on support trenches and supporting points. Enemy retaliated and G and F trenches, but few rounds effective.	
	Flash of German gun ~~[illegible]~~ observed roughly between O 25 a 38 and N 30 b 65. Only 2 rounds fired from it ~~So~~ exact position not located. 3 observers are on the look out for it.	
	The infantry in G2 trench successful blew up German mine being ~~[illegible]~~ driven under G2 trench. 100th Battery stood by, but their fire was not needed.	KR

Instructions regarding War Diaries and Intelligence Summaries are contained in F. S. Regs., Part II. and the Staff Manual respectively. Title pages will be prepared in manuscript.

WAR DIARY
or
INTELLIGENCE SUMMARY.
(Erase heading not required.)

Army Form C. 2118.

862

Hour, Date, Place	Summary of Events and Information	Remarks and references to Appendices
22nd	Weather much improved and the light for observation excellent. Aeroplanes of both sides very active all day, particularly British. Reconnaissance of prepared backward defences of Kemmel Hill and Scherpenberg completed by officers of the Brigade. Small red balloon observed by 69th Battery very high travelling S.E. at about 5.30 pm. (first observed by other individuals) near a German aeroplane.	
23rd	A German trench mortar firing a 30 lb shell (sausage shape) active on G1 trench at about 9.0 am. B/89 and 100th Battery retaliated. Small field gun also shelling G1 in the afternoon. 100th Battery retaliated on PECKHAM - 3 rounds and 69th Battery on Black Redoubt (N 30 a 33) - 2 rounds - with desired effect. A misty day bad for observation. 69th Battery report much work done by enemy at N 30 a 56 near PECKHAM where communication trench from front line.	
24th	Minenwerfer at PECKHAM started firing at 2.7 am. 100th Battery fired 7 rounds in all in retaliation from 2.30 am to 3.20 am. B/89 fired 2 lyddite which quieted the Germans immediately.	

(9 29 6) W 4141—463 100,000 9/14 H W V Forms/C. 2118/10

Instructions regarding War Diaries and Intelligence Summaries are contained in F. S. Regs., Part II. and the Staff Manual respectively. Title pages will be prepared in manuscript.

WAR DIARY
or
INTELLIGENCE SUMMARY.
(Erase heading not required.)

Army Form C. 2118.

863

Hour, Date, Place	Summary of Events and Information	Remarks and references to Appendices
	Tests calls from the trenches were replied to satisfactorily except from 69th Battery. F S Trench unable to get a reply, as the instrument in the trenches had a very weak buzzer and the Battery operator was engaged sending a long message.	R.G.M.
	At 12 noon B/87 Battery put 13 rounds of lyddite into Black Redoubt, 8 rounds being direct hits. The enemy retaliated with field guns on G2 in the evening and with 6 or 8 with H.E. at 8 to 7 pm. near SP10. No damage was done but 100th Battery replied with 12 rounds.	
	OC. 100th Battery reports that the field gun which fires on G2 is almost certainly in enemy's front trench at MEDELSTEDE farm salient.	Attached [illegible] of 87th [illegible] [illegible]
25th	B/87 Battery ordered to keep a gun laid and loaded with lyddite to retaliate for "whizzbang" on point of MEDELSTEDE salient.	
	Registration carried out by 103rd and 115th Batteries on a communication trench and Sap head respectively. Enemy retaliated with field gun, and 4.2 Howitzer. The 100th, 103rd and 115th replied on enemy trenches firing 23 rounds in all between 5.40 pm. & 6.5 pm.	

Instructions regarding War Diaries and Intelligence Summaries are contained in F. S. Regs., Part II. and the Staff Manual respectively. Title pages will be prepared in manuscript.

WAR DIARY
or
INTELLIGENCE SUMMARY.
(Erase heading not required.)

Army Form C. 2118.

864

Hour, Date, Place	Summary of Events and Information	Remarks and references to Appendices
26th	Wind East to North-east, brilliant sunshine, warm and dry.	
	At 11.0 am the 103rd Battery observer saw a flag hoisted in German trench. A round or two were fired, and position of flag was moved: this was repeated until the flag was taken down.	
	At 3.40 pm 103rd Battery fired on a working party in communication trench North of SPANBROEKMOLEN and dispersed it. Enemy retaliated on G2 with field gun. 100th Battery replied at 3.50 pm firing 6 rounds on PECKHAM. The B/87 observer did not notice the shelling of G2 and when they were called up to fire their laid gun it was too late to be of any value for the purpose and the gun was not fired.	
	At 10.15 pm an aeroplane passed over ~~[illegible]~~ North of KEMMEL flying N.E. This might have been an airship at great height, but sounded more like an aeroplane.	
	The infantry called on 69th Battery to fire at a working party on Spanbroekmolen at 10.30 pm and at 11.35 pm. 14 rounds were fired and reported effective.	
27th	Weather remains brilliant.	
	Pointed out to infantry that their sniping of working parties probably more effective and certainly less expensive than asking a battery to disperse	

Instructions regarding War Diaries and Intelligence Summaries are contained in F. S. Regs., Part II. and the Staff Manual respectively. Title pages will be prepared in manuscript.

WAR DIARY
or
INTELLIGENCE SUMMARY.
(Erase heading not required.)

Army Form C. 2118.

565

Hour, Date, Place	Summary of Events and Information	Remarks and references to Appendices
	them at night.	
	Situation regarding the mine under G2 trench still precarious. 84th Brigade did not support suggestion that 9.2" How[rs] should shell PECKHAM farm and break up the mine entrances.	
	About 10 rounds 5.9" shrapnel fired by enemy at about 1.30 pm near ROSSIGNOL - objective unknown.	
	Several German aeroplanes about in the morning. Otherwise all very quiet.	KJ?
28th.	Very dull and misty - Signs of change in weather. OC. 100th Battery discovered that position prepared for WULVERGHEM SWITCH line was unsuitable as the guns would not clear the crest of Little KEMMEL when firing on left of Battery zone. No other zone of the Brigade front was as favourable - New position therefore necessary. Reconnaissance taken in hand.	
29th	Bad light in morning, and heavy rain all afternoon - 69th Battery only fired in morning to re-register points behind enemys trenches - B/47 How[rs] registered left Section on PETIT BOIS (3rd Brigade zone) and No. 4 gun on trench opposite G3.	

Instructions regarding War Diaries and Intelligence Summaries are contained in F. S. Regs., Part II. and the Staff Manual respectively. Title pages will be prepared in manuscript.

WAR DIARY
or
INTELLIGENCE SUMMARY.
(*Erase heading not required.*)

Army Form C. 2118.

866

Hour, Date, Place	Summary of Events and Information	Remarks and references to Appendices
30th	Daily registration carried out. Enemy's activity for some time past proved to be conversion of front line parapet into shell-proof glacis. 69th dispersed a working party at 3. pm Weather changeable	KH
31st	9.55 am. 100th Battery dispersed a working party near PECKHAM Farm. This produced retaliation on G2 support trench. The 118th and 365th Batteries replied the 118th getting in very successful burst in enfilade of MAEDELSTEDE trenches which settled the matter. Our infantry appear at last to be copying the Germans in the obvious namely making parapet irregular and of multi-coloured sandbags. They may soon be able to have some loop-holes. This copying campaign appears to be meeting with much success to the advantage and peace of all concerned.	2/Lieut J. C. Cunliffe on posting to 31st Brigade R.F.A. joined 31st Bde A.C. yesterday (30th inst.)
		KH Roland Lt RFA

28th Division

121
7145.

31st Bde R.F.A.

Vol IX.

Sept 15.

Army Form C. 2118.

Instructions regarding War Diaries and Intelligence Summaries are contained in F. S. Regs., Part II. and the Staff Manual respectively. Title pages will be prepared in manuscript.

WAR DIARY
or
INTELLIGENCE SUMMARY.
(*Erase heading not required.*)

Hour, Date, Place	Summary of Events and Information	Remarks and references to Appendices
KEMMEL September 1st	10.30 a.m. An 8" Heavy gun opened fire on a working party 200 yards from Brigade H.Qs. 7 rounds fired - no damage. 6/87 ordered to fire 6 lyddite on SPANBROEKMOLEN in reply.	
	Later some 5.9" Shrapnel were fired onto KEMMEL Hill - objective unknown.	
	At 5.30 p.m. our 8" How: ranged on PECKHAM farm. Out of 20 rounds fired only 5 hit the ruins and a few [illegible] did not appear to detonate properly. The 69th, 100th and 118th Batteries cooperated effectively with shrapnel, the 69th Battery accounting for a party of Germans apparently endeavouring to extricate something from the ruins. The enemy's 8" How: fired in retaliation apparently at Support 10, but had evidently made a mistake in [illegible] position. They also fired one salvo of shrapnel from 5.9" gun over 103rd Battery position - no casualties.	
	The 100th Battery dropped one round short into 92 trench.	KGI.
2nd	Noticeable that our aircraft are no longer fired at by German guns from behind WYTSCHAETE.	
	At 5.0 p.m. the 100th and 117th Batteries attacked	

Instructions regarding War Diaries and Intelligence Summaries are contained in F. S. Regs., Part II. and the Staff Manual respectively. Title pages will be prepared in manuscript.

WAR DIARY
or
INTELLIGENCE SUMMARY.
(Erase heading not required.)

Army Form C. 2118.

Hour, Date, Place	Summary of Events and Information	Remarks and references to Appendices
	a German in full view – He escaped, but doubtful if whole or not.	
	Between 5.30 pm. and 6.30 pm. the enemy searched round the lower slopes of KEMMEL Hill – The first 6 rounds were 8" inch, 5 falling within 150 yards of Brigade Headquarters. Then followed a salvo of 5.9 inch then 4 of 4.2" inch. Two telephone airlines (alternate) broken. At 6.45 pm the enemy exploded a mine <u>under</u> and heavily shelled G2 trench	The 69th and 100th Batteries replied to their fire until requested by the infantry to stop. Apparently no damage had been done. This proved to be the long-expected mine. KGl
3rd	Heavy rain fell all day. No firing done.	KGl
4th	Weather improving. Saddler of 100th Battery slightly wounded in head by a groom cleaning an officer's revolver which was loaded and went off.	
	At 7.15 pm. our 8" Howrs put a few rounds into Black Redoubt. One or two appeared to be blinds. Enemy retaliated on F4, F5 and F6 trenches. B/89 Battery replied with lyddite (6 rounds) on Spanbroek-molen and Peckham (4 rounds)	KGl.
5th	Brigade Commander accompanied G.O.C. R.A. and an R.E. representative round KEMMEL observing stations to discuss making the dug-outs "crump-proof"	

Instructions regarding War Diaries and Intelligence Summaries are contained in F. S. Regs., Part II. and the Staff Manual respectively. Title pages will be prepared in manuscript.

WAR DIARY
or
INTELLIGENCE SUMMARY.
(Erase heading not required.)

Army Form C. 2118.

Hour, Date, Place	Summary of Events and Information	Remarks and references to Appendices
	Orders received that the 4.5" Hows were to fire 2 rounds lyddite and 2 of Shrapnel daily into Black Redoubt.	
	B.S.M. Deeks, Sergt Roberts, Fitter S. Sgt. Bates, and 2 gunners 69th Battery R.F.A. injured by the explosion of a German fuze, which the B.S.M. and Fitter had removed from a blind 77mm. shell (contrary to all standing orders). Injuries to B.S.M. and Sergeant Roberts serious. The fuze was a high explosive one, the shell a shrapnel.	B.S.M. Deeks, 69th Battery R.F.A. commissioned Lieutenant from
	Between 4 p.m. and 5.0 p.m. the 100th and 103rd Batteries registered 2 points - cross roads - by balloon. Both had very successful results.	
	At 5.50 p.m. the 9.2" Hows fired several rounds over SPANBROEKMOLEN at a steam trench digger supposed to be working there. The 118th Battery cooperated with Shrapnel. No movement was seen however.	K.G.I.
6th.	Weather much improved.	
	B/87 shelled Black Redoubt as usual, firing 6	

Army Form C. 2118.

Instructions regarding War Diaries and Intelligence Summaries are contained in F. S. Regs., Part II. and the Staff Manual respectively. Title pages will be prepared in manuscript.

WAR DIARY
or
INTELLIGENCE SUMMARY.
(*Erase heading not required.*)

Hour, Date, Place	Summary of Events and Information	Remarks and references to Appendices
	rounds of lyddite and 2 Shrapnel. The 118th Co-operated. All very effective.	
7th	B/89 Battery renumbered "B" Battery, 130th Brigade.	
	B/130 carried out daily bombardment of Black Redoubt at 3.30 pm in co-operation with 118th Battery. B/130 fired 5 Lyddite, all effective and 118th Battery 12 shrapnel.	KGL
	A fine day but no movement observed.	
8th	Major Ramsden acting Brigade Commander, during Colonel Bond's absence on leave (from 4/9/15 to 11/9/15) accompanied G.O.C. R.A. and Brigade-Major in a reconnaissance for ~~[illegible]~~ position for 100th Battery for WULVERGHEM switch. No suitable position was found for the zone allotted; change of zones of Batteries will be necessary to suit positions as now decided on. KEMMEL Hill renders the subsidiary lines extremely difficult to support effectively with artillery fire	R.S.M. J.P. Adams Commissioned Lieut. from 31/7/15 – leaves Brigade on admission to hospital.

(9 29 6) W4141—463 100,000 9/14 H W V Forms/C. 2118/10

Army Form C. 2118.

WAR DIARY
or
INTELLIGENCE SUMMARY.
(Erase heading not required.)

Instructions regarding War Diaries and Intelligence Summaries are contained in F. S. Regs., Part II. and the Staff Manual respectively. Title pages will be prepared in manuscript.

Hour, Date, Place	Summary of Events and Information	Remarks and references to Appendices
	Method of extracting time detonator from No 80 and 44/80 fuzes in H.E. shell explained. This to be done with all H.E. until further orders.	
	At 3.30 pm. B/130th Battery and 118th Battery fired on Black Redoubt – effective.	
	69th, 100th and 103rd Batteries all fired on and dispersed working parties in the morning –	KJ.
9th	2.45 pm 100th Battery shelled buildings where movement was observed – near work O 25 a 98 – but owing to 3 premature in 8 rounds, series was not a success	Lieut. E.C. Williams on posting to 31st Brigade joined 31st Bde Amm. Col.
	3.0 pm 103rd Battery registered machine gun emplacement with help of infantry.	
	At 5.15 pm the 100th, 69th B/130th Battery and 118th Battery bombarded BLACK REDOUBT for 10 minutes. 10 rounds of H.E. were allotted to 18 prs. (fired by 69th and 100th Btys) and B/130 fired 5 lyddite. 18 prs. cooperated with shrapnel – All appeared effective. Distinguished gathering looked on including G.O.C. & G.O.C. R.A. 25th Division, C.R.E. IInd Corps, G.O.C. R.A. 12th Division and attendant staffs. The enemy replied	

Instructions regarding War Diaries and Intelligence Summaries are contained in F. S. Regs., Part II. and the Staff Manual respectively. Title pages will be prepared in manuscript.

WAR DIARY
or
INTELLIGENCE SUMMARY.
(Erase heading not required.)

Army Form C. 2118.

Hour, Date, Place	Summary of Events and Information	Remarks and references to Appendices
	feebly with 3 or 4 H.E. over F6 trench.	K.G.A.
10th	The 69th Battery put 5 rounds amongst a working party at O.25 a.9.8½ at 4.0 p.m. and the 100th Battery fired at 2 parties at BLACK REDOUBT at 12.30 pm. and at 1.30 pm. at O.19 d.15 (Quarry redoubt).	
	B/130 shelled Black Redoubt at 4.0 pm.	K.G.A.
11th	Orders received for a further bombardment of BLACK REDOUBT with lyddite and H.E. to take place on 12th at 4.0 pm. Two mountain guns to take part, one on BLACK REDOUBT and one on houses in N30 c between German trenches and ours – a sniper's haunt – in destruction of which 25th trench mortar Battery were to assist.	
	The usual bombardment of BLACK REDOUBT by B/130th Battery and 118th Battery took place at 3.30pm. The enemy retaliated on F4 trench – 103rd Battery replied on SPANBROEKMOLEN – 20 rounds 18pr. shrapnel 3 4.5" lyddite & 2 4.5" shrapnel for 3 H.E. by Germans (about 4")	

(9 29 6) W4141—463 100,000 9/14 H W V Forms/C. 2118/10

Army Form C. 2118.

Instructions regarding War Diaries and Intelligence Summaries are contained in F. S. Regs., Part II. and the Staff Manual respectively. Title pages will be prepared in manuscript.

WAR DIARY
or
INTELLIGENCE SUMMARY.
(Erase heading not required.)

Hour, Date, Place	Summary of Events and Information	Remarks and references to Appendices
	O.C. left Section No 2 Mountain Battery put in his two guns at night. The embrasures were built into the parapet in the evening and completed in the night. The guns were not actually put together in the platform.	K.P.
12th	Between 11 am and 12 noon the 69th Battery shelled 3 working parties in rear of SPANBROEK MOLEN and South of WYTSCHAETE, dispersing them: 23 rounds in all fired.	
	The Germans apparently located the mountain gun in E2 trench as they shelled the emplacement with a field gun at 2.0 pm. The 103rd Battery retaliated and stopped the enemy's fire.	
	At 4.0 pm. the Bombardment of Black Redoubt commenced: the mountain gun in F4 trench also opened fire on machine gun emplacements between the Redoubt and Spanbroekmolen & fired 20 Shrapnel.	
	All fire appeared effective though 5 rds. 4.5" lyddite, 10 rds. 18 pr. H.E. and 20 rds. 18 pr. Shrapnel did not damage the parapets appreciably.	

(9 29 6) W 4141—463 100,000 9/14 H W V Forms/C. 2118/10

Army Form C. 2118.

WAR DIARY
or
INTELLIGENCE SUMMARY.
(Erase heading not required.)

Instructions regarding War Diaries and Intelligence Summaries are contained in F. S. Regs., Part II. and the Staff Manual respectively. Title pages will be prepared in manuscript.

Hour, Date, Place	Summary of Events and Information	Remarks and references to Appendices
	The mountain gun in F 4 obtained 2 hits on the machine gun emplacement and many on the trench and enemy's wire. The gun in E 2 had to cease fire after 6 rounds owing to collapse of embrasure as result of enemy's shelling previously. The 25th Trench How: obtained several hits on the ruins in N 30 c, setting fire to one and destroying the other.	
	The enemy replied with 3 rounds of H.E. behind F 4 trench.	KJL
13th	Enemy still hard at work on their defences. 69th Battery dispersed a working party at 5.30 pm.	
	B/130 How: Battery and 148th Battery shelled BLACK REDOUBT at 3.0 pm.	KJL
14th	A steam engine of some kind is undoubtedly behind Spanbroekmolen – the 69th Battery confirm report of infantry.	Captain T.F. Sandeman on posting leaves for 130th How: Brigade.
	Registration with Balloon observation carried out satisfactorily by 69th Battery on 3 points	Lt. C.H.L Penney posted to 100th Battery R.F.A. from 130th Brigade vice Capt. Sandeman
	Flash observation by night in conjunction with the	

Army Form C. 2118.

Instructions regarding War Diaries and Intelligence Summaries are contained in F. S. Regs., Part II. and the Staff Manual respectively. Title pages will be prepared in manuscript.

WAR DIARY
or
INTELLIGENCE SUMMARY.
(*Erase heading not required.*)

Hour, Date, Place	Summary of Events and Information	Remarks and references to Appendices
14th (cont'd)	Canadians at PLOEGSTREET arranged. Hostile fire too far north during night. Canadians unable to see the flashes angled from KEMMEL.	KGA
15th	The 68th Battery registered trenches near WULVERGHEM satisfactorily with balloon observation. The C/130th How. Battery being unable to take on a machine gun emplacement in their zone (N. of 31st Brigade) with safety to our own trenches, the task was given to B/130th Battery, who shelled the emplacement located in W edge of PETIT BOIS with 7 lyddite and 9 shrapnel. Observation from the trenches and from KEMMEL. The emplacement was not destroyed though several rounds burst within a few yards of it. The 69th Battery also registered with balloon, on a point behind MESSINES-WYTSCHAETE ridge invisible from O.P. Flash observation in conjunction with Canadians continued - No gun fire on front WYTSCHAETE-MESSINES during night - Some flashes angled East of YPRES.	

(9 29 6) W 4141—463 100,000 9/14 H W V Forms/C. 2118/10

Instructions regarding War Diaries and Intelligence Summaries are contained in F. S. Regs., Part II. and the Staff Manual respectively. Title pages will be prepared in manuscript.

WAR DIARY
or
INTELLIGENCE SUMMARY.
(Erase heading not required.)

Army Form C. 2118.

Hour, Date, Place	Summary of Events and Information	Remarks and references to Appendices
16th	Very little firing done. The 100th Battery retaliated on German trenches opposite G 2 for whizz bangs on the G trenches at 11.30 a.m. The Shoot arranged to take place at 4.0 p.m. was postponed owing to insufficient light for observation. No forward observing Officer in the trenches had been arranged for, and BLACK REDOUBT was not sufficiently visible from KEMMEL HILL owing to mist.	~~Lieut Griffin posted to 21st Brigade R.F.A.~~ [illegible]

(9 29 6) W 4141—463 100,000 9/14 H W V Forms/C. 2118/10

Army Form C. 2118.

WAR DIARY
or
INTELLIGENCE SUMMARY.
(*Erase heading not required.*)

Instructions regarding War Diaries and Intelligence Summaries are contained in F. S. Regs., Part II. and the Staff Manual respectively. Title pages will be prepared in manuscript.

Hour, Date, Place	Summary of Events and Information	Remarks and references to Appendices
17th	In accordance with R.A. Orders the 9.2" Hows. having commenced to bombard BLACK REDOUBT at 4.0 pm the 69th and 100th fired a round of gun fire each, after each of the first 4 rds. of 9.2". The 118th Battery were ordered to fire a few rounds on MAEDELSTEDE Fm. during the shoot in the hopes of catching a careless and inquisitive Hun. B/130 were also ordered to fire 5 rounds lyddite at the ruins in N 30 C at which the 25th Trench Hows. also fired 9 heavy bombs at 4.20 pm. The 9.2" Hows. subsequently turned onto steam engine South-east of SPANBROEKMOLEN: the 146th F.A. Brigade co-operated with shrapnel. General effect of shoot appeared good. The 9.2" were slightly over and did not succeed in putting a round into the front trenches, but appeared to blow up some dug-outs from the debris thrown up. The enemy replied with 8" and smaller H.E. but did no damage - 2 rounds fell into F2 and blew in a Bay - no Casualties	2/Lieut. H.T. Griffin on posting to 31st Brigade R.F.A. joins 31st Brigade Amm. Col. KJ.A.

(9 29 6) W 4141—463 100,000 9/14 H W V Forms/C. 2118/10

Army Form C. 2118.

WAR DIARY
or
INTELLIGENCE SUMMARY.
(Erase heading not required.)

Instructions regarding War Diaries and Intelligence Summaries are contained in F. S. Regs., Part II. and the Staff Manual respectively. Title pages will be prepared in manuscript.

Hour, Date, Place	Summary of Events and Information	Remarks and references to Appendices
18th	Wind changing to N and N.E. At 1.30 pm. the enemy commenced to put H.E. from 8", 5.9" and 4.2" onto the F trenches presumably in retaliation for 9.2" shoot yesterday. The enemy fired about 60 H.E. and about 150 whizz-bangs on the F and G trenches between 1.30 pm. and 4.30 pm. 8" came in salvos of 2, 5.9" in salvos of 2 or 3, and 4" in salvos of 3 or 4. All our Batteries replied, firing 70 shrapnel in all and 15 lyddite 4.5 inch. The 4.7 guns were also turned on to shell gun positions, the 9.2" Howr being otherwise engaged. Our last 10 lyddite and 14 shrapnel on MAEDELSTEDE farm appeared to stop the enemy's fire. Casualties to infantry 1 killed 3 or 4 wounded, and parapet blown in in 3 places.	
19th.	The houses in N 30 C were inspected by Brigade Commander ~~at~~ from E3 trench Bay 5 in the morning. Nothing remains but a shell of the walls, which are not worth firing at. Owing to shortage of grenades our infantry asked us to assist in retaliation opposite 15 trench	KGL

Instructions regarding War Diaries and Intelligence Summaries are contained in F. S. Regs., Part II. and the Staff Manual respectively. Title pages will be prepared in manuscript.

WAR DIARY
or
INTELLIGENCE SUMMARY.
(Erase heading not required.)

Army Form C. 2118.

Hour, Date, Place	Summary of Events and Information	Remarks and references to Appendices
	While this was being arranged, the enemy again began to shell E and F trenches (2.30 pm) B/130 fired rounds lyddite on Spanbroekmolen in retaliation, and our 18pr. batteries fired on German trenches in their zones. The 4.7 inch guns also turned onto the enemy emplacements and firing ceased at about 4.0 pm. B/130 fired 6 rounds lyddite opposite 15 trench with trench observation - 2 hits on parapet obtained.	
	Orders for relief by 2 batteries of 80th Brigade, 17th Division received; the 100th and 103rd each withdrawing a section at 8.30 pm. tonight.	
	Reliefs completed at 10.15 pm. and 11.45 pm respectively.	K.G.
20th	Registration by newly arrived sections of A and C Batteries, 80th Brigade carried out during the day. Zones allotted for registration A Battery BLACK REDOUBT to MAEDELSTEDE Farm, C Battery N 30 c 2 4 to BLACK REDOUBT.	
	Orders received from G.O.C.R.A. re turn-out and march discipline; also with regard to exercise in back area at PRADELLE: no horse exercise on roads, and men to be given physical training.	
	Relief of 84th Brigade by 3rd Canadian infantry	

Instructions regarding War Diaries and Intelligence Summaries are contained in F. S. Regs., Part II. and the Staff Manual respectively. Title pages will be prepared in manuscript.

WAR DIARY
or
INTELLIGENCE SUMMARY.
(Erase heading not required.)

Army Form C. 2118.

Hour, Date, Place	Summary of Events and Information	Remarks and references to Appendices
	Brigade carried out during the night.	
	Orders received and issued that 31st Brigade relief would be completed on night 22nd/23rd and the Brigade would march from LOCRE at 10.0 am. 23rd instant.	KGA
21st	Arrangements for handing over continued. Airlines reeled in, leaving complete duplicated system of buried wires to hand over.	
	No firing done by 31st Brigade Batteries.	KGA
22nd	Officers Commanding A and C Batteries 80th Brigade assumed command at 12 noon vice O.C. 100th and 103rd (relieved).	
	O.C. 80th Brigade and Staff arrived 1.0 pm. to take over.	
	Handing over completed during afternoon.	
	No firing during the day except by B/130 How. Battery in retaliation for crumps on F 4 trench.	
	69th, 118th and B/130th Battery withdrawn at 8.0 p.m. Relief of 103rd completed 8.15 pm. and of 100th 8.20 p.m.	KGA

(9 29 6) W 4141—463 100,000 9/14 H W V Forms/C. 2118/10

Army Form C. 2118.

Instructions regarding War Diaries and Intelligence Summaries are contained in F. S. Regs., Part II. and the Staff Manual respectively. Title pages will be prepared in manuscript.

WAR DIARY
or
INTELLIGENCE SUMMARY.
(Erase heading not required.)

Hour, Date, Place	Summary of Events and Information	Remarks and references to Appendices
23rd	31st Brigade marched off at 9.15 a.m. at the head of Divisional Artillery - Baggage reduced to a minimum. Road badly blocked between LOCRE and BAILLEUL causing delay of 10 to 15 minutes. PRADELLE reached at 2.30 p.m. Weather fine throughout. 7.0 p.m. orders received to be ready to move at one hour's notice - Amended shortly afterwards to read one Battery to be held in readiness to move at one hour's notice. 118th Battery detailed.	K.G.1.
~~24th~~ 24th	Weather changed - Wind South - Rain in the evening. Units employed cleaning and overhauling vehicles and equipment - Horses exercised in draught. 6.0 pm Programmes of work wired for - To be submitted daily -	K.G.1.

Instructions regarding War Diaries and Intelligence Summaries are contained in F. S. Regs., Part II. and the Staff Manual respectively. Title pages will be prepared in manuscript.

WAR DIARY
or
INTELLIGENCE SUMMARY.
(Erase heading not required.)

Army Form C. 2118.

Hour, Date, Place	Summary of Events and Information	Remarks and references to Appendices
25th	Wind S.W. – Considerable amount of rain. Inspection of billets by G.O.C. R.A. did not take place in the morning, but afternoon – Parades not interfered with.	
	Draft of 9 remounts received – 5 L.D., 4 Riders.	
	6.55 p.m. 3 telegrams received. – One ordering units to be ready to move at 2 hour's notice, one calling for programme of work for tomorrow and one calling for names of men qualified for drivers of steam rollers.	
	8.0 p.m. Wire from R.A. – "move not likely to take place before daybreak.	KGI
26th	2.0 a.m. Orders received that the Brigade would move at 7.30 a.m.	
	2.55 a.m. Wire from 28th R.A that orders for march would be received from 84th Infantry Brigade.	(Ref. Map HAZEBROUCK 5A)
	4.30 a.m. March orders received from 84th Infantry Brigade. 31st Brigade to follow infantry and 85th Field Ambulance, leaving PETIT SEC BOIS at 9.5 a.m. and march to MERVILLE.	

Army Form C. 2118.

Instructions regarding War Diaries and Intelligence Summaries are contained in F. S. Regs., Part II. and the Staff Manual respectively. Title pages will be prepared in manuscript.

WAR DIARY
or
INTELLIGENCE SUMMARY.
(Erase heading not required.)

Hour, Date, Place	Summary of Events and Information	Remarks and references to Appendices
	Billetting parties (N.C.O. or officer & 2 men per battery under Brigade Orderly officer) met Staff Captain 84th Bde at 7.30 a.m. at NEUF BERQUIN.	
	Brigade passed through MERVILLE at 1.30 pm and reached billets near BOIS DE PACANT (2 miles N.W. of HINGES) at 2.0 pm. – Billets not to be occupied	
	On arrival orders by Despatch Rider received to move at once after watering, feeding and dinners. Orderly Officer sent to 84th Brigade H.Q. at once – Orders brought back from 84th Brigade that billets would be occupied and march not continued.	System of A.S.C. in issuing rations in bulk to the Brigade causing much extra work to Q.M.S. on duty – no success on the march. KJ.1.
	6.0 pm Orderly sent to R.A.H.Q. at MERVILLE – returned 11.30 pm saying HQS. R.A. had moved no one knew where. 84th Brigade could not inform us.	
27th	Orders to move as soon as possible received by D.R. from 8th R.A. at 1.0 pm – R.A. orders sent out at 9.0 a.m. to move at 12 noon were not received till 1.35 pm.	
	Move consisted in a march to HINGETTE	

(9 29 6) W4141—463 100,000 9/14 H W V Forms/C. 2118/10

Instructions regarding War Diaries and Intelligence Summaries are contained in F. S. Regs., Part II. and the Staff Manual respectively. Title pages will be prepared in manuscript.

WAR DIARY
or
INTELLIGENCE SUMMARY.
(Erase heading not required.)

Army Form C. 2118.

Hour, Date, Place	Summary of Events and Information	Remarks and references to Appendices
	of 3 miles - New billets considerabley worse than those at BOIS DE PACANT, which were poor. No cover available for men, and very little for officers. In addition rain fell in torrents in the evening.	
	Endeavoured to get A.S.C. of Indian Corps moved from billets in our area through S.C.R.A.	K.f.1
28th.	A.S.C. ordered to move - Clear by 2.30 pm. More room available, so that all officers have a billet, and most of the men get cover.	
	4.0 pm. Orders received that 31st Brigade would come under orders of IInd Division to-morrow. Brigade and Battery Commanders to meet C.R.A. IInd Division at 8.0 a.m. tomorrow.	
	One section of each Battery to go into action on the night 29/30.	
	At 5.30 pm. rain began to fall in torrents and fell all night.	K.f.1
29th.	Brigade Commander and Battery commanders with small staffs left for H.Q. R.A. IInd Division at 7.0 am. Raining heavily at 10.0 am.	

(9 29 6) W4141—463 100,000 9/14 H W V Forms/C. 2118/10

Army Form C. 2118.

WAR DIARY
or
INTELLIGENCE SUMMARY.
(Erase heading not required.)

Instructions regarding War Diaries and Intelligence Summaries are contained in F. S. Regs., Part II. and the Staff Manual respectively. Title pages will be prepared in manuscript.

Hour, Date, Place	Summary of Events and Information	Remarks and references to Appendices
	The 69th 100th and 103rd Batteries moved off independently, the 69th to take up a fresh position the 100th and 103rd Batteries to take over from Batteries of the Guards Divisional Artillery.	
	The 69th and 100th Batteries only ~~come~~ to come under the ~~31st~~ O.C. 31st Brigade. The 103rd and 118th Batteries were placed under the orders of O.C. 41st and 34th Brigades respectively.	KGJ
30th	69th and 100th Batteries having come into action last night, were busy laying telephone lines during the morning.	
	Brigade Headquarters moved to ANNEQUIN mines 31st Brigade Ammunition Column to Farm Du Roi BETHUNE	
	118th Battery occupies a position under orders of O.C. 34th Brigade.	
	31st Brigade supporting infantry of 5th Brigade, 2nd Division	
	Communications from Batteries to Infantry Battns and their O.P.'s & from Brigade Headquarters to Batteries and Infantry Brigade H.Q.S established and both	

Appendix 4

Operation Order No 26 — Copy No. 1

by Major R.C. Ramsden

Cmdg 31st Brigade R.F.A.

1. Commencing at 5.15 pm this evening the 31st Brigade R.F.A. and B/130 Battery will bombard Black Redoubt in accordance with the following programme.

2. B/130 Battery will open fire at 5.15 pm and will fire 5 rounds of lyddite between 5.15 pm and 5.25 pm. The 118th Battery will co-operate by firing shrapnel after each round of lyddite bursts.

3. The 69th and 100th Batteries are each allotted 5 rounds of H.E. for the bombardment and for the sake of accuracy one gun of each Battery will be told off to fire it.

4. The 69th Battery will fire from 5.15 pm to 5.20 pm and the 100th Battery from 5.20 pm to 5.25 pm, following up each round of H.E. with a round of shrapnel.

5 The intervals between the rounds of H.E. should be as irregular as possible.

6 Time will be checked at 4.0 pm.

7 Any registration necessary on Black Rebutt will be carried out before 4.0 pm.

8. Acknowledge

9.9.15.

K. [illegible] Lt R.A.
Adjt 31st Bde R.F.A.

Copy No. 1 to 69th Battery R.F.A.
2 100th
3 103rd
4 118th
5 B/130
6 84th Infantry Brigade
7 Retd

458 B

SECRET.

Operation Order No 27 Copy No. 1

by Lt. Col. A.H. Bond

Cmdg, 31st Brigade R.F.A.

Appendix II

1. The Bombardment of Black Redoubt by 31st Brigade R.F.A. and B/130th How. Battery will be continued to-morrow the 12th instant, commencing at 4.0 pm.

2. The 69th Battery will fire from 4.0 pm. to 4.5 pm. the 100th Battery from 4.5 pm. to 4.10 p.m. and B/130th Battery from 4.0 pm. to 4.10 pm.

3. The 69th and 100th Batteries will each fire 5 rounds of H.E. following up each round with a round of shrapnel.

B/130th Battery will fire 5 rounds of lyddite, the 118th Battery following up each round of lyddite with a round of shrapnel.

4. O.C. Left Section No. 2 Mountain Battery will bring into action to-night (11/12) one gun to engage BLACK REDOUBT and one gun to engage the houses at

N 30 c 2.3½ - opposite E 2 trench

5. Each mountain gun will fire 20 rounds between 4.0 pm. and 4.10 pm. at the targets mentioned in 4.

6. Time will be checked at 2.30 pm.

7. The Brigade Commander will be at Brigade Observing Station at 3.45 pm to which place reports will be sent.

11.9.15.

K G Ireland
Lt. R.F.A.
Adjutant 31st Bde R.F.A.

Copy No. 1 to 69th Battery R.F.A.
2 " 100th "
3 " 103rd "
4 " 118th "
5 " Left X'n No 2 Mount'n Bty.
6 " 84th Inf Bde.
7 " B/130th How'r Bty
8 " 25th Trench How'r Bty
9 Filed

Appendix III Operation Order No 28 — Secret

by Lt. Col. H.H. Bond R.F.A. — Copy No. 1

J 22 — Cmdg 31st Brigade R.F.A.

(1) At 4.0 pm. tomorrow, the 16th instant, the 9.2" Hows. will fire a series of 20 rounds on the BLACK REDOUBT - Duration of series probably 45 minutes.

(2) During the bombardment the 69th and 100th Batteries will cooperate by firing one round of gun fire each, after each of the first 4 rounds from the 9.2" Hows. on the communication and support trenches in rear - i.e. 16 rounds each Battery.

(3). At the same hour SPANBROEKMOLEN will be shelled by A/130th How. Battery together with 18 pr. Shrapnel from guns of 146th and 3rd F.A. Brigades.

(4) At 4.20 pm B/130th How. Battery will fire 5 rounds of H.E. at the houses in N 30 C. The 25th Trench How. Battery will assist if possible in the destruction of these houses

(5) Any rounds required to check range and line should be fired in the morning.

(6) The 31st Brigade H.Q. will be at the

Appendix

XV Brigade observing station from 3.45 pm. to the end of the bombardment.

15.9.15.

K G Ireland Lt RFA
Adjt. 31st Bde RFA.

4.5 x 4

Copy No 1 to 69th Battery RFA.
2 100th "
3 103rd "
4 118th "
5 367th "
6 B/130 "
7 84th Inf. Bde
8 Filed.

28th Division

121
7493

31st Bde R.F.A.

Oct 1915

Vol X

Instructions regarding War Diaries and Intelligence Summaries are contained in F. S. Regs., Part II. and the Staff Manual respectively. Title pages will be prepared in manuscript.

WAR DIARY
or
INTELLIGENCE SUMMARY.
(Erase heading not required.)

Army Form C. 2118.

Hour, Date, Place	Summary of Events and Information	Remarks and references to Appendices
October 1st 1915 ANNEQUIN	19th Infantry Brigade relieved 5th Infantry Brigade (2nd Div.) during the night. 31st Brigade Headquarters established at ANNEQUIN and telephone line laid to 19th Brigade Headquarters by 8.0 am. Registration by Batteries continued – 69th Battery ordered to fire intermittently on MAD ALLEY (about 2900) throughout the day and 100th Battery on LONE FARM (about 2600)	Kg1.
2nd	At 3.0 pm heavy bomb fighting in LITTLE WILLIE heard observed. Our infantry seen to withdraw across open. British Artillery immediately opened a hot fire on LITTLE WILLIE At 5.30 pm. Royal Welsh Fusiliers asked for 9th Battery to fire on LITTLE WILLIE; this they were unable to do (not registered and emplacements would not allow switch). Message passed to R.A. 2nd Division and 9th Division and 14th Brigade (covering South) 19th Battery fired on their extreme right lines viz. where LITTLE WILLIE joined Front trench (North)	
[illegible]	19th Brigade (2 Battalions) relieved by 22nd Bde. with 4 Battalions of R.W. Fusiliers, Queens, Royal Warwicks, ~~Glasgow Highlanders~~, S. Staffords.	Kg1.

(73989) W4141—463. 400,000. 9/14. H.&J.Ltd. Forms/C. 2118/10.

Army Form C. 2118.

Instructions regarding War Diaries and Intelligence Summaries are contained in F. S. Regs., Part II. and the Staff Manual respectively. Title pages will be prepared in manuscript.

WAR DIARY
or
INTELLIGENCE SUMMARY.
(*Erase heading not required.*)

Hour, Date, Place	Summary of Events and Information	Remarks and references to Appendices
3rd	At request of Royal Welch Fusiliers 69th Battery	
7.0am	fired at 7.0 a.m. on North end of LITTLE WILLIE.	
	Queens reported through 100th Battery (supporting them)	103rd Battery returned to the Brigade - Supporting the trenches held by R. Warwicks and Glasgow Highlanders. (left zone)
8.0am to 12 noon	that shells fell short opposite MADAGASCAR trench at 8.0 a.m., 11.0 a.m. & later. Battery could not be traced. Message passed to R.A. 2nd & 25th Divisions.	
12.30am & 1.10am	100th Battery at request of Queens fired on working parties of Germans in their front at 12.30 a.m. & 1.10 a.m.	
3.0pm	At 3.0 p.m. 84th Brigade (on our right) launched apparently successful counter-attack on Little Willy.	
5.5pm	Heavy bomb fighting in Little Willy (84th Brigade subsequently reported to have been driven out)	
	Throughout the afternoon enemy shelled our trenches as far south as HULLUCH heavily - F.O.O.s warned against attack	
2.10pm	100th Battery engaged and silenced a trench mortar firing on Warwick's trenches	
4.25pm	100th Battery registered more points in enemy's trenches.	
8.2pm	A heavy burst of rifle fire in South of Brigade zone (Little Willy and Hohenzollern Redoubt). 69th Battery immediately opened barrage fire on trenches in their zone and subdued part of the fire - All quiet then in our front. 69th Battery fired for 5 minutes	K.G.I.

(9 29 6) W4141—463 100,000 9/14 H W V Forms/C. 2118/10

Instructions regarding War Diaries and Intelligence Summaries are contained in F. S. Regs., Part II. and the Staff Manual respectively. Title pages will be prepared in manuscript.

WAR DIARY
or
INTELLIGENCE SUMMARY.
(Erase heading not required.)

Army Form C. 2118.

Hour, Date, Place	Summary of Events and Information	Remarks and references to Appendices
4th	22nd Infantry Brigade relieved by 21st Infantry Brigade during the night. Front now held by 2nd Bedfords and 4th Camerons. 69th & 100th Batteries support 2nd Bedfords, and 103rd Battery 4th Camerons.	
	Orders issued for an officer to be at each Battn. HQS. by night as Liaison officer (at Infantry's request)	
	Brigade Headquarters changed billet 300 yards E. of Annequin mines to be nearer Infantry HQS.	
1.5pm	103rd Battery retaliated on German trenches N of AUCHY - VERMELLES railway for a few light shell on our trenches.	
2.30pm	69th Battery observed and fired on a party of Germans behind CORONS DE MARONS. Party took cover in house which 69th Battery shelled with HE. No more movement seen.	
5.0pm	~~69th and~~ 103rd Battery ~~ordered to~~ fired on German trenches to stop rifle fire from them on one of our aeroplanes. The 69th Battery observer located by sound approximate position of a machine gun firing on our aeroplane and opened fire on the point. Machine gun fire stopped.	
	About 7.0pm considerable rifle fire heard near Hohenzollern Redoubt. R.A. 2nd Division ordered 2 Batteries to fire for ½ an hour on German trenches to keep enemy quiet. 69th and 100th Batteries ordered to	

Instructions regarding War Diaries and Intelligence Summaries are contained in F. S. Regs., Part II. and the Staff Manual respectively. Title pages will be prepared in manuscript.

WAR DIARY
or
INTELLIGENCE SUMMARY.
(Erase heading not required.)

Army Form C. 2118.

Hour, Date, Place	Summary of Events and Information	Remarks and references to Appendices
	to fire up to 40 rounds apiece on MADAGASCAR trench and LONE Farm respectively.	KGA
5th	Communication between 69th Battery and 2nd Bedfords by direct line was broken all night - The fact had not been reported to an officer of the Battery.	
	From 8.30 am. onwards Germans fired a considerable number of shell round VERMELLES, and appear to have brought up more heavy guns, as previously practically no shell appeared to have been fired into our lines.	
	Raining all day - light impossible for observation	
	No rounds having been fired by Batteries up to 3. pm. all were ordered to fire up to 30 or 40 rounds and display more offensive spirit	KGA.
6th	The infantry worked all night on their wire in front of their trenches.	
7.45am	69th. Battery fired H.E. into HAISNES in retaliation for German shell in VERMELLES.	
	Verbal orders received with regard to proposed attack on FOSSE 8, and Batteries ordered to register the houses CORONS de MARON and de PEKIN N. of Rly N. of the dump.	

(73989) W4141—463. 400,000. 9/14. H.&J.Ltd. Forms/C. 2118/10.

Army Form C. 2118.

Instructions regarding War Diaries and Intelligence Summaries are contained in F. S. Regs., Part II. and the Staff Manual respectively. Title pages will be prepared in manuscript.

WAR DIARY
or
INTELLIGENCE SUMMARY.

(*Erase heading not required.*)

Hour, Date, Place	Summary of Events and Information	Remarks and references to Appendices
6th (Contd) 11.30 am	69th Battery fired on a dispersed small hostile working party S.W. of AUCHY.	
	103rd Battery shelled German trenches opposite 4th Camerons at 11.30 am. and 1.30 pm. in retaliation for rifle grenades.	
	In the afternoon registration by Batteries as under –	
	69th Battery – Power House FOSSE 8. / CORONS de MARONS. / CORONS de PEKIN. } about 2400x	
	100th Battery CORONS de MARONS.	
	103rd Battery CORONS de PEKIN / Power House FOSSE 8 } about 2000x / HAISNES ALLEY (comm. trench) about 2300x	
	At about 4.0 pm. Germans shelled our trenches opposite HOHENZOLLERN Redoubt heavily – Batteries answered replied – not in 31st Brigade zone –	
	At 7.30 pm. the 103rd Battery fired some rounds on AUCHY – HAISNES road where transport was heard to be moving – This battery completely enfilades the road – movement of Transport stopped –	KB.
7th –	Arrangements made for support of Brigades on either flank if required and necessary registration carried out. Support Trenches only can be shelled in these zones.	

Instructions regarding War Diaries and Intelligence Summaries are contained in F. S. Regs., Part II. and the Staff Manual respectively. Title pages will be prepared in manuscript.

WAR DIARY
or
INTELLIGENCE SUMMARY.
(Erase heading not required.)

Army Form C. 2118.

Hour, Date, Place	Summary of Events and Information	Remarks and references to Appendices
7th (contd)	103rd Battery registered HAISNES - AUCHY road with aeroplane - Message from R.A. 2nd Division giving instructions as to preparations for this not received, so that verbal instructions had to be given and arrangements rushed through. In the course of the day some complaints received from Infantry that shell were falling short - Probably anti-aircraft, which were firing, as no battery could be found responsible.	KJA.
8th	In accordance with orders from R.A. 2nd Division the area N.E. of Rly at FOSSE 8 subdivided into areas in consultation with 41st Brigade R.F.A., who were also given task of keeping the houses in this area under fire during proposed attack on FOSSE 8 on the 12th. In the morning the 100th Battery located approximately a machine gun emplacement near AUCHY - VERMELLES railway - As infantry reported this was believed heavily concreted, 100th Battery only fired a few rounds and a report was forwarded to R.A. 2nd Division asking for heavy shell to be put onto it. Batteries attempted to verify registration on houses in allotted area, but owing to activity of British Artillery it was difficult to identify their shell. The houses meanwhile are being very much knocked about	KJA.

(73989) W4141—463. 400,000. 9/14. H.&J.Ltd. Forms/C. 2118/10.

Instructions regarding War Diaries and Intelligence Summaries are contained in F. S. Regs., Part II. and the Staff Manual respectively. Title pages will be prepared in manuscript.

WAR DIARY
or
INTELLIGENCE SUMMARY.
(Erase heading not required.)

Army Form C. 2118.

Hour, Date, Place	Summary of Events and Information	Remarks and references to Appendices
9th	103rd Battery fired during the night on German trenches in their zone to check hostile rifle fire on our working parties. They also fired on AUCHY-HAISNES road when transport was heard moving.	
	Day too misty for observation.	
	104th Battery fired 50 rounds on German trenches intermittently during the afternoon in aggression.	
	At 7.30 pm. Infantry listening post reported movement of transport on AUCHY-HAISNES road. 103rd Battery opened fire on it, and assisted by the infantry observations scattered the transport, which retired at the gallop, followed up by the fire of the Battery. The Battery fired about 80 or 90 rounds.	
	At 11.30 pm. the transport was again heard and dispersed by 103rd Battery, which fired about 40 more rounds. Effect could not be observed in darkness, but the shrapnel bursts could be seen among the trees in the road	K.G.A.
11th	Orders received at noon from R.A. 2nd Division to commence cutting enemy's wire in our front with HE as a demonstration, and to judge the effects of HE on wire and parapets.	
	At the same time Batteries continued	

(73989) W4141—463. 400,000. 9/14. H.&J.Ltd. Forms/C. 2118/10.

Army Form C. 2118.

Instructions regarding War Diaries and Intelligence Summaries are contained in F. S. Regs., Part II. and the Staff Manual respectively. Title pages will be prepared in manuscript.

WAR DIARY
or
INTELLIGENCE SUMMARY.
(*Erase heading not required.*)

Hour, Date, Place	Summary of Events and Information	Remarks and references to Appendices
10th contd	successfully knocked down the houses N. of FOSSE 8. 21st Brigade (7th Division) relieved by 5th Brigade (2nd Division) during the afternoon; RA. 2nd Division ordered 31st Brigade to support 5th Brigade. Front taken over by 5th Brigade (with 2 Battalions) much narrower than that previously held by 21st Bde - 103rd Battery zone taken over by 41st Brigade Group. LITTLE WILLIE trench being opposite the front held by Glasgow Highlanders (right Btn. 5th Bde.) arrangements made for 149th and 75th Batteries, 146th Bde, to support them for defence only as our Batteries could not switch so far South and those two Batteries had the front well registered. These was agreed upon on condition that 31st Bde found the Liaison officer at the QUARRY (Btn. HQs Glasgow Highlanders) which was arranged - Previous zones of 69th + 100th Batteries divided up between 69th 100th + 103rd Batteries. All three connected to Btn. HQs. of Queen's (left Btn. 5th Bde.) - Officer for liaison purposes found at night by 100th Battery who have 4 subalterns. Wire cutting demonstration apparently successful, as Germans displayed esttosness	

(73989) W4141—463. 400,000. 9/14. H.&J.Ltd. Forms/C. 2118/10.

Instructions regarding War Diaries and Intelligence Summaries are contained in F. S. Regs., Part II. and the Staff Manual respectively. Title pages will be prepared in manuscript.

WAR DIARY
or
INTELLIGENCE SUMMARY.
(Erase heading not required.)

Army Form C. 2118.

Hour, Date, Place	Summary of Events and Information	Remarks and references to Appendices
	by unusual rifle fire and a large number of flares.	
	103rd Battery again disturbed German transport in HAISNES.	KJ
11th	Wire cutting continued - morning light misty. German aeroplane brought down by our aeroplanes near SAILLY LA BOURSE at 9.0 a.m. apparently unhurt.	
	Orders regarding attack on FOSSE 8 received and issued as per attached. Attack arranged for 12th.	
	Results of wire cutting very difficult to observe, as the German wire consisted only of loose coils.	
	Several H.E. burst in air after graze (new 100 fuze - no particulars received to-date) - Each Battery took a front of about 50 yards. Many posts seen blown into the air, and considerable gaps made in German parapet.	
	Wire laid to observing station selected by G.O.C. 5th Brigade for the attack.	
	R.A. 2nd Division at 5 p.m. [illegible] by message on telephone that attack was postponed 24 hours.	KJ

(73989) W4141—463. 400,000. 9/14. H.&J.Ltd. Forms/C. 2118/10.

Instructions regarding War Diaries and Intelligence Summaries are contained in F. S. Regs., Part II. and the Staff Manual respectively. Title pages will be prepared in manuscript.

WAR DIARY
or
INTELLIGENCE SUMMARY.
(Erase heading not required.)

Army Form C. 2118.

Hour, Date, Place	Summary of Events and Information	Remarks and references to Appendices
12th	Bombardment of houses N. of FOSSE 8 continued. Batteries during the last week have fired about 400 rounds a day – mostly H.E.	
	The enemy in the morning fired a few 5.9" and 4.2" shell round the gun positions N. of VERMELLES.	
	In the afternoon the 103rd Battery knocked down the upper storey of the "Manager's house" FOSSE 8.	
	On the order of R.A. 2nd Division, the 69th Battery maintained a "barrage" of 12 rounds per hour on MAD ALLEY (commt. trench running S.W. from AUCHY)	K.g.1
13th	Brigade Headquarters occupied Battle Station at 9.30 a.m.	
	Bombardment commenced at 12 noon. FOSSE 8 obliterated by smoke. Effective round from 15 inch How. struck Power House, FOSSE 8 and destroyed it. German shell fire appeared very ineffective on our trenches.	
	1.0 p.m. Heavy guns lifted, 18 prs remained on trenches. Gas and smoke started.	
	2.0 p.m. Assault launched. Our troops appeared to take HOHENZOLLERN redoubt without a casualty.	

Army Form C. 2118.

Instructions regarding War Diaries and Intelligence Summaries are contained in F. S. Regs., Part II. and the Staff Manual respectively. Title pages will be prepared in manuscript.

WAR DIARY
or
INTELLIGENCE SUMMARY.
(Erase heading not required.)

Hour, Date, Place	Summary of Events and Information	Remarks and references to Appendices
	At 3.0pm. advance checked on chord of Hohenzollern. Little Willie trench seemed to be offering considerable resistance. Germans could be seen standing up but apparently flanking fire not arranged for as they remained unhurt for some time.	
	3.20pm. Our troops seen withdrawing from CHORD.	
	3.25pm. Advance continued, followed by small reinforcements.	
	No further movement above ground observed, but from bursts of bombs, our troops appeared to have reached the dump. All very quiet round Little Willie.	
	Telephone lines along communication trenches (pegged in) held very successful, but shell fire in our trenches very slight.	
	Barrage on MAD ALLEY and HAISNES road maintained all night.	K.G.A.
14th	Bomb attack on Little Willy by 5th Brigade made no progress owing to hostile rifle fire. Germans apparently still in possession of all Little Willy and the CHORD.	

Instructions regarding War Diaries and Intelligence Summaries are contained in F. S. Regs., Part II. and the Staff Manual respectively. Title pages will be prepared in manuscript.

WAR DIARY
or
INTELLIGENCE SUMMARY.
(Erase heading not required.)

Army Form C. 2118.

Hour, Date, Place	Summary of Events and Information	Remarks and references to Appendices
14th contd.	Attack seemed a failure through lack of co-operation and higher control, as casualties did not appear excessive.	
	5th Brigade dug new trench (GUILDFORD trench) towards Hohenzollern to connect with 46th Division but dug too far North –	
	Batteries meanwhile maintained barrage day and night on MAD ALLEY (100th Battery), and junction of Little Willy and Fosse trench (69th Battery) Our immediate front very quiet	
	A misty day, bad for observation. Considerable artillery activity on both sides, and bomb fighting in Hohenzollern Redoubt.	
	Guards Division took over from 46th Division on our right during the evening.	K.J.I.
15th	5th Brigade attempted to join up with Hohenzollern Redoubt ~~with~~ by sapping during the night, but were unsuccessful. – GUILDFORD trench converted into a fire trench and wired.	
	Day again very misty and useless for observation Under orders from R.A. 2nd Division barrage maintained by 100th Battery all day.	

Instructions regarding War Diaries and Intelligence Summaries are contained in F. S. Regs., Part II. and the Staff Manual respectively. Title pages will be prepared in manuscript.

WAR DIARY
or
INTELLIGENCE SUMMARY.
(*Erase heading not required.*)

Army Form C. 2118.

Hour, Date, Place	Summary of Events and Information	Remarks and references to Appendices
	Relief of 46th Division by Guards Division completed.	
	1 man of 118th Battery and 2 horses (Major Hudson's groom & chargers) killed by shell at BEUVRY while on exercise.	
	A few minor casualties from prematures from other Batteries sustained in 69th Battery – none serious enough for admission to hospital.	
	Headquarters moved back to ANNEQUIN.	K.G.1.
16th	After a rather quiet night, day broke misty as usual – Enemy's field guns active on our support trenches for which retaliation was made by 69th and 103rd Batteries.	
	VERMELLES shelled daily & intermittently by German field guns ~~with~~ occasional heavy shell.	
	Barrage on MAD ALLEY and HAISNES road still maintained day and night.	
	100th Battery alternate position practically complete –	K.G.1.
17th	10.0 a.m. Barrage on MAD ALLEY and HAISNES road stopped by order R.A. 2nd Division.	
	Many orders and counter-orders received	

Army Form C. 2118.

WAR DIARY
or
INTELLIGENCE SUMMARY.
(Erase heading not required.)

Instructions regarding War Diaries and Intelligence Summaries are contained in F. S. Regs., Part II. and the Staff Manual respectively. Title pages will be prepared in manuscript.

Hour, Date, Place	Summary of Events and Information	Remarks and references to Appendices
	from RA. 28th Division reference "dumping" Ammunⁿ. Last order, dump of 100 rounds per gun may be maintained	
	More complaints of shell falling short, which cannot be traced - No accurate times kept, so there is no means of checking.	
	Batteries only fired a few rounds in retaliation for some light shell on our trenches.	KGI
18th	5th Brigade still unsuccessful in joining up sap to Hohenzollern redoubt with Guards Division - Saps reconnoitred by C.O. and Adjt. 31st Bde, found to be still 50 yards apart having been dug parallel to each other - Reported to 5th Brigade.	
	Orders received that the 28th Division would be relieved on the nights 20/21 and 21/22, and would take over from Meerut Division N. of LA BASSEE Canal on the nights 21/22 and 22/23.	
	31st Brigade R.F.A. to relieve the 9th Brigade R.F.A. and support the sector CANAL to GIVENCHY.	
	Preliminary reconnaissance of positions and details carried out during the afternoon by O.C. 31st Brigade R.F.A.	KGI

Instructions regarding War Diaries and Intelligence Summaries are contained in F. S. Regs., Part II. and the Staff Manual respectively. Title pages will be prepared in manuscript.

WAR DIARY
or
INTELLIGENCE SUMMARY.
(*Erase heading not required.*)

Army Form C. 2118.

Hour, Date, Place	Summary of Events and Information	Remarks and references to Appendices
19th	O.C. 31st Brigade and representatives from each Battery went to reconnoitre positions and observing stations of the 9th Brigade R.F.A. preparatory to taking over.	
1.30pm	Orders received from R.A. 2nd Division that the 36th Brigade would take over 31st Brigade front.	
2.31pm	Previous orders cancelled - 28th Division to be prepared to move out at once - Arrangements for relief to be made as soon as possible.	
4.45pm	Orders received by wire that relief would continue as originally ordered.	
5.30pm	Reports received of Germans massing near the QUARRIES and heavy shelling & bomb fighting heard in HOHENZOLLERN Redoubt. All quiet after 40 minutes.	
6.0pm	All reports to be handed over to relieving Brigades.	
6.15pm	All men to be recalled from leave	
11.20pm	Wire from 28th Divl Artillery, that rest area CANTRAINNE 1½ miles N E of LILLERS has been allotted to 31st Brigade. The Brigade Ammn Col. to move at 10.0 am. via BETHUNE - CHOCQUES - LE HAMEL - BUSVETTES - CANTRAINNE. Billetting parties under Orderly Officer to set out at 9.0 am from BEUVRY.	

W.S.

Instructions regarding War Diaries and Intelligence Summaries are contained in F. S. Regs., Part II. and the Staff Manual respectively. Title pages will be prepared in manuscript.

WAR DIARY
or
INTELLIGENCE SUMMARY.
(Erase heading not required.)

Army Form C. 2118.

Hour, Date, Place	Summary of Events and Information	Remarks and references to Appendices
20th.	69th and 118th Batteries to be relieved in bulk by 2 batteries 36th Brigade RFA; the 100th and 103rd Batteries to be withdrawn. Arrangements made for early relief (by 2.0 pm.) of 69th and 118th Batteries owing to the length of march to be carried out that evening – The guns of the 69th and 118th Batteries had to be left in position and guns to replace them taken over from 62nd Brigade, 12th Division. The 118th Battery obtained 4 guns, but the 69th Battery were only able to obtain 3 and those not earlier that 8.0 pm. Arrangements for this three-cornered exchange were not good; the guns taken over were mainly new but very incomplete in fittings. Relief also considerably delayed owing to a break down in telephone communication at the critical moment – wire broken – 100th Battery withdrew at 2.0 pm. 69th and 118th Batteries were clear at 3.0 pm. 103rd Battery withdrawn at 3.50 pm. O.C. 41st Brigade RFA took over the front at 4.0 pm. Headquarters 31st Brigade marched away at 5.30 pm.	

(73989) W4141—463. 400,000. 9/14. H.&J.Ltd. Forms/C. 2118/10.

Instructions regarding War Diaries and Intelligence Summaries are contained in F. S. Regs., Part II. and the Staff Manual respectively. Title pages will be prepared in manuscript.

WAR DIARY
or
INTELLIGENCE SUMMARY.
(Erase heading not required.)

Army Form C. 2118.

Hour, Date, Place	Summary of Events and Information	Remarks and references to Appendices
	Brigade Headquarters reached CANTRAINNE at 10.0 pm. 69th Battery marched in at 11.30 pm. being the last unit to reach their billets.	
	Orders received at 12 midnight regarding return of all smoke helmets, & collection and packing in bulk of grocery portion of iron rations, and a request for a return of deficiencies in rifle covers.	K.G.I.
21st –	3.40 am. Orders received reference entraining at LILLERS on the 21st/22nd and 23rd as per attached programme	
	Energies expended throughout the morning to obtaining another gun for the 69th and making up deficiencies in gun stores on those taken over.	
	A fourth gun for the 69th Battery was obtained from the 10th M. 1st Corps at MERVILLE. A new gun, without breech fittings or gun stores.	
	Deficiencies partly made up during the afternoon by R.A. 12th Division whose representative brought them in a cart. A gun reported to have been sent in the morning from BETHUNE did not arrive.	
	69th and 1/2 100th Battery marched at 10.0 pm to entraining station, the 69th Battery gun being still deficient of carrier, extractor & trigger besides many other small stores.	

Instructions regarding War Diaries and Intelligence Summaries are contained in F. S. Regs., Part II. and the Staff Manual respectively. Title pages will be prepared in manuscript.

WAR DIARY
or
INTELLIGENCE SUMMARY.
(Erase heading not required.)

Army Form C. 2118.

Hour, Date, Place	Summary of Events and Information	Remarks and references to Appendices
	Ration arrangements for journey – First day consume iron ration: 2nd and 3rd day's rations to be drawn at entraining point – also forage for 3 days.	KH.
22nd	69th and ½ 100th Battery left LILLERS at 2.51 am. ½ 100th and 103rd Battery " at 6.51 a.m. 118th Battery and Brigade Staff " at 9.51 am. Only 2 long halts arranged per day where water for men and horses was provided. – Train accomodation very scarce. Journey extremely slow with numerous halts of short duration when water for horses had to be obtained when possible –	Each unit handed over its Baggage wagon complete to A.S.C. at entraining station. KH.
23rd	31st Bde Ammn Col. less 40 horses and 20 men (under an officer) entrained and left at 15.51. from LILLERS. Details of Bde. Ammn Col. entrained 2.35 a.m. 24.10.15 at FOUQUEREUIL. Train route followed was unknown but was not main line. French inhabitants, as the fighting area was left behind, displayed great enthusiasm – All appeared to know our destination. At MOULINS Brigade Commander was presented with a bottle of champagne by a kind Frenchman on the platform.	KH
24th	MARSEILLES reached at 4.50 pm (16.50) On arrival, no Staff officer or guide	

Instructions regarding War Diaries and Intelligence Summaries are contained in F. S. Regs., Part II. and the Staff Manual respectively. Title pages will be prepared in manuscript.

WAR DIARY
or
INTELLIGENCE SUMMARY.
(Erase heading not required.)

Army Form C. 2118.

Hour, Date, Place	Summary of Events and Information	Remarks and references to Appendices
	met the train, and no transport was ready for Baggage. Subsequently a R.T.O. and S. and T. Sergeant appeared, who sent for necessary transport and informed us that the train had arrived at the wrong station and the Camp provided for the Brigade was 5 miles distant.	
	Brigade Staff, less details left in charge of Baggage to await transport, marched from the station at 6.0 pm and arrived Camp BORELY at 8.30 pm.	
	118th Battery and transport arrived at 11.0 pm.	
	69th, 100th and 103rd Batteries already encamped.	KJ1
25th	Re-adjustment of allotment of ground to units.	
	Requirements in clothing and equipment made up to a large extent. 69th Battery received the important parts required for their 4th gun.	
	Strict measures as regards leave for the men to avoid crime will be necessary.	
	At 10.30 pm 12 men of the 69th Battery and about 20 men of the 118th Battery found to be absent without leave.	KJ1
26th	Brigade Ammunition Column arrived and reached camp at 4.30 am.	
	A draft of 17 men received from the Base	

Instructions regarding War Diaries and Intelligence Summaries are contained in F. S. Regs., Part II. and the Staff Manual respectively. Title pages will be prepared in manuscript.

WAR DIARY
or
INTELLIGENCE SUMMARY.
(*Erase heading not required.*)

Army Form C. 2118.

Hour, Date, Place	Summary of Events and Information	Remarks and references to Appendices
	completing the Batteries to Establishment, but leaving the Ammunition Column still deficient of 8 men (in hospital and left behind at BETHUNE)	
	A draft of 26 horses - Whalers - received - completing establishment	KJI
27th	No prospect of embarkation at present - A large number of men awarded Field punishment for absence and drunkenness, necessitating the pitching of a Brigade guard tent and appointment of Brigade Provost Sergeant to control them. Hours for tying up 7.0 am to 8.0 a.m. and 5.30 p.m. to 6.30 p.m.	KJI
28th to 31st	Training, overhaul of equipment and clothing carried out - Weather very wet and state of camp suffering in consequence - Number of men undergoing field punishment for absence and drunkenness increased to 24 in the Brigade. The large number of fatigues and guards to be found interferes with training and care of horses. Arrangements for forage and supplies unsatisfactory - 118th Battery and Brigade Ammunition Column being without oats for 24 hours.	

K J Ireland
Capt. RFA

(73989) W4141—463. 400,000. 9/14. H.&J.Ltd. Forms/C. 2118/10.

Copy No 3

8th Divisional Artillery
Operation Order No 5

20 x 15

(1) The Divisional Artillery will entrain according to appended programme

(2) Bde Cmdrs will notice that entraining will commence at 3 hours before the scheduled time in the table = which is the hour at which the train will start

(3) The Staff Captain will be the representative referred to in para 8

(4) Acknowledge by bearer

Copy No 1 to [illegible]
2
3
4
5
BAC

[illegible]
Maj RFA

31st

SECRET.

General Instructions for move of 28th Division.

---

1. Units will not take with them any articles of Government property in excess of Mobilization Store tables.

2. All surplus stores not handed over to D.A.D.O.S will be collected in a Brigade dump; in the case of 83rd and 84th Brigades these dumps will be left in charge of their Territorial Battalions. In the case of 85th Brigade, O.C. Train will arrange for a guard.

The situation and contents of these dumps will be notified early to the Division.

3. Surplus horses and vehicles will be handed over to affiliated Train Companies.

4. Men useless and unable to march will be handed over to O.C. Train.

5. No man belonging to another Division will accompany 28th Division under any circumstances.

6. French interpreters will not accompany the Division.

7. No bombs except those in boxes which have never been opened will be taken under any circumstances whatever.

8. Vehicles will not be loaded beyond their authorised weight. S.A.A. will be dumped if necessary at Brigade dumps.

9. No Second Line Transport vehicles will accompany the Division, all Supply and Baggage wagons being returned to Train Co. concerned.

10. The following A.S.C. personnel will accompany each Infantry Brigade Headquarters :-

Supply details.	2 Officers and 10 Rank and File.
Transport details.	1 Officer and 2 Rank and File.
	5 horses and 1 G.S.Limbered Wagon.

11. The following A.S.C. personnel will accompany Divisional Headquarters :-

Supply details.	2 Officers and 10 Rank and File.
Transport details.	1 Officer and 2 Rank and File.
	5 horses and 1 Limbered G.S.wagon.

P. T. O.

12. The length of the journey will be about 60 hours.

13. Instructions as to places of halts etc., will be handed to Officers Commanding Railway Trains.

R. HENVEY, Lieut. Colonel,

20th October 1915. A.A.& Q.M.G., 28th Division.

S E C R E T.

1. The 28th Division will entrain at FOUQUEREUIL and LILLERS in accordance with attached time tables.

2. In order to make more room for men in the closed trucks which have a maximum capacity of 40 men or 8 horses each, Infantry Brigades should arrange to divide the horses of 1st Line Transport of Battalions so as to have the full number of 8 horses per truck as nearly as possible. Thus each battalion is taken to have 81 horses and the total for the 4 battalions of a Brigade would thus be 324 horses for which 41 trucks are necessary, i.e. 10 trucks for each battalion except one which has 11 trucks, instead of 11 trucks for each battalion.

3. Transport and strong working parties (1 company) for Infantry battalions will arrive 3 hours and remainder of battalion 1 hour before time of departure of train. All other units 3 hours before.

4. The flat sided trucks provided should take four pairs of wheels except in cases of large vehicles such as G.S. Wagons, motor ambulances, etc., and a small vehicle such as a water cart can be loaded with a G.S. Wagon.

5. Units will entrain with 3 days preserved rations, exclusive of the unexpired portion of the day's ration and the iron ration.

6. Straw for trucks will be available at the entraining station.

7. Blankets will be taken. They will be handed in at the detraining station.

8. A Divisional representative and an A.S.C. Officer will be present at the entrainment.

9. A statement showing number of Officers, N.C.O's and men, horses and vehicles entrained and the name of the Commanding Officer of the train will be handed to the Divl. representative.

10. The first halting place for tea and water is at LONGUEAU. Details as to others will be communicated en route.

R. HENVEY, Lieut. Colonel,

20th October 1915. A.A. & Q.M.G., 28th Division.

SECRET.

28th DIVISION.

PROGRAMME OF ENTRAINING

FOUQUEREUIL STATION.

Number of Train.	Distinguishing No. of Unit.	Date.	Time	Units.
1.	2821.	21/10/15.	12.35	2/Northd. Fusiliers.
2.	2822.	21/10/15.	15.35	1st Suffolk Regt.
3.	2823.	21/10/15.	18.35	2nd Cheshire Regt.
4.	2824.	21/10/15.	22.35	1st Welsh Regiment.
5.	(2820. (2825. (2803.	22/10/15. --- ---	2.35 --- ---	H.Q. 84th Inf. Brigade. No.3 Sec: Div. Signal Co. "B" Sqdn. Surrey Yeom:
6.	2831.	22/10/15.	6.35.	2nd East Kent R.
7.	2832.	22/10/15.	9.35.	3rd Royal Fusrs.
8.	2833.	22/10/15.	12.35.	2nd East Surrey Regt.
9.	2834.	22/10/15.	15.35.	3rd Middlesex Regt.
10 10.	(2830. (2835. (2810. (2815. (2895. (2896.	22/10/15. --- --- --- --- ---	18.35. -- -- -- -- --	85th Bde. Hd. Qrs. No.4 Sect: Div. Signal Co. 83rd Bde. Hd. Qrs. No.2 Sect: Div. Signal Co. 15th Sanitary Section. No.17 Mob: Vet. Sect, and Salvage Co.
11.	2811.	22/10/15.	22.35.	2nd K.O. R. Lancs.
12.	2812.	23/10/15.	2.35.	2nd East Yorks.
13.	2813.	23/10/15.	6.35.	1st K.O.Y.L.I.
14.	2814.	23/10/15.	9.35.	1st York & Lancs.
15.	2880.	23/10/15.	12.35.	H.Q. Div. Ammn. Column.
16.	2881.	23/10/15.	15.35.	No.1 Sect. D.A. Col.
17.	2882.	23/10/15.	18.35.	No.2 Sect. D.A. Col.
18.	2883.	23/10/15.	22.35.	No.3 Sect. D.A. Col.
19.		24/10/15.	2.35.	(Surplus Vehicles D.A.C. (and 40 horses from each (18 pr. Bde. Ammn: Col. (and 2 closed trucks for (D.A.D.O.S. stores.

SECRET.

28th Division.

PROGRAMME OF ENTRAINING.

LILLERS STATION.

No. of Train.	Distinguishing No. of Unit.	DATE.	TIME.	UNITS.	REMARKS.
1.	(2841) (½2842)	21st Oct.	12.51	(75th Bty.RFA. (½149th Bty.RFA.	
2.	(½2842) (2843)	do.	15.51	(½149th Bty. RFA. (366th Bty. RFA.	
3.	(2801) (2802) (2804) (2805)	do.	18.51	(Divl. Headquarters) (H.Q. Divl.Artillery) (Divl.Cyclist Coy. (H.Q.& No.1 Sec.Div.Sig.Co.	
4.	(2840) (2844)	do.	22.51	(H.Q. 146th Bde.RFA. (367th Bty. RFA.	
5.	(2851) (½2852)	22nd Oct.	2.51	(69th Bty. RFA. (½ 100th Bty. RFA.	+ Staff
6.	(½2852) (2853)	do.	6.51	(½ 100th Bty. RFA. (103rd Bty. RFA.	
7.	(2850) (2854)	do.	9.51	(H.Q.31st Bde. RFA. (118th Bty. RFA.	
8.	(2861) (½2862)	do.	12.51	(18th Bty. RFA. (½ 22nd Bty. RFA.	
9.	(½2862) (2863)	do.	15.51	(½ 22nd Bty. RFA. (62nd Bty. RFA.	
10.	(2860) (2864)	do.	18.51	(H.Q.3rd Bde. RFA. (365th Bty. RFA.	
11.	(2870) (2871) (½2872)	do	22.51	(H.Q.130th (How) Bde.RFA. ('A' Bty do. (½ 'B' Bty do.	
12.	(½2872) (2873)	23rd Oct.	2.51	(½ 'B' Bty. do. ('C' Bty. do.	

2.-

13.	(2886)	23rd Oct.	6.51	2/1st Northbn.Fd.Co. R.E.
14.	(2884) (2885)	do.	9.51	(H.Q. Divl.Engineers. (38th Field Coy.R.E.
15.	(2845)	do.	12.51	146th Bde.RFA.Amm.Col. (less 40 horses.)
16.	(2855)	do.	15.51	31st Bde. RFA. Amm.Col. (less 40 horses.)
17.	(2865)	do.	18.51	3rd Bde. RFA. Amm.Col. (less 40 horses.)
18.	(2892) (½2874)	do.	22.51	(84th Field Ambulance. (½ 130th Bde.RFA.Amm.Col.
19.	(½2874) (2893)	24th Oct.	2.51	(½ do. do. (85th Field Ambulance.
20.	(2894)	do.	6.51	(86th Field Ambulance. (Field Amb.Workshop Unit.

www.ingramcontent.com/pod-product-compliance
Lightning Source LLC
Chambersburg PA
CBHW080534250426
43668CB00052B/2157